CW00956497

MURDER
ON THE
MIND

MURDER
ON THE
MIND

AN INSIGHT INTO THE MINDS OF SERIAL KILLERS AND THEIR CRIMES

AMANDA HOWARD

NEW HOLLAND

Books by Amanda Howard

Non-Fiction

A Killer in the Family: When Murder Waits at Home (2013, New Holland)

Serial Killers and Philosophy: Being and Killing (2010, ed Sara Waller, Wiley & Sons)

Predators: Killers Without Conscience (2009, with Paul Wilson, New Holland)

Innocence Lost: Crimes that Changed a Nation (2009, New Holland)

Terror in the Skies (2007, ticktock/Bearport)

Million Dollar Art Theft (2007, ticktock/Bearport)

The Lottery Kidnapping (2007, ticktock/Bearport)

River of Blood: Serial Killers and Their Victims (2004, Universal)

Fiction: Detective Kate Reilly Ritual Series

Ritual: A Thousand Cuts (forthcoming 2014, Killing Time Books)

Ritual: The Elements of Murder (2013, Killing Time Books)

Ritual: The Blood of Many (2013, Killing Time Books)

Fiction: Novellas and Short Stories

The Cicadas Roar (2013, Killing Time Books)

Writer's Block (2013, Killing Time Books)

Charlotte's One of a Kind Cakes (2013, Killing Time Books)

For Yvonne Jamieson
The Matriarch
and the strongest person I will ever know

First published in 2014 by New Holland Publishers Pty Ltd
London • Sydney • Cape Town • Auckland

The Chandlery Unit 114 50 Westminster Bridge Road London SE1 7QY United Kingdom
1/66 Gibbes Street Chatswood NSW 2067 Australia
Wembley Square First Floor Solan Road Gardens Cape Town 8001 South Africa
218 Lake Road Northcote Auckland New Zealand

www.newhollandpublishers.com

Copyright © 2014 New Holland Publishers Pty Ltd
Copyright © 2014 in text: Amanda Howard
Copyright © 2014 in images: Amanda Howard

All rights reserved. No part of this publication may be reproduced, stored in a retrieval system or
transmitted, in any form or by any means, electronic, mechanical, photocopying, recording or otherwise,
without the prior written permission of the publishers and copyright holders.

A record of this book is held at the British Library and the National Library of Australia.

ISBN: 9781742575698

Managing Director: Fiona Schultz
Publisher: Alan Whiticker
Project Editor: Emily Carryer
Designer: Peter Guo
Proofreader: Julie King
Production Director: Olga Dementiev
Printer: Toppan Leefung Printing Ltd (China)

10 9 8 7 6 5 4 3 2 1

Keep up with New Holland Publishers on Facebook
www.facebook.com/NewHollandPublishers

ACNOWLEDGEMENTS

This book is a culmination of more than twenty-three years of work in the field of serial murder and violence. I have certainly looked into the abyss and seen it staring back at me. I have had death threats from killers as well as cookbook recipes that include me in the list of ingredients. However, there is not a day that goes by that I regret being a writer of true crime. It is my set path in life. Writing for me is like eating and breathing, I do it because without it I would feel empty.

I am pleased to say that my writing has now crossed genres and fields. I have written several fiction crime thrillers as well as a horror novella and many short stories. The freedom of the various genres has meant that whatever the mood is, I am able to pick up pen and paper, my trusty broken laptop or my new tablet PC and madly bash out another story or search out that elusive article on a killer that died more than two hundred years before my birth.

Writing, as many describe it, is a very isolating career. It is one of those jobs that no one can do for you; you cannot delegate others to put your words on paper. Yet, in saying that, writing cannot be done in a vacuum, either. I am extremely grateful to many people who listened to my ideas, offered suggestions, critiqued my work, gave me ideas, pointed me towards different stories and even helped me with a title for this book when I put it to them. I would like to name every single person who has offered and given input into putting together this book, or even given me a shameless plug:

Cheryl Langdon-Orr	Terri Chappell
Laura Barnes	Amanda Durley
Debra Betts	Andrea Black
Danielle Barrett	Emma Burbidge
Jodie Toon	Richard Halcomb
Robert McKnight	Karen Carlisle
Lisa Ryder	Alexia Sewastenko
Adam Holstein	Helen Curl
Robyn Ryan	Joan Dunleavy
Danielle Gilles	Tegan Barber
Nigel Fortescue	Cathy Alesbrook
David Russell	Michael Szucko
Don White	Amy Wright
Clay Cosner	Jennifer Cunningham

I am sure that there are dozens more names I can add, and if I missed you this time, I am sure you will get an inclusion in the next book. I am really thankful for my friends and family as well as my readers who support me and encourage me in my career.

In addition to those who have offered assistance, I must always include my gratitude to my husband Steve and our two loving children who allow me to be the mad and frantic writer that I am. They know when to leave me alone to crazily bash out slabs of text; they also know when to tell me to take a break; my husband also knows when it is time to bring me a glass of wine. I would never replace my little family for anything in this world. They feed my very soul.

I would also like to thank my parents, Brenda and Gordon. They taught me to fight hard and work hard for my dreams. I have been a writer since I was six years old, when, from the moment I could write a sentence, I started writing stories. I have not stopped since that very first story. My parents give honest advice, and nothing in my life was sugar coated. If it wasn't good enough I learned that it was imperative that I did it again, making it better or making it grander. I guess that is why I now strive to do everything to the absolute best of my skill and ability. I am truly grateful for their honesty and integrity that has made me the strong and successful woman I am today.

I would also like to thank those writers who inspire me every day to continue on my journey. I look to Edgar Allan Poe and Ernest Hemingway who seem to share my tortured soul. I aspire to be as good as Stephen King in my fiction work. I love his conversational style and strive to create works worthy of his status. There are also a pile of books that I keep near at all times, John Douglas' *Mindhunter*, Anne Rule's *Small Sacrifices*, Thomas Harris' *Silence of the Lambs* and Donald Rumbelow's *The Complete Jack the Ripper*. Those four books and their authors changed the direction of my life.

I would also like to thank the very good team at New Holland, to whom I am always indebted. To Alan Whiticker my commissioning editor and mentor, he has guided and shaped my writing over the past six years. He has given me a lot of valuable advice and pushes me to produce a large volume of work—that for some would be impossible—but he knows I can do it. To my editor, Emily Carryer, who has suffered through my repeated errors and incoherent sentences to make everything read as it should.

Finally, my last thank you goes to you, the reader. It is for you that this book is written. It is you that makes me return to my keyboard each and every day and visit the stories that pour from my mind and fingers. I am grateful that you chose to pick up my book and go with me on the journey. So let's begin, shall we?

Amanda Howard

March 2014

CONTENTS

DEFINING THE SERIAL KILLER

A ttempting to define who is truly a serial killer, when looking at murderers who have killed more than one victim, is an issue often met with dissent and leaves many killers in a 'grey area' of the definition. The theories do differ, and it is to this extent that here I have attempted to show that the singular term of 'serial killer' is too vague to encapsulate the varying types of multiple murderers, as well as provide possible subcategories that are more definitive than the umbrella term of serial killer.

Most experts do agree that a serial killer murders three victims or more; the victims are killed separately and in sometimes different places with a 'cooling off' period between kills. Though this generalised definition is a good theory, such killers as John Gacy would not be included as all of his victims were killed in the one place—his home. Jeffrey Dahmer falls into the same category. Though he did move several times, he killed all of his victims at his own residence.

Therefore, the definition needs an adjustment. Steven Eggar in *The Killers Among Us* (1998)[1] used a more definitive description to pigeonhole serial killers. Eggar states that 'a serial murder occurs when:

- one or more individuals (in many cases, males) commit(s) a second murder and/or subsequent murder;
- there is no general prior relationship between victim and attacker (if there is a relationship, such a relationship will place the victim in a subjugated role to the killer);
- subsequent murders are at different times and have no apparent connection to the initial murder; and
- are usually committed in a different geographical location and
- the motive is not for material gain and is for the murderer's desire to have power or dominance over his victims,
- Victims may have symbolic value for the murderer and/or are perceived to be prestigeless and in most instances are unable to defend themselves or alert others to their plight, or are perceived as powerless given their situation in time, place or status within their immediate surroundings, examples being vagrants, the homeless, prostitutes, migrant workers, homosexuals, missing children, single women (out by themselves), elderly women, college students and hospital patients'.

Eggar's highly developed definition covers the more 'classic' type of serial killer, that of the sexually motivated murderer; however, his definition does not lend itself completely to the variants that can come under the serial killer umbrella.

A key point that Eggar omitted was the cooling off period between murders that separates the serial killer from the mass murderer. The cooling off period is, however, part of the FBI's classification and the 'Crime Classification Manual' defines serial murder as 'three or more separate events in three or more separate locations with an emotional cooling off period in between the homicides'. Many criminologists, however, tend to disagree that three or more murders are required for a killer to be categorised as a serial killer. Today, two murders are sufficient to see a pattern and signature and the propensity for further, future possible violent acts.

When the term 'serial killer' was penned in the 1970s by the FBI's then called Behavioural Science team, there had been a spate of sexually motivated multiple homicides that were almost a phenomena and, though sexually motivated 'stranger' crimes were uncommon, they were not completely unheard of but still the spate of serial crimes gave rise to the new field of behavioural analysis. It was only after the capture and study of serial killer Ted Bundy that FBI's Robert Ressler came up with the term serial killer.

It was around that time that the FBI began a study of incarcerated multiple murderers and compiled a list of common traits. At the time, a high percentage of serial killers were white men. Many were aged between twenty and thirty-five and most of them had some form of sexual dysfunction. Victims were usually females, with prostitutes as the most likely and easily accessible victims.

A three-point checklist, now called the 'serial killer triad' were childhood development indicators that were common amongst serial killers. The three common points were:

- Cruelty to animals
- Enuresis: bed-wetting beyond the age of twelve
- Pyromania: the lighting of fires

It must be noted that people that have any or all of these traits do not necessarily go on to become killers but of those killers studied, many like

John Gacy, Ted Bundy, Henry Lee Lucas, Ed Kemper and David Berkowitz all possessed the triad indicators, making the traits a common theme.

Beyond the 1970s as we head into the twenty-first century, the classification of serial killers has gone through a metamorphosis and recent killers, though still classed a serial killer, require a more defined classification.

The differences in the cooling off periods, motives, signatures and modes of murder of serial killers are becoming rather diversified. Where such killers as The Hillside Strangler, Ivan Milat and Dr H. H. Holmes would once have all been classified as serial killers, today the labels are outdated and need to be re-addressed.

Before discussing the different categories of serial murderer, first it is imperative to understand the definition of a mass murderer, which in itself also needs further defining.

The mass murderer, unlike the serial killer, often kills in an explosion of violence in a very short period of time. According to the FBI's definition, mass murder is described as 'a number of murders (four or more) occurring during the same incident, with no distinctive time period between the murders. These events typically involved a single location, where the killer murdered a number of victims in an ongoing incident'.[2]

Over the next ten chapters, I will look at several of the sub-species of serial killers, namely those who murder children, killers who murder in pairs, thrill killers, poisoners and those who murder family members. Though they fit under the umbrella of serial killers, you will see that there are distinct differences under that broad title. In subsequent books in the series, other sub-species such as the torturers, cannibals, sex killers, spree killers as well as others will be examined to help build the larger picture of those murderers known usually only as serial killers.

CHILD KILLERS

The worst category of serial killers, if there were such a thing, is the category of child sexual predator. Child killers usually prey on children for sexual gratification and the murders are often an attempt to conceal the paedophile's sex-crime. Killers such as Michael Laurance in Australia and Colin Pitchfork in England are examples of this type of serial killer. Each killer lured their victims away from safety for the sole purpose of sexually assaulting them. The victim's subsequent death is often to silence and prevent them from identifying the killer.

The killer is usually weak in the presence of other adults. They are often shy and often those around them are unaware that they have a lustful desire to rape children. However, there are also those like Marc Dutroux and Gordon Northcott who were protected by family members who knew of their shocking desires.

The child killers in the section were mostly not known to their victims, they were what is commonly referred to as stranger abductions that often prove hard to unearth until it is too late for the victims.

Marcelo Costa de Andrade

'The soul and spirit of these children will go to live with God in heaven'

Brazilian Marcelo de Andrade was arrested at his Copacabana home in December 1991 for the murder of 6-year-old Odair de Abreu. When police arrived the killer simply asked them why they had not come sooner.[3] The man's arrest came after Odair's 10-year-old brother Altair was able to escape from the man's clutches and go to the police, where he told them of his abduction and of the murder of his younger brother that he had been forced to witness. The young boy told police that de Andrade had raped and then murdered the six year old on a deserted Rio beach.

Altair told police how de Andrade approached the brothers at a bus station in Santa Isabel, promising to give them money if they helped him at the local church.[4] Eager for some money, the brothers agreed and followed the man towards the local church, where de Andrade grabbed Odair around the throat and strangled him. He 'did not notice whether he was alive or dead when [he had] raped him …' According to Andrade in his confession, '[he] could not satisfy me. [I] squeezed his throat once more to ensure that his soul would go to heaven'.[5] After he killed the six year old, de Andrade then hugged Altair and professed his love for him. Scared for his life, Altair agreed to spend the night with his brother's killer. As soon as de Andrade was asleep, Altair escaped and ran straight to the local police station.

Once in custody de Andrade confessed to the murder of 6-year-old

Odair as well as a 9-month killing spree that commenced in April 1991. The first victim was a small boy whom de Andrade enticed home with the promise of money. Once he had the boy alone he raped him before stoning him with large rocks. The boy was then strangled and de Andrade again raped the boy's beaten and broken body. His second victim was 11-year-old Anderson Goulart. The boy was raped on a soccer field by de Andrade before being decapitated. In his confession de Andrade stated that when he decapitated the boy he was not sure if he was already dead. De Andrade had 'sawed off his head so that the children would make fun of him when he arrived in heaven'.[6]

The 24-year old man told police of his troubled childhood, including his own rape and time spent working as a male prostitute. De Andrade claimed that he had killed fourteen young boys, ranging from six to thirteeen years of age. He confessed to raping his victims before beheading them with a machete or bludgeoning them to death.

De Andrade claimed he became excited by the blood that poured from his victims' necks, before each time filling a cup with the blood and drinking it, believing it would make him beautiful.[7] It was his blood-drinking antics that earned him the nickname of 'o Vampiro de Niteroi', the Vampire of Niteroi.

In his confession he told police that 'the Soul and spirit of these children will go to live with God in heaven'.[8] With the information detailed in the killer's confession police were able to locate twelve of his victim's bodies. Born in January 1967, de Andrade claimed that he was a victim of his own brutal childhood and was not guilty of the crimes as he claimed to not know any better. His religious rants also added weight to his claims of mental illness. During his committal hearings in 1993 de Andrade was found to be mentally incompetent and was sent to a psychiatric hospital for the criminally insane to serve out his sentence.

Four years after his incarceration he escaped from the hospital. He was recaptured two weeks later while trying to make his way to Mecca.

Arthur Bishop

'I realised that I allowed myself to be misled by Satan and as a result my life was marked by wicked, perverse and depraved actions'

Arthur Bishop was born in Hinckley, Utah. Bishop was a dedicated Mormon who had spent time in the Philippines as a missionary, doing the work of God. However, the man was excommunicated by the church after being arrested for forgery in July 1978, and promptly disappeared. The short, overweight man with the thick brown hair and bushy eyebrows reappeared in October 1979 using the alias Roger Downs.

Four-year-old Alonzo Daniels disappeared while playing in the front yard of his home in Salt Lake City on the afternoon of 16 October 1979. Arthur Bishop was a neighbour of the Daniels family. Bishop enticed the boy away from his yard and took him to his own home where he attempted to rape the boy. When he was finished with the child he took the boy to the bathroom where he drowned him in the bathtub. Bishop then dumped the boy's body, burying it in a shallow grave on the sandy outskirts of Cedar Fort.

On 9 November 1980, 11-year-old Kim Peterson vanished. He was last seen on his way to sell his roller skates to a man he had met the previous day. Witnesses came forward describing the man seen with Kim as tall, with short, dark hair and bushy eyebrows, a description that matched Bishop's appearance. But again, no arrests were made. The man had again abducted the child. After sexually abusing the child he bludgeoned the boy to death and buried his body near Alonzo's grave.

Almost a year after Kim's disappearance another young boy vanished. On 20 October 1981, 4-year-old Danny Davis was on a shopping trip with his grandfather in Salt Lake City. Sometime during the trip, the pair became separated and Danny disappeared into the crowd with Bishop. The boy was again sexually assaulted before being murdered.

A fourth child disappeared on 22 June 1983. Troy Ward was seen walking off with an adult male at a park on his sixth birthday. Graeme Cunningham was the fifth boy abducted. He disappeared while on a camping trip on 14 July 1983. Graeme's trip was with a school friend and a man called Roger Downs. Downs was interviewed by police but released. However a second interview saw the man confess. He told police his name was Arthur Bishop and he was responsible for the murders of five missing boys. He told police, 'I'm glad you caught me, because I couldn't stop. I get around little kids and I start shaking'.[9] Following his confession, Bishop took the officers to the burial sites of his young victims. Buried near trees in Cedar Fort lay the bodies of Alonzo Daniels, Danny Davis and Kim Peterson. The bodies of Troy Ward and Graeme Cunningham were uncovered in Big Cottonwood Creek. Bishop confessed that he killed the boys so that they could not tell of the sexual assaults after their abductions. After his arrest, those who knew the killer called him 'strange … a split personality. Everything was really right. Even his pencils were in the right place. … But he turned into a different person when he left [work] at five. He had a lot of good times at night'.[10]

When Alonzo Daniels disappeared, investigators discovered that Bishop was living in the apartment opposite and in the other cases Bishop resided within a block of the family homes. Additional checks on Bishop uncovered other aliases and numerous sexual attacks on young children, particularly young boys. In his home Bishop kept a folder containing hundreds of photographs of naked and semi-naked boys.

At his trial, the jury found Bishop guilty of five counts of murder, five counts of kidnapping and one count of sexual abuse. During sentencing, the jury listened to sections of his taped confessions in which Bishop stated that had he not been caught, the sexual attacks and murders would have continued. Bishop was sentenced to death. Under Utah law the choice of method of execution is left to the defendant. Bishop chose lethal injection over firing squad. By his own admission Bishop wanted to die. He waived all appeals by his lawyer, refused his last meal and was executed by lethal injection on 9 June 1988. His final words were, 'I realised that I allowed myself to be misled by Satan and as a result my life was marked by wicked, perverse and depraved actions. Though perhaps a little too late, I am doing the right thing now'.[11]

Marc Dutroux

'I am not a murderer, I am not asking for forgiveness. I can't do much to change the irreversible'

Marc Dutroux was born in Brussels on 6 November 1956 and was the eldest of school-teachers Jeannine and Victor's five children. In court, Dutroux blamed his mother, Jeannine Lauwens, for the direction his life had taken. He claimed that rather than sending him to secondary academic school, she had forced him to go to an agricultural school, where, he claimed, he was destined to a life as a stable hand—a job he saw as well below his own delusions of grandeur. He claimed that most of his childhood was accented with beatings at the hands of both parents. According to his father, Dutroux was a 'difficult child' and was beaten regularly as punishment. He was sent to live with his grandmother when he was young after his parents had given up trying to control him. Dutroux left his grandmother's home in 1971 at the age of fifteen and spent most of his time living on the streets, turning to prostitution to make enough money to survive.

At the age of twenty, Dutroux married his first wife. Together they had two sons before they divorced due to spousal violence and the sexual abuse of the children by Dutroux. He began an affair with a young woman called Michelle Martin, who became his second wife.

In 1979, Dutroux was sent to prison for the first time. He had been found guilty of a variety of charges including trading in stolen cars, drugs and theft. His incarceration did little to deter him from continuing as a career criminal.

During the 1980s Dutroux fed his penchant for young girls by stalking children at swimming centres around Belgium in his white van, often in the company of his new wife Michelle Martin and associates Michel Lelièvre and Michel Nihoul. He would watch for the perfect victim, one that met his precise taste, and once a girl was found, Dutroux or one of his gang would grab the girl, bundle her into the van and then, once incapacitated, the victim would be raped before being released.

According to his criminal record his first official victim was an 11-year-old girl who was abducted and raped before being released. His second victim was a 15-year-old student, who was riding her bike to school when she was grabbed by Dutroux and forced into the back of his car. The girl's mouth and eyes were taped closed and she was savagely raped.[12]

In total Dutroux raped at least five girls, often in the company of his wife. But in early 1989 the couple were arrested and sent to prison, where Dutroux was sentenced to serve thirteen years for the attacks. Martin's sentence was suspended as she had young children.

In April 1992, only weeks after his release from prison, Dutroux abducted his next victim. The girl was fortunate enough to fight off her attacker and manage to escape.

The rapist returned to his poisonous fantasies and began the excavation of large amounts of dirt beneath several of the homes he owned. He stole large earth-moving equipment to manage the job without the police taking any notice. The bunkers were built in a labyrinth of tunnels that were to connect several of the criminally-obtained homes owned by Dutroux that peppered the railway tracks through the rundown suburb of Chaleroi. As his concrete sex cells neared completion, Dutroux abducted a number of girls.

In July 1994, a young girl named Eva was abducted and raped by Dutroux before being released. In May and June of 1995 several other girls were grabbed. A young girl, Aurelie, managed to escape the man's clutches in Gerpinnes in May or June 1995. In Slovakia, Dutroux raped another girl, Henriata in June 1995. The young girl was lucky to escape with her life following the attack. In Kortrijk in the north west of Belgium, another little girl, Sylvia, managed to escape Dutroux's clutches. Thyfene escaped him when he tried to abduct her in June in Spy, a city north of Dutroux's Charleroi home. Dutroux attempted to abduct two more girls in June in Jupile, but thankfully, both Lindsay and Stephanie were able to escape.

On 24 June 1995, Dutroux headed to Ougree near the border of Belgium and Germany and attempted to grab two young girls. The victims, Dikana and Vanessa, managed to escape but the next two would not be so lucky.

Julie Lejeune and Melissa Russo, two 8-year-old school friends, disappeared on the outskirts of Liège while waving to cars driving past and were taken to the home of Dutroux. According to Dutroux he played no part in the actual kidnapping of the two young girls, but arrived home and 'found' Melissa and Julie in his kitchen being raped by their abductors and Dutroux's closest friends Michel Nihoul, Michel Lelievre, Bernard Weinstein and Michelle Martin. Day after day, the two little girls were brought out of the dark, dank bunkers to the main house where they were raped and beaten by Dutroux and others. The girls' bodies were tortured physically and sexually by their abusers, who took pleasure in the daily attacks.

Almost two months after the disappearance of Julie and Melissa, 17-year-old An Marchal and 19-year-old Eefje Lambrecks were abducted by Dutroux on 22 August 1995. The girls were drugged and raped for the next several weeks before being drugged and buried alive in the yard of his house, leaving only Melissa and Julie alive to continue being tortured and raped repeatedly.

Dutroux was arrested and imprisoned for theft at the end of 1995. He told his wife to ensure his two little captives were kept alive during his sentence as he planned to use them as part of his welcome home celebrations. However, his wife claimed she was too scared to go near the girls and they starved to death in their dungeon.

On 4 November 1995, Dutroux drugged his friend Bernard Weinstein and buried him alive next to the bodies of An and Eefje after he botched an abduction of three more victims.

On 28 May 1996, Dutroux found his next victim, 13-year-old Sabine Dardenne, who was taken off the streets of Kain, Belgium by Dutroux and accomplice Michel Lelievre. The young girl documented her captivity and her rape and torture, using little symbols in her schoolbooks to note down what brutality her captor inflicted upon her. With Sabine already held captive, Dutroux and Michelle decided to abduct another girl in the last week of July 1996. Sixteen-year-old Yancka was grabbed by the couple on 22 July 1996 and raped. Yancka's sister had also been an assault victim of Dutroux's two years earlier. Yancka escaped from the violent killer on 1 August.[13] No investigation was ever made of her complaint.

Dutroux decided to abduct another little girl. On 9 August 1996, Dutroux, Michelle and Michel Nihoul abducted Laetitia Delhez. Several people witnessed the abduction and a police investigation was mobilised quickly. A man recalled the numberplate of the white van, giving police their best lead, and it led them straight to Marc Dutroux. On 13 August 1996, Dutroux and Michel Nihoul were arrested for the abduction of Laetitia Delhez.[14] Both men denied any knowledge of the girl's whereabouts. However, after two days of questioning, Dutroux finally revealed the hidden location of Laetitia's prison cell. He also confessed to holding Sabine Dardenne in the dungeons as well.

Later, Dutroux also led police to the graves of four of his victims, as well as that of accomplice Bernard Weinstein. Police also confiscated hundreds of video-tapes that showed the killer sexually abusing and torturing his victims.[15]

At his trial Dutroux admitted to the charges of kidnap and rape but said he was not responsible for the deaths of the two 8-year-old girls nor the two women who were found in the gardens of his home.

In the final stage of the explosive trial, Dutroux made a final impassioned speech. He said that he felt sincere regret for what had happened, yet his part was only a small element of a larger organised paedophile ring. In a hushed courtroom Dutroux continued, 'I am not a murderer … I am not asking for forgiveness. I can't do much to change the irreversible'.[16]

In June 2004, after almost a decade, millions of Belgians watched, on live television, the sentencing of Marc Dutroux. He was found guilty of the abduction and rape of six of his victims in 1995 and 1996, as well as the murders of An and Eefje and Bernard Weinstein. He was also found guilty of imprisoning and raping the two surviving girls. Dutroux was sentenced to life imprisonment without the possibility of parole. The judge called him a danger to society. Dutroux's wife, Michelle Martin was sentenced to thirty years imprisonment, Michel Lelievre received a 25-year sentence. Michel Nihoul was acquitted of all charges; he was however sentenced to five years for drug related charges.

Sergey Golovkin

'I had such a good feeling that I did something good. I had done my duty'

Sergey Golovkin was born on 26 November 1959 in Moscow. He was born with a defect of his spine and was often beaten by his alcoholic and abusive father. He was a sickly child who also suffered from a weak bladder. His afflictions also made him extremely shy and he stayed away from other children as he was terrified that he would be teased for having a weak bladder and always smelling like urine. He was often a victim of school-yard bullies who found the sickly boy an easy target. He preferred to spend his time alone and would torture small animals, skinning cats and pulling apart road kill. He claimed that being beaten up at school as a teenager was a trigger for the murders.

He left school and after graduating from an agricultural school he took a job as a livestock expert and horse breeder. He was also a pederast and serial killer who preyed on young boys between 1986 and 1992. His victims were mostly boys aged ten to twelve. Golovkin terrorised Moscow for six years, killing eleven known victims and many more unknown victims.

After he attempted to rape and kill older victims in the early 1980s, Golovkin killed his first victim in April 1986. Sixteen-year-old Andrei Pavlov was strangled and raped after he was abducted from Savelovsky train station in Moscow. A second boy, 14-year-old Andrei Gulyaev was abducted and raped only a few months later in July 1986. The boy had been disembowelled and his head cut from his body. There were at least fifty-three stab wounds to the boy's body when it was later found. In 1989 another boy was abducted and raped. Again, his body was dumped in woods on the outskirts of the town where Golovkin lived.

Between 1990 and 1992 Golovkin purchased a garage that he converted into a torture chamber where he murdered eight more victims after raping and torturing them. Golovkin would rape and sodomise the boys for days while he mutilated them, cutting their genitals, torso and throats.

Finally, in October 1992, Golovkin was arrested when police discovered that he owned a garage near the locations where the boys disappeared. The man, dubbed 'The Fisher' because of a tattoo on his hand, confessed to the killings, even though police had all the evidence they needed in the man's torture chamber to convict him. In his confessions he did complain that he did not get the full experience of empowerment over his victims. The ultimate pleasure of consuming the flesh of his victims eluded him. He claimed that though he had tried it, he did not like the taste of human flesh.[17] Nonetheless he was not apologetic for the crimes, stating, 'I had such a good feeling that I did something good. I had done my duty'.[18]

The man was found guilty of eleven murders. Golovkin's execution was carried out on 2 August 1996. His death was by a single gunshot wound to the back of the head. His death was the last execution in Russia before the abolition of the death penalty.[19]

Michael Laurance

'It gave me a thrill watching them die. I got an erection watching them drown in the bath tub'

On 29 September 1984, friends, 12-year-old Mark Mott and 11-year-old Ralph Burns disappeared while walking home from the Griffith Show in country Australia. The two boys found themselves in the hands of paedophile 35-year-old Michael George Laurance. Laurance had seen the boys walking past his home and seized the opportunity. Once Laurance had enticed the boys inside his house, things turned sinister. Laurance forced the Mark and Ralph to strip down to their underwear and then put each boy in a different room. Laurance then moved from room to room and sodomised each boy, ignoring their crying pleas to be released. For two days, the boys were subjected to repeated attacks. The frightened boys were forced to perform oral sex on their captor and made to perform other acts on each other to suit their captor's pleasure before Laurance murdered them by drowning them in the bathtub.[20] The body of Ralph was then burned and buried in Laurance's back yard until he later dug it up and dumped it under a wild cactus bush near Lake Wyangan.[21] Laurance kept Mark's body for another week and subjected the corpse to further abuse before he dumped the dead body in Lake Wyangan, just a few meters from Ralph. The bodies remained hidden for nearly twelve months.

On 21 June 1986, 8-year-old John Purtell retired to the showers to change out of his football gear. Laurance was also at the toilet block. Laurance offered to take him to a nearby takeaway shop to buy him a burger.[22] The man left with the small child, which was witnessed by two of John's football teammates. Once at his home, Laurance told the boy to come inside where they would play a game of 'tie-ups'. John had his clothes removed and then had his hands and feet taped together. Laurance raped the boy several times.

Laurance then put the boy back in the car and drove to a secluded area at Darling Point where he raped the boy again. When John tried to struggle against his binds, screaming in fear and agony, Laurance put a large piece of tape over the boy's nose and mouth and the boy suffocated.[23] Laurance hid the boy's body under a fallen log. By that time, police had been called in and a massive search was already underway. The two boys who had seen Laurance with John gave police a precise description of the man. An identikit picture of the suspect was released to the public. It gained a massive response and many people identified Michael Laurance as the boy's abductor.

On 2 September 1986, police arrived on the doorstep of Michael George Laurance to question him about the disappearance of John Purtell. The man denied any knowledge of the boy and police soon left. The following morning, Laurance attempted suicide. After he was released from hospital, Laurance was taken back to the police station where he confessed to the murders of all three boys. He told police, 'Poor little Burnsie and Mottie, I killed them too'.[24] He also told police where they could find John's body. He also confessed to playing with hundreds more boys over an 18-year period.[25] The man began to discuss his life as a predator in detail, telling police everything they wanted to hear and more. When asked why he murdered the boys, he claimed 'It gave me a thrill watching them die. I got an erection watching them drown in the bath tub'.[26] The answer sent shockwaves through the community when it was released to the press that they had caught the serial predator and killer. The public called for the man's blood. People wanted to see Laurance dead.

Laurance stood trial on 21 September 1987. He pleaded not guilty by reason of insanity for the murders of all three boys. He claimed that he had been raped by a police officer as a boy and was a male prostitute by the age of thirteen and it had turned him towards a life as a pederast and killer.[27] Nevertheless the killer was found guilty of the murders of Mark, Ralph and John and sentenced to life imprisonment. The sentencing judge recommended that Laurance should never be released. On 17 November 1995, Laurance finally succeeded in taking his own life by hanging himself after two failed attempts.

Michael Lockhart

'My first thought was this is a perfect day to die ... and if I was going to die then I was going to kill somebody too'

Michael Lee Lockhart murdered two girls in 1987 before gunning down police officer Paul Hulsey Junior who was attempting to arrest the killer in Beaumont, Texas in March 1988.

According to the police profile given at trial, Lockhart was a dreamer, who hoped to one day become a police officer.[28] He told his mother-in-law of his plans to be wealthy and provide his wife-to-be with a lovely home and new car. Yet his delusions of grandeur were far removed from reality. He was an unemployed transient who travelled through state after state using many aliases. He could turn on the charm to match his good looks to get him what he wanted.[29] His family described him as flighty; he rarely finished a task nor completed any job he had started. [30]

Lockhart's first victim was 16-year-old Windy Gallagher.[31] Lockhart broke into the Gallagher home having pulled up outside in a stolen red Corvette.[32] Once inside he tied the girl's hands behind her back, tore the clothes from her lower body and brutally raped her. She was then stabbed 21 times in the neck and body. The killer then pulled her intestines out of the wounds in her stomach. He left her on her bed where her younger brother found her[33] in her home in Griffith, Indiana in October 1987.

Three months later, 14-year-old Jennifer Colhouer was raped before being stabbed by her killer. Lockhart had left the teenager bleeding to death in her home in Land O'lakes in Florida in January 1988.

Two months later, police officer Paul Hulsey attempted to arrest the man in Beaumont, Texas, for speeding in a stolen car when Lockhart gunned him down. The killer claimed that he was feeling suicidal that day and the officer was in the wrong place at the wrong time. 'My first thought was this is a perfect day to die ... and if I was going to die then I was going to kill somebody too'.[34] The killer was quickly apprehended by other officers and told police that he would have continued on a countrywide killing spree if he had not been caught. While in custody Lockhart confessed to twenty-nine murders, including the murders of several children in 1987 and 1988 before recanting the statement.[35] At his trial Lockhart was found guilty of the murder of Paul Hulsey and sentenced to death.

On 10 December 1997, Michael Lockhart was executed in Texas for the death of officer Hulsey. He was also found guilty of the two murders in Florida and sentenced to two further death sentences. As Lockhart was executed, the crowd of police officers outside the prison applauded. Jennifer Colhouer's younger brother Jeremy, who had found her body, graduated from the police academy in 1998 and became a County Sheriff Deputy.[36]

Gordon and Sarah Northcott

'If you ever get any of my family members to talk, you will hear one of the most weird tales you even listened to'

Gordon Northcott was born on 9 November 1906 in Bladworth Saskatchewan. He was one of two children born to Sarah and Cyrus Northcott. His family moved to Los Angeles in 1924 and they purchased the farm for their son where the murders would occur. Northcott raised chickens and with the help of his young nephew, turned a profitable farm. However he soon turned to more brutal pursuits. Over two years, Northcott abducted several boys and took them to the farm where he would rape and abuse them before letting them go again.

The first murder victim was a Mexican boy, Alvin Gothea.[37] Northcott had picked up the boy and taken him back to the farm. After raping him, he murdered him. He then decapitated the victim and burned his head in the farm's fire. He then had his nephew, Sanford Clark, crush the skull into small fragments. The bone pieces were then buried near one of the fence posts that dotted the perimeter of the farm. The rest of the body was dumped on the side of the road.

The second victim was 9-year-old Walter Collins. The boy was abducted by Northcott on 10 March 1928 and raped several times. Between assaults the boy was hidden in the chicken coop. When Northcott's mother arrived at the farm she was suspicious of her son's behaviour and found the boy hiding in the chicken pen. Sarah Northcott knew the boy and decided that the three of them, Gordon, Sanford and her, would need to kill the boy. All three of them—so that they were all guilty—struck the sleeping boy with the blunt edge of the axe. The boy's body was then cut up and buried near the chicken yards.

The next victims were brothers, 12-year-old Lewis and 10-year-old Nelson Winslow. The victims were sexually assaulted prior to their axe deaths. Their bodies were interred next to that of Walter Collins. He also claimed to have murdered a boy called Richard and another whose name he did not know.[38]

In 1926 the 19-year-old killer travelled to California with his 13-year-old Canadian nephew, Sanford. Once Northcott had his nephew away from the farm, he added the boy to his list of victims. Northcott proceeded to abuse and rape the young boy repeatedly. For Sanford the repeated attacks were the final straw. The boy had witnessed horrific things at the farm and once the pair had returned to Wineville the boy told his older sister, who had come to visit, everything he had witnessed.

After leaving the farm and returning to Canada, Sanford's sister called police to tell them her brother's story. Police handed the case over to the immigration officials, believing that Sanford, a Canadian, was in the country illegally. The case stalled for two years until, on 31 August 1928 immigration services arrived to arrest the now 15-year-old boy. Upon seeing the officials, Northcott demanded that the boy stall them while he made his escape along with his mother, Sarah. After two hours in custody, Sanford told them about Northcott and what had occurred on the farm. Sanford showed the authorities where to find the bodies and within moments the first body was found.

Gordon and Sarah Northcott were arrested in September 1928 in Canada. During their wait for extradition to Los Angeles, Sarah Northcott confessed to the murders of the three boys, while Gordon confessed to five deaths, claiming that he was in fact innocent but he had tried to shield his 'poor little mother' from the horrible things that people were saying about him.[39] His father claimed, 'there is something wrong with that boy mentally',[40] and he refused to help his son in fighting against the charges.

Northcott was eventually charged with 11 murders and confessed to nine victims.[41] He took police on a journey across the Mojave Desert to look for several of his victims. On the trip, he told police, 'if you ever get any of my family members to talk, you will hear one of the most weird tales you even listened to'.[42]

Back in America, Sarah again confessed to the crimes and was given a life sentence. She tried to sway the court in her son's defence stating that he was innocent of the crimes and that he had had a tough upbringing that had contributed to what they had done.

Gordon Northcott was sent to trial and found guilty of the murders of the Winslow brothers and the unidentified Mexican child. He was sentenced to death and was executed on 2 October 1930. Northcott began his last day on earth screaming. He was terrified of the hangman's noose and kept asking if it will hurt. He had to be dragged up the stairs to the gallows. His last words were 'A prayer … please, say a prayer for me' as the trapdoor opened.

Sarah Northcott was released twelve years into her life sentence. She died in 1994. Sanford Clark was declared innocent of the crimes. He was enrolled in a program at Whittier Boy's School where he graduated and went on to live a productive and good life. He died in 1991.

Colin Pitchfork

'She was there and I was there'

The husband of a social worker, Colin Pitchfork attempted to understand some of the mania that compelled him to rape and murder two teenage girls but it did little to comfort him with his compulsions to expose himself and rape young girls.

Colin Pitchfork was the second of three children born to parents that had little time for their middle child. He grew up in the village of Newbold Verdon in Leicestershire, England and felt devoid of parental affection and love for most of his childhood. His parents preferred to give their attentions to his older sister and young brother, leaving Pitchfork resentful.

He attended the local schools where he achieved average results. He was bullied in his mid-schooling years for his early onset of puberty.[43] Leaving school at the age of sixteen he gained an apprenticeship as a baker at Hampshire in Leicester, where he remained employed until his arrest at the age of twenty-three.

During his teenage years, the first signs of Pitchfork's sexual perversions were noticed; he liked to expose himself to fellow students. By seventeen he had exposed himself several times to teenage girls.

In February 1979, at the age of nineteen he crept up behind a 16-year-old girl and forced her into a nearby field where he 'undid her clothing and put his hand down the front of her jeans'.[44] He fled quickly when he thought he had heard someone coming, leaving the girl to flee home where police were called. Pitchfork was arrested for the attack but was not punished. Instead he was scheduled to attend Woodlands outpatient treatment program to help him deal with his 'illness', the lack of deterrent was enough to encourage him to continue to expose himself to young girls until the moment that the flashing turned to murder.

Two years after his arrest for flashing he married Carole and by 1983 the couple had their first son. Babysitting his young son on the evening of 21 November 1983 while his wife Carole attended a course, Colin Pitchfork decided to go for a drive to help put the baby to sleep. While travelling through Narborough the man spotted 15-year-old Lynda Mann walking along the Black Pad footpath traversing the short distance between the homes of two friends. Black Pad path was a tree-lined back lane that locals used often, but it was by fluke that other locals were not walking their dog or using the laneway the evening that Pitchfork struck.

Pitchfork drove past the girl and parked his car near the footpath where Lynda was heading a little after 7.15 p.m. He left his baby sleeping in the back seat and headed out into the evening. Pitchfork would later assert that the attack and murder was an opportunistic crime. He saw her and wanted her. In the dark he doubled back towards the unsuspecting teenager and from a distance asked her for directions, pretending to be lost. Obligingly she tried to explain to him how to get back to the main road. As she got closer to him Pitchfork exposed his genitals, causing the girl in shock to scream and run away. In her panicked state she ran towards an open field rather than towards nearby houses. Pitchfork grabbed her as she tried to flee. He dragged Lynda towards the vacant block of land and away from the well-traversed footpath and stripped off her clothing from the waist down.[45] He then raped her as she struggled against him. She tried to fight him off, even telling him that she had noticed his wedding ring and asked him how his wife would feel knowing that she was married to a rapist. In his later confession Pitchfork explained what happened: 'She turned and ran into the dark footpath. She backed herself into a corner. Her two big mistakes where running into the footpath and saying "What about your wife?" She'd seen my wedding ring'.[46] He tried to explain himself to her before realising he had told her a lot about himself as he raped her that could prove helpful in identifying him later. He would later admit during his police interview that Lynda had been terrified of him as he stripped her clothes from her body. She had done most of the undressing herself as she was too terrified to try to fight him as he menaced her. He then strangled her with her own scarf as he continued to rape her.

The following morning Lynda's body was found, but police had little to go on as the hours turned into weeks and then months without an arrest. To assist with attempting to catch Lynda's killer a profile was created by criminal psychologist Paul Britton.[47] Britton claimed that the killer was a local man, having known the terrain of the Black Pad path. He was in a stable heterosexual long-term relationship but driven by a sexual fantasy cycle that saw him target younger girls. The profile was partially accurate, Pitchfork was not a local, but what police did not know was that the man had been to Littlethorpe many times as he and his social worker wife were looking to move to the little borough. Pitchfork was also a local baker and had made birthday and celebratory cakes as a side business for many of the town's people.

A month after the murder, Pitchfork, his wife and baby moved to nearby Littlethorpe, a town that was within the constabulary's net. In a door-to-door investigation, police arrived at the Pitchforks' home and while police officers waited in the man's living room, the killer took his time in the attic to calm himself before facing the officers. Pitchfork was one of many people interviewed following the murder but though he did not have an alibi, he was not suspected as the teenager's killer. Police assumed that a man that was home alone with his baby would not have ventured far, and certainly would not leave his baby son to rape and murder a teenage girl.

As time passed, Pitchfork realised that he had gotten away with the murder and again commenced exposing himself to teenagers without being caught. In October 1985 he sexually assaulted a teenage girl whom he threatened with a screwdriver, telling her he would hunt her down if she reported the assault. He had grabbed her from behind and pulled her into a dark corner near a row of lock-up garages. He was arrested for indecent exposure and avoided incarceration, instead being given a probationary term.

Shortly after his non-custodial sentencing, his wife gave birth to their second son in January 1986. With two small children to dote on—a life that he himself had been denied as a child—he momentarily lost his drive to expose himself. That feeling would last only a few months.

Pitchfork struck again on 31 July 1986. This time he was careless. He attacked his next teenage victim in broad daylight. Dawn Ashworth has collected her wages from her newsagency job and made plans with a girlfriend to go out that evening. However, when she arrived home, Dawn's parents asked her to babysit her younger sibling for the evening. Dawn obliged, letting her mother know that she would walk to her friend's home to cancel their plans. Heading home after being unable to find her girlfriend, Dawn took the short-cut that would have sliced a significant distance from her trip. It was a trip that her father had begged her not to make, particularly after the murder only two years earlier of Lynda Mann.

Like he had done to Lynda, Pitchfork spotted the girl as she walked along the Black Pad pathway. Pitchfork stopped his car nearby and got out. He doubled back to where he knew the teenager would cross his path. Once she was near him, he exposed himself to the teenager before dragging her into the scrub to rape and strangle her. She had tried to fight him off and she had been punched several times in the face to subdue her during the attack. In what was described in court as a 'brutal sexual attack',[48] Pitchfork had left significant bruises over the girl's body where he had grabbed her violently. Her perineum and anus were torn during the attack and he strangled her while he raped her before covering her dead body with fallen foliage. Her body was found where he had left it, two days later.

With no leads after weeks of investigation, police turned to a new technique of DNA testing. A first in Britain, more than five thousand men were DNA tested in the hopes that they would find a match to the semen found at both murders. While the laboratories worked tirelessly to run every DNA sample that came in, police arrested a possible suspect. A teenager confessed to the murder of Dawn Ashworth but was quickly discredited when his DNA sample did not match that found at the two crime scenes.

As weeks and months passed, police were no closer to catching Pitchfork and he was able to attack another girl in June 1987. Fortunately for her, she was able to escape from her attacker.

By August 1987, as a majority of men had had their blood samples done, Pitchfork began to falter, as several letters arrived requesting that he visit his local police station to give a blood sample. He convinced a friend to go in his place and give the sample. Pitchfork told his friend that he had given a sample himself for another friend who was in a bind, and if he gave blood he would be arrested for another crime. Obligingly, the friend believed the cunning man's story and took the test in his place. Pitchfork believed that his plan was faultless. He had convinced a naive friend of his innocence.

While having drinks with other co-workers from the bakery, the friend boasted how he had taken the sample for Pitchfork. One of the co-workers, who always believed that Pitchfork was a little strange and overly sexual in the workplace, called police. Police were quick to check the man's background and found that he had been arrested several times for indecent exposure.

On 19 August 1987, police waited for Pitchfork to arrive home from work. He was arrested and submitted a blood sample that proved that he was the killer of both Lynda and Dawn. When asked by his wife, why he had attacked the girls, his answer was honest and brutal. 'Opportunity. She was there and I was there'.[49] Paul Britton, in his book *The Jigsaw Man*, would describe the interview and confession by Pitchfork as 'cold."[50]

Pitchfork pleaded guilty to both murders and was sentenced to two life sentences. He was also found guilty of the other rapes and assaults. The psychological report submitted at trial stated that Pitchfork was diagnosed with a 'personality disorder of psychopathic type accompanied by serious psychosexual pathology … [and that he] … will obviously continue to be an extremely dangerous individual while the psychopathology continues'.[51]

At sentencing, Justice Otten stated that 'the rapes and murders were of a particularly sadistic kind',[52] and recommended no minimum sentence for his crimes. There was no doubt that Colin Pitchfork would have continued to rape and murder had he remained out of prison. At his trial, he was declared dangerous and a threat to women. Even at his sentence re-determination in 2009, where a reduction of two years was made, the judge declared that the reduction did not mean that Pitchfork would be free. He was not to be released until it could be proven that he no longer posed a risk to society.

John Straffen

'What would you do if I killed you? I have done it before'

John Staffen was born in Hampshire, England on 27 February 1930. He was the youngest of three children born to an army officer and a housewife. The family moved often due to the nature of his father's career in the military and included six years in India during one overseas posting. While the family were in India, Straffen suffered a serious bout of encephalitis at the age of six that caused significant damage to his brain. The family returned to Bath in England two years later and the move seemed to unsettle the small child further; he commenced stealing and missed many days of school. A year after their return John Straffen, at the age of nine, found himself in court for stealing a girl's purse. He was given a two-year probationary sentence for the offence. He was also assessed by the court and found to be 'mentally defective'.[53] A year later, further tests were conducted and Straffen was noted to have an IQ of 58. Though he was ten he had the mental age of a six year old. He was sent to a special school, St Joseph's, Sambourne. He had by now attended at least four schools, with many more to come. After being moved on again to Besford Court School he was suspected of strangling two geese at the school. However he was never charged with the killings. By the age of sixteen his IQ was 64, putting him at the developmental level of a nine year old. He left the court school and returned to the family home in Bath, but remained under a mental deficiency Act requiring regular monitoring and management.

At seventeen he started working as a machinist and also began burglarising local homes. At one home, he attacked a 13-year-old girl. He stifled her cries with his hand before asking her, 'What would you do if I killed you? I have done it before'.[54] The girl managed to escape and report the attack to police. However it would be years before police realised that Straffen was the culprit.

Straffen again killed livestock in 1947. After having a fight with a neighbourhood girl, he strangled the family's five chickens. He was arrested for the killings and sentenced to Hortham Colony after being certified as feeble minded.

After two years in custody he was released for good behaviour to a low-security halfway house. However, after being caught stealing a bag of walnuts he was returned to Hortham. Further tests of the man's mental capacity showed that he had serious brain injuries and had the mental capacity of a ten year old. He was released again in 1951 into the care of his mother.

On 15 July 1951, 5-year-old Brenda Goddard was picking wildflowers in Bath when Straffen tried to strike up a conversation with her.[55] When the girl ignored his questions, he tried another tact and accused her of stealing the flowers. He then told her that it would be okay if she picked flowers on the other side of the nearby fence. He then helped her over the wall. Straffen claimed that when he had helped her over the wall, she had fallen and hit her head. He had then panicked and strangled her.[56] He left her body and went to the movies where he claimed to have not felt anything for the dead girl.[57] Police were quick to believe that Straffen, who had been seen with the child, was responsible for the child's death. He was arrested and questioned, but released when police did not have enough evidence to charge him with the crime.

On 8 August, in what Straffen called revenge for being arrested for Brenda's murder, he killed again. He again had been at the movies when he spotted 9-year-old Cecily Batstone. He convinced the little girl to watch a film with him before taking her to pick flowers in a nearby field. The pair were seen several times by witnesses as they travelled to a field on the outskirts of Bath. Once he had the girl alone he strangled her to death. Police again arrested the man after witnesses had come forward following the search for the missing girl.

Once in police custody, Straffen confessed to both murders, saying, 'the other girl, I did her the same'.[58] The killer was charged and sent to trial for the two murders, however experts examined the young man and testified that he was mentally unfit for trial and was instead declared insane and sent to Broadmoor.

Six months into his custodial sentence Straffen escaped and grabbed another child. Police were quick on his trail but were too late to save 5-year-old Linda Bowyer from being strangled. The girl's body was found in Berkshire soon after she had been killed. Straffen was found two miles away with another little girl in his company.

Once in custody, Straffen was asked why he had escaped from Broadmoor, to which he replied, 'to prove I could be out without killing any children'.[59] For the third murder he was found competent to stand trial and his motives were again addressed. 'He wanted to annoy the police because he hated them because they shadowed him and followed him about and had been doing so since he left the mental defectives'.[60]

Straffen was found guilty of Linda's murder and sentenced to death. His execution was set for 4 September 1952 after his various appeals were denied.[61] Six days before his execution he was given a reprieve by the home secretary when concerns were raised about the man's mental capacity. His sentence was subsequently commuted to life. Since 1952 there have been numerous attempts to have the case reheard regarding concerns about the man's mental acuity. Yet the case had been repeatedly denied. He was recommended for parole in 2002 however the Home Secretary refused his release. The killer died on 19 November 2007 of natural causes following an illness. He had served fifty-five years in prison.

Huang Yong

'I've always wanted to be an assassin since I was a kid but I never had the chance'

In a scene reminiscent of the Gacy home in 1978 Chicago, the bodies of seventeen boys were found beneath the house of 29-year-old Huang Yong in Henan, China in December 2003. Between September 2001 and his arrest, Yong lured boys away from various Internet cafes in the province and took them home.

Once Yong had the boys in his home, he would tie them to a machine that was designed to make noodles and then suffocated them. He buried the bodies under his house and in his garden. He kept the belts of his victims as trophies.[62]

The killer was arrested on 22 November 2003 after his eighteenth victim escaped and went to police. Once in custody Yong told police that he had committed the crimes to feel the thrill of being a killer. He claimed that he had 'always wanted to be an assassin'.[63]

The killer was found guilty of the seventeen murders on 9 December 2003. On 26 December 2003 the killer was executed by a single gunshot.

Child killers are people who haunt our nightmares. Parents hug their children closer to them whenever a story hits the headlines of a child who has been abducted and murdered. If there were indeed a list of the worst categories of serial killer, the child sexual predator would be at the top of the list. As shown in this chapter, the child killer often grabs vulnerable children; sometimes the child goes willingly with their killer, or sometimes they are violently snatched. The child killer preys on children for sexual gratification, with the assault the primary crime for the killer. The murder is used to conceal the paedophile's crimes and to prevent their detection. Many child sexual predators are caught after they allow a victim to escape. Their crimes are usually crimes of opportunity rather than organised, planned attacks.

The child killers in this section were mostly not known to their victims; their crimes were what is commonly referred to as 'stranger abductions' that often proved hard to unravel until it was too late for the victims.

The next chapter, that of the 'known stranger', gives rise to a whole new type of child sexual predator. The known stranger are those killers who are known to their victims, albeit loosely, are often active in their community and are generally the last person people would expect to be horrific sexual predators.

THE KNOWN STRANGER

When a mass killer is discovered, those who knew them often show confusion and horror. There is an attempt to try and find those hints at the true horror of what the known person was capable of. The killers in this chapter were well known in their community. Some, like Dean Corll had innocuous nicknames like 'The Candyman'. They were known and often loved in their community as someone who showed leadership. John Gacy was a member of many community groups and even entertained sick children in the local hospitals dressed as a clown. These killers, often murderers of children, are what can be referred to as 'Known Strangers'. They are known to some of their victims; they are unlikely to commit high-risk abductions. They are more likely to befriend their victims and/ or their victim's families. They use their community standing or ability to gain trust to get their victims into a vulnerable position. These 'known strangers' are able to kill a high number of victims as they are unlikely suspects.

Dean Corll

'I was tired of him doing things like that. And it was either me or him right then'

Dean Arnold Corll was born in Waynesdale, Indiana on Christmas Day, 25 December 1939 to an over-affectionate mother, Mary and a father, Arnold, who did not like children. Early family life was not happy for Dean and his brother Stanley, with their parents constantly arguing. Arnold and Mary eventually divorced in 1946. Around 1950, Dean was diagnosed with a congenital heart ailment after a bout of rheumatic fever and was told that he should avoid sports wherever possible. Dean, not being a sporting type, found this good news. At school he preferred music and was a keen trombone player. Teachers remembered him as a quiet and polite student.

After a suggestion from a candy sales representative, Mary Corll set herself up with a little candy shop to help support the family. Dean was a runner for the candy shop that had its humble beginnings in the garage of the family home. Dean often found himself exhausted from running orders to people in town, but never complained.

After high-school graduation, Corll got a job with the Houston Lighting and Power Company during the day and still helped make candies with the family at night.

In 1964, Dean was drafted into the US Army. Life in the army caused a change in the young man. Dean found himself desiring the fellow officers with whom he shared his quarters and soon realised he was gay. Until then Dean had known something about his life felt wrong but until his realisation about his homosexuality, he had been unsure what had been missing.

Returning home after eleven months in the army, Dean found himself an apartment near his now twice divorced mother and started hanging out with teenage boys from the neighbourhood. One day in 1969, Dean learned that some of these boys would give oral sex in exchange for money. This is how Corll met 14-year-old David Brooks.

Brooks enjoyed the older man's company and looked up to him as a big brother—someone to ask for guidance. Soon David became completely emotionally dependent on Corll and spent most of his time with him rather than at home.

When he turned thirty Corll became depressed and soon started harassing Brooks for oral sex. The relationship changed and Brooks, still eager to be in the man's company, obliged. Corll remained morose, unsure why he still had a yearning in his life that was unfulfilled by the young man's sexual acts. Soon the depressive change in Corll turned deadly when he started to pick up more and more hitchhikers, from whom he demanded sex.

University of Texas student, Jeffrey Konen, left campus to hitchhike home to Houston on 25 September 1970. He was picked up by Corll, who took him to his apartment where he was bound by his hands and feet and gagged. Corll sodomised the student before killing him and dumping his body.

A second unnamed victim accepted an offer to smoke marijuana at Corll's apartment. When the man, along with Brooks, arrived at the unit, Corll tied the boy to his torture rack in his bedroom and sodomised him. Corll then strangled the boy while Brooks watched.

On 15 December, 15-year-old Danny Yates and 14-year-old James Glass were quickly tied to Corll's torture rack and sodomised. Danny and James were then strangled. On 27 January 1971, Dean Corll decided he needed to commit another double murder to satiate his appetite. Brothers, 13-year-old Jerry and 14-year-old Donald Waldrop, were taken back to Corll's apartment where they were raped and strangled.

On 29 May 1971, 13-year-old David Hilligiest and 16-year-old George Winkle accepted a lift from Corll. They were last seen climbing into Corll's white van. At Corll's apartment the two boys were tied to the bed before being sodomised, tortured and strangled. They were then buried with the others at the boat shed storage container that Corll had rented for the specific purpose of burying bodies in the shed's soft dirt floor.

Seventeen-year-old Ruben Watson was last seen on his way to the cinema on 17 August 1971. Brooks and Corll picked him up along the way and took him back to Corll's apartment where he was brutalised for hours until Corll grew bored of his victim and killed him. The next victim that Brooks bought to the house was Elmer 'Wayne' Henley.

The first time Corll met Henley, it was as a potential victim, but Corll saw him as a better procurer than Brooks had been. He therefore arranged a test for the new young man. Henley was asked to knock Brooks unconscious, which he did without hesitation. When Brooks woke, he found himself tied to Corll's bed and bleeding. Corll had sodomised him while he was unconscious. Brooks did not tell anyone about the incident until after Corll's death and remained in the man's servitude as a procurer.

Another victim was abducted on 24 February 1972. Frank Aguirre was a little older than most of Corll's victims, being nineteen when he disappeared. He had a girlfriend at the time, 14-year-old Rhonda Williams, who would later return to Corll's home. Frank's body was found with his entire head wrapped in duct tape and a noose around his neck.[64]

On 21 May 1972, Dean grabbed another two victims. Sixteen-year-old Johnny Delome and 17-year-old Billy Baulch were taken to the apartment where they were tortured and raped for hours before being killed. Like Frank, they also had duct tape placed over their eyes and mouth. Inside Johnny's mouth was a gag; his arms had been tied together and a single gunshot wound to his forehead had killed him.[65]

On 3 October 1972, Corll again chose a double murder. The victims were 13-year-old Richard Hembree and 14-year-old Wally Simoneux. The teens were taken back to Corll's apartment on the premise of a party. The boys sniffed paint fumes and other substances that rendered them unconscious. Once the boys were unconscious, Corll took them to his room and strapped them to his torture rack, a board that was later described as eight feet long and three feet wide.[66] The victims were repeatedly raped.

According to Brooks, the boys, like the others, were kept alive for days of torture. Most of the victims were procured in the same way. Brooks or Henley would lure victims to Dean's house with the promise of an 'alcohol party'. The victims would then be allowed to drink, smoke or sniff themselves unconscious. Dean would then tie them up and molest them. Once Corll was done with his victims they were strangled and dumped.

During November 1972, fifteen-year-old Michael Baulch, the younger brother of previous victim Billy Baulch, became the next victim. The boy was subjected to days of torture, including having his pubic hairs pulled out one by one, Corll brutalised the boy with foreign objects and glass rods were shoved into his penis. Finally he was murdered and buried in the boat shed.

On 11 June 1973, 15-year-old Billy Lawrence was taken to Corll's apartment for a party. Billy was kept alive and tortured for days. According to Henley, at his trial, 'Billy Lawrence was kept about three days because Dean Corll particularly liked him'.[67]

A month later, 15-year-old Homer Garcia joined the list of Corll's sexually tortured and murdered victims. On 27 July, less than three weeks after Homer's murder, 17-year-old Charles Cobble and 18-year-old Marty Jones were murdered after being tortured by Corll. A 9-year-old boy disappeared around the last day of July, followed by the murder of 13-year-old James Dreymala during the first week of August 1973. To ferry the bodies to the boat shed, Corll had made a 'body box' in which he hid the bodies during transport to prevent them being detected if they were pulled over by police.[68]

On the afternoon of 8 August 1973 Henley arrived at Corll's apartment with two victims. He had brought 16-year-old Timothy Kerley for Corll and Rhonda Williams—the girlfriend of one of Corll's previous victims for himself. When Corll saw Rhonda, a girl, with Henley he was furious, but kept his temper under control. He would punish Henley later.

After a glue-sniffing session, Henley, Timothy and Rhonda all passed out. Corll seized the opportunity to teach Henley a lesson for bringing a girl.

Corll tied all three of them up, when Henley woke and saw his predicament he begged Corll to let him live. He pleaded with Corll saying he would rape and kill Rhonda while Corll did the same to Timothy. Corll took Timothy to the bedroom and stripped him of his clothes, gagged him and tied him to the torture board. Corll then demanded that Henley do the same to Rhonda.

Henley grabbed Rhonda and took off her clothes as Corll looked on. However, Henley was unable to get an erection, which Corll found funny. The killer began calling Henley names and Henley was furious. He picked up Corll's .22 calibre pistol and aimed it at the killer. Corll laughed and egged on the young man, daring him to shoot him. He mocked him: 'Go on Wayne, kill me, why don't you?'[69] As Corll lunged towards Henley, the boy fired six bullets into Corll's chest, killing him instantly. Henley untied his friends and called the police. He told them he had shot Corll in self-defence. He told police, 'I was tired of him doing things like that. And it was either me or him right then'.[70] Henley told police that Corll's house contained a torture room that included a wooden board with handcuffs fitted at each top corner and rope knots at each bottom corner. He told them then about the victims. The young man's monotone story continued with details of Corll's parties, where the killer would tie the victims up and sodomise them on his torture board before murdering them.

Then Henley told the officers where they would find most of the victims. He took them to the Silver Bell Street boat shed rented by Corll in Houston. At the boat shed, police scientific officers began the dig. In no time, lime and the telltale smell of decay were uncovered. The first body was found. The naked body of the 13-year-old boy, James Dreymala was in a plastic bag. As each body was brought out Henley cried more. When police finished their search they found the bodies of seventeen boys under the floor of the boat shed, and ten others were found at various other sites. As the scene was later described, there were 'wall to wall bodies'.[71] David Brooks watched the news reports as the body count grew and decided it was time to talk to police. When he arrived at the police station, the officers interviewing Henley told him that Brooks had just arrived. Henley looked relieved and said, 'That's good, now I can tell you the whole story'. Henley admitted to murdering some of the victims himself, while Brooks claimed his involvement had been far less. He said he had helped with several murders but it was not until Henley joined the group that Corll lost complete control of the situation and the murders escalated.

'Most of the killings that occurred after Wayne came into the picture involved all three of us. Wayne seemed to enjoy causing pain'.[72] Both boys were charged with a variety of murders and sent to trial. Henley claimed, 'I killed several of them myself. With Dean's gun and helped him choke some others. Then we would take them and bury them in different places'.[73]

Brooks was tried and sentenced to life imprisonment for his involvement in at least six murders. Henley was tried for murder in July 1974. He was found guilty of the murders of six victims and sentenced to six 99-year terms of imprisonment. His killing of Dean Corll was declared to be a justifiable homicide. In December 1978, Henley's conviction was overturned on the grounds that the trial had suffered from pre-trial publicity. He was convicted a second time in June 1979 and remains in prison.

Albert Fish

'I do not think I am altogether right'

Albert Fish was born Hamilton Fish on 19 May 1870, in Washington, DC. His father was seventy-five when Albert was born and died when he was five. Fish, along with his eleven siblings, was placed in St John's Orphanage in Washington by his mother soon after his father's death. He blames his years at the orphanage for his later problems. 'We were unmercifully whipped. I saw boys doing many things they should not have done'.

Fish was never adopted from the orphanage and only left when he reached maturity, at which time he got an apartment and lived with his mother. In 1896 at the age of twenty-six, he married a young woman of nineteen and had six children in quick succession. When the youngest was three, his wife ran off with another man, leaving Fish to raise the children.

He 'married' again three more times, however the subsequent marriages where bigamous as he had not divorced his first wife.

In 1910, Fish attacked Thomas Bedden in Wilmington. He claimed the 14-year-old was 'witless'.[74] The teen was kept prisoner by Fish for almost a week, where he was beaten and raped. Fish fled the apartment leaving the boy tied up. He had no idea if the boy survived the attack.

He also claimed that sometime between 1915 and 1920 he had kept an African boy prisoner on a boat in the District of Columbia for more than two weeks as a sex slave. He fled again, leaving the boy trapped when he thought he heard another boat approaching.[75]

On 11 July 1924, 54-year-old Albert Fish murdered his first confirmed victim. 8-year-old Beatrice Kiel was playing in her yard as Fish came upon her, but her mother appeared and shooed the unkempt-looking man away. Three days after the altercation at the Kiel's homestead, Fish tried again and this time he succeeded in finding a victim,

On 14 July 1924, 8-year-old Francis McDonnell was playing on the front porch of his home on Staten Island when he was called inside. It was then that his family noticed he was missing. The 8-year-old's sexually brutalised and mutilated body was found in the woods near the Kiel's farm, haphazardly concealed under some wooded brush. The boy had been choked to death.[76]

On 11 February 1927, 4-year-old Billy Gaffney was playing in the hallway outside his apartment with his 3-year-old neighbour Billy Beaton when Fish abducted him. When Billy Beaton's father asked him where Billy Gaffney had gone, the young boy answered, 'The boogey man took him'. Billy was never seen alive again.

Another victim disappeared in 1927. 11-year-old Yetta Abramowitz was strangled and tortured in the Bronx area shortly after the murder of Billy Gaffney.

On 3 June 1928, as her older brothers prepared to go and work for Albert Fish, who, using an alias, had agreed to hire the boys, 10-year-old Grace Budd washed up and put on her Sunday best. The man had said he would take her to her niece's party before he took the older boys. After lunch Gracie quickly took the old man's hand and was led away with the promise of a birthday party. The killer took Grace to an abandoned two-story building called Wisteria Cottage. He stripped off his clothes and called her. When she saw the old man naked, she screamed and tried to escape. Fish grabbed the small girl by her throat and choked her to death. He then decapitated her and cut the body in two.

In November 1934, six years after the little girl's abduction, the case remained open and Delia Budd received a letter. Mrs Budd was completely illiterate but could read her own name on the front. The letter was abhorrent in its detail, describing Grace's death and how the killer had consumed her over more than a week.

The stationery used for the letter and the envelope gave the detective the break he had waited nearly seven years for and Fish was arrested on 13 December 1934.

At the police station Fish confessed. Fish told him that in the summer of 1928 he had been overcome by what he called his 'blood thirst'—his need to kill.

Albert Fish faced murder charges in Manhattan and Westchester County. First Westchester County indicted him on a charge of first-degree murder, while Manhattan was preparing an indictment for kidnapping.

The media went into a frenzy over the arrest of Fish for Grace Budd's murder. The press brought forward many new leads about other children and accounts of Albert Fish being seen with children. One lead proved extremely fruitful. The trolley-driver on the Brooklyn tram-line saw a picture of Fish in the newspaper and came forward to identify Fish as the nervous old man that he had seen on 11 February 1927, seven years earlier. The man was trying to quiet a little boy sitting with him on the trolley. The little boy, who didn't have a jacket or coat, was crying for his mother continuously and had to be dragged by the old man on and off the trolley. The little boy, as it turned out, was the kidnapped Billy Gaffney. Ultimately, Fish confessed to murdering and eating Billy Gaffney.

More cases came to light, including the 1932 murder of a 15-year-old girl named Mary O'Connor in Far Rockaway. The girl's mauled body was found in some woods close to a house that Fish had been painting. With all of those indictments in different counties, there was very little chance that Albert Fish was going to be acquitted. His only opportunity to beat the death penalty was to be declared insane.

Fish was ready for the doctors. Fish's attitude towards his situation was one of complete detachment. 'I have no particular desire to live. I have no particular desire to be killed. It is a matter of indifference to me. I do not think I am altogether right'. [77]

Dr Wertham considered Fish's unparalleled perversity unique in the annals of psychiatric and criminal literature. 'Sado-masochism directed against children, particularly boys, took the lead in his sexually regressive development'. [78]

Fish told him: 'I had a desire to inflict pain on others and to have others inflict pain on me. I always seemed to enjoy everything that hurt'. [79] Wertham, enthralled by his subject's sexual habits, wrote down explicitly what the man had done: 'Experiences with excreta of every imaginable kind were practiced by him, actively and passively. He took bits of cotton, saturated them with alcohol, inserted them into his rectum, and set fire to them. He also did that with his child victims'.

Fish confided in Dr Wertham a long history of preying on children— 'at least a hundred'. Fish would bribe them with money or candy. He usually chose African-American children because he believed that the police did not pay much attention when they were hurt or missing.

He never went back to the same neighbourhood twice. He said that he had lived in at least twenty-three states and he had killed at least one child in each state.

He had also had a compulsion to write obscene letters and did so frequently. According to Dr. Wertham, 'they were not the typical obscene letters based on fantasies and daydreams to supply a vicarious thrill, they were offers to practice his inclinations with the people he wrote his graphic suggestions to'. Initially, Dr Weitham had some concerns about whether Fish was lying to him, especially when he told the psychiatrist that he had been sticking needles into his body for years in the area between the rectum and the scrotum: 'He told of doing it to other people too, especially children. At first, he said, he had only stuck these needles in and pulled them out again. Then he had stuck others in so far that he was unable to get them out, and they stayed there'. The doctor had him X-rayed and sure enough, there were at least twenty-nine needles in his pelvic region. Some had begun to decay, proving they had been there for an extended period of time [80]

At about the age of fifty-five, Fish started to experience hallucinations and delusions. Fish's children had seen him 'hitting himself on his nude body with a nail-studded paddle until he was covered with blood. They also saw him stand alone on a hill with his hands raised, shouting: "I am Christ"'.[81] Dr Wertham believed that Fish was legally insane. He also believed that Fish had actually killed fifteen children and mutilated about a hundred others. 'That figure was verified many times to me by police officials in later years'. [82]

The trial for the murder of Grace Budd began on Monday, 11 March 1935, and lasted ten days. The jury took less than an hour to reach its verdict of guilty. The killer was sentenced to death by electric chair. Fish was executed on 16 January 1936 in Sing Sing Prison.

John Gacy

'I've been a bad boy. I killed thirty people, give or take a few'

John Wayne Gacy Jnr was born to John and Marion Gacy on 17 March 1942. He was the middle child of three siblings, having two sisters, one younger and one older. John Gacy Jnr was adored by his mother but was picked on by his father, who was not impressed by his effeminate son's character. The short, pudgy John was not good at sport—a fact that infuriated his macho, sports-crazy father and became a source of resentment between the two. At school, Gacy was an unexceptional child, doing the bare minimum to scrape through. When he was eleven years old, he fell off a set of swings hitting his head quite hard. After the incident he complained of headaches often and later had several blackout episodes that he blamed on the swing incident.

At the age of sixteen, after a severe fainting episode, he was diagnosed with a blood clot and he also told people that he suffered from a heart condition. Gacy would avoid strenuous activities and spent a great deal of his spare time stealing from local stores or homes. The young man was a compulsive liar and boaster, telling people bizarre tales in an attempt to gain their sympathy or to get something he was after. He left school without graduating and went to a local business college where he found his ability to spin strange stories useful and he succeeded in becoming a successful salesman and, later, a businessman.

Gacy left home after finishing his college certificate and headed to Las Vegas. He was hired as a funeral-home assistant for six months but failed to gain any other significant work. So he returned to the family home in Chicago. By the time he was a young adult, confused about his sexuality, he dated a string of young women before marrying Marilyn Myer in 1964. He got a job working for Marilyn's father at a local Kentucky Fried Chicken and joined the local chapter of the Jaycees.

While at work at the restaurant early in 1967, Gacy chained up one of his young male employees, Edward Lynch, and strangled him into unconsciousness before raping the boy. Edward was fired soon after the attack and went to police to tell them about Gacy. When Gacy was interviewed by police he told them that Edward had been making up the story out of revenge for being fired. The police believed Gacy's story and the matter was forgotten.

In August 1967, Gacy again attacked one of his employees. Fifteen-year-old Donald Vorhees was forced to perform fellatio on his boss after work one evening, but Gacy paid the young boy substantially to silence him before forcing the boy to fellate him several more times. By March 1968, Donald could no longer hide the sexual abuse he was suffering at the hands of Gacy and told his father about the attacks. The pair went to police. Gacy was arrested for the sexual assault of the teenager and was charged on 10 May 1968 with sodomy[83] and sentenced to prison. While in prison, Gacy's wife Marilyn divorced him and the couple never spoke again.

On his release, Gacy was again arrested after interfering with a young boy on 12 February 1971. He was charged with disorderly conduct, but when the boy refused to testify the charges were dropped.

On 1 January 1972, John Gacy killed for the first time. Gacy wanted to take his mother home around 12.30 a.m. on New Year's Day after a rowdy party. When Mrs Gacy refused, her son left alone. Gacy began prowling the street searching for anyone in the need of company. He eventually picked up a young man from the Greyhound Bus Station at Chicago's Civic Centre. According to Gacy, back at his home the boy attacked him with a knife and Gacy killed him in self-defence. He put the body down into the space under his house. A few days later he buried it there before covering the area with lime.

On 22 June, 1972 Gacy was arrested by police on charges relating to sexual misconduct against another boy, but again the charges were dropped and Gacy continued his sexual conquests. Gacy's second murder victim was 16-year-old John Butkovich. John told his father that he had been underpaid by two weeks by Gacy and was rather bitter with his employer. John's father told him to go and see Gacy and remind him that if he did not correct the pay that he would tell the taxation department about Gacy not paying correct taxes. So, on 31 July 1975, 'Little John' went to see Gacy and the two had an argument. Later that evening, as Gacy cruised the streets for a victim, he spotted John, who was inebriated, getting out of his car at the corner of Sheridan and Lawrence Streets in Chicago. John got into Gacy's car and returned home with him, leaving his car behind. Back at Gacy's house the pair drank alcohol and shared a joint. After showing the boy a magic trick where he was handcuffed, he sodomised the boy and forced him to fellate him. Then Gacy strangled him using a rope as a garrotte. According to Gacy, John had threatened to kill him if he released him from the handcuffs. In a bizarre stretch of the imagination, Gacy believed the killing was justifiable.[84] Once John was dead, Gacy dragged the body to the garage, before retiring for the few remaining hours of darkness. The next day Gacy spent his time digging a ditch in a corner of the garage floor. Once he had dug quite a large hole he dragged the rigid body of John Butkovich into it. There, 'Little John' Butkovich's body remained until after Gacy's arrest in December 1978.

On 6 April 1976, Gacy killed his third victim, Darrell Sampson. The young man had accompanied Gacy back to his home, possibly with the lure of a job and a bit of a party. Darrell was raped and abused before being strangled by Gacy.

On 14 May 1976, a little over five weeks after the murder of Darrell Sampson, Randall Reffett and Samuel Stapleton both disappeared. Randall was the first to disappear, with Gacy picking the boy up in broad daylight and taking him to his home, where he was subjected to acts of sexual abuse and violence. Fourteen-year-old Sam Stapleton was walking home from his sister's house at 11 p.m. that same night when he was also picked up. The boy had been only a block from his own house when Gacy pulled up beside him and offered him a lift. Gacy took the boy instead to his house where the teenager was strangled and raped. Both Randall and Sam were interred in the same grave under Gacy's house.

Gacy's next victim luckily survived being attacked by the killer. Sixteen-year-old Mike Rossi met John Gacy on 22 May 1976. The pair spent the night at Gacy's home, drinking and smoking drugs. The following day, Gacy threw Mike to the ground, sat on the boy's chest and forced his penis into the young man's mouth, demanding that Mike perform fellatio on him. For some reason, Gacy did not kill the boy. Mike never reported the attack to the police and continued to visit Gacy at his home. He was given a job by the killer and threatened with the sack if he ever told anyone about the attack. Later, Mike moved in with Gacy, and after the killer's arrest became a suspect in some of the killings.

Seventeen-year-old Michael Bonin told his mother he was going to help a friend with a painting job on 3 June 1976. The painting job was for Gacy, and after the young man had finished work for the day he went home with the older man for a few drinks. He was never seen alive again. Later, after the killer's arrest, several of Michael's personal items were found in Gacy's possession.

On 10 June 1976, teenager William 'Billy' Carroll Jnr was working part time as a prostitute when he was picked up by Gacy and taken to the killer's home. Once alone in the house, Gacy raped and tortured the boy before strangling him to death. Billy was then pushed down into the crawlspace under Gacy's house, where he joined the other six bodies in various stages of decomposition.

The eighth murder victim was 18-year-old Rick Johnson on 6 August 1976. His mother dropped him off at concert on the other side of Chicago that evening. He told her that he would find his own way home as several of his friends were going to be at the concert and he would catch a lift home with them. The killer saw Rick heading away from the concert alone and offered him a ride. As he had done so often before, Gacy took the boy home where he tied him up, raped him and killed him, burying him away from the others in the floor under the laundry.

Nineteen-year-old David Cram was luckier than most. He was able to escape from Gacy. The young man moved into Gacy's house in August 1976 after starting work at his construction company, PDM, the previous month. On 11 August 1976, after spending the day celebrating his birthday, David returned to Gacy's house where he was attacked. Gacy did not expect the young man to be strong, yet even with his arms cuffed behind his back David was able to overpower Gacy by shoulder-charging him and escaping. The would-be victim later committed suicide.[85]

On Saturday 11 December 1976, 17-year-old Gregory Godzik had been on a date with his girlfriend Judy. After dropping Judy home, Greg decided to visit his boss, John Gacy, at home. Gacy opened his front door and happily invited Greg inside. Gacy plied the young man with alcohol before deciding to show Greg the rope trick he used in his clown act at various hospitals. Gacy tied Greg's hands behind his back. Gacy then grabbed Greg around the throat and squeezed. He watched the boy pass out, helpless against Gacy and the ropes around his wrists. The killer then sexually abused Greg for hours before strangling him and reviving him, over and over again, before finally killing him. Greg's body was pushed down into the crawlspace.

Gacy murdered 19-year-old John Szyc on 20 January 1977. Gacy picked up the young man at Bughouse Nightclub. After having sex, Szyc was bound by Gacy and strangled.

It was less than two months after the murder of John Szyc that Gacy murdered again. Victim eleven was 20-year-old Jon Prestige. Jon Prestige had been feeling bored on the evening of 15 March 1977, and told his flatmate that he was going to head to the Bughouse, a place he had heard about from friends. This was the place where John Szyc also disappeared. Jon had been enjoying himself at the nearby nightclub when he accepted an offer from Gacy of a party at his house. Gacy offered the young man drugs and free alcohol to go with him. So Jon happily agreed and like many of the young men before him, did not leave Gacy's home alive. The young man's body was the first to be exhumed after Gacy's arrest during Christmas 1978.

The twelfth victim of John Gacy was 19-year-old Matthew Bowman. The young man had been dropped off by his mother at a Chicago railway station on 5 July 1977. Moments later, Gacy arrived and offered the young man a lift. Matthew got into Gacy's car and was driven back to Gacy's home. Once inside the house, Matthew was drugged, raped and sexually abused before being strangled to death and buried under the house with the others.

Robert Gilroy met Gacy a little over two months after the murder of Matthew Bowman. The eighteen year old had set off on 15 September

1977 to meet with friends for a horse-riding trip when he was picked up by Gacy. The young man died after hours of sexual torture.

On 25 September 1977, 19-year-old John Mowery became the fourteenth known victim. On the day of his murder John had gone to visit his mother. Gacy offered him a ride. Gacy drove the nineteen year old to his own house. Repeating his usual murderous routine, he tied the young man up and raped him before strangling him to death and putting the remains with the others in his crawlspace.

The next victim was 21-year-old Russell Nelson on 17 October 1977. The man had been out at a disco on the night of his murder when Gacy offered him a lift home. Once at the Gacy home, he too was murdered and buried in the crawlspace under the killer's home.

Robert Winch, a sixteen year old, had run away from Kalamazoo, Michigan and was picked up by Gacy on 11 November 1977 and taken back to the killer's house. Robert was systematically raped and strangled until he died. He was interred with the other bodies in the rapidly filling crawlspace of Gacy's home where he remained for thirteen months.

The killings were escalating and the next victim was murdered on 18 November 1977, only a week after Robert Winch. The seventeenth known victim of Gacy was 20-year-old Tommy Baling. Gacy offered him a ride. Tommy accepted the lift and ended up at Gacy's home. Tommy was subjected to various sex acts before being shown Gacy's rope trick, where he was strangled to death as he struggled against the loops around his wrists and throat. Like the others, Tommy was buried in the graveyard under Gacy's house.

The next to die was 19-year-old marine David Talsma on 9 December 1977. Gacy took the man home where he was raped and strangled and buried under the house with the others. By the end of

1977, as the victim tally continued to grow, Gacy was diagnosed with syphilis.

Around 30 December 1977 another victim escaped with his life. Nineteen-year-old Robert Donnell was picked by Gacy. According to Gacy, he propositioned the young man, offering money to accompany him home. Robert agreed and Gacy drove to his house. Until morning, Gacy raped and sodomised Robert using dildos. Gacy also tied up Robert and whipped him with chains. Gacy pushed the man's head into the water-filled bath and held his head under until Robert stopped fighting and loss consciousness. Gacy then revived the victim and started the torture again. He urinated on his victim and also held a gun to Robert's head and spun the barrel, firing when it stopped, playing the sick game of Russian Roulette. The torture continued for eight hours. For some unknown reason, Gacy decided not to kill the nineteen year old. He drove to the street where he had picked up his victim and dumped the man, bruised and battered on the side of the road. Robert memorised the number plate and stumbled to the police station to report the attack. A week later, on 6 January 1978 Gacy was arrested for the brutal attack on Robert, yet after interviewing the killer the officers believed Gacy's side of the story and he was released.

The nineteenth known victim, Billy Kindred, was not as lucky as Robert. He was last seen on 16 February 1978 by his fiancé. Billy found himself in Gacy's torture house, handcuffed and begging for his life as he was beaten and raped by Gacy. Like the other victims, Billy's body was interred in the crawlspace the next morning, when Gacy had finished with him.

On 21 March 1978, Jeff Rignall stormed out of the apartment he shared with his girlfriend. Gacy pulled up beside the twenty-six year old and offered him a ride. Once Gacy had Jeff inside the car, he lit up a marijuana joint and the two men shared it. As Jeff relaxed, Gacy pounced, grabbing the man around the head and shoving a chloroform-soaked cloth over Jeff's nose and mouth. Jeffrey woke inside Gacy's home, his head buzzing. Gacy raped Jeff, then pushed the rag with chloroform over the man's face again to render him unconscious repeatedly before waking him each time to sexually abuse him, screaming 'you love it' each time he did.[86] Jeff was woken a final time near the street where he had first encountered the killer. The man, though battered and disoriented, made his way home before being taken to the hospital and then the police station.

The police believed the man's story—his battered and swollen face testament to what he had told them—however he was unable to give a clear description of his attacker nor the location of the assault. Police were helpless to do anything. Jeff decided to take the matter into his own hands. He sat on the side of the road where Gacy had picked him up and waited in the hope that Gacy would again drive by. Though unsure of the number plate, Jeff did remember that it was a vanity plate with only three letters on it. Finally, Gacy drove past Jeff. The man knew it was his attacker and wrote down the number plate—PDM—and took it to the police. He was certain his attacker would face justice. Yet as time went on and Jeff was not called to provide further testimony or evidence he knew that nothing had been done. Like the other boys who had told police about Gacy his report was noted but not followed up nor investigated.

One of the final victims was Tim O'Rourke. He remained nameless for quite some time after his body was discovered. It was only through a tattoo that Gacy remembered who the boy was. Tim met Gacy around 14 June 1978 and was never seen alive again. The young man had left his apartment to buy cigarettes when Gacy made him a better offer of free marijuana at his home. The boy with the 'Tim Lee' tattoo gladly accepted the killers' offer and returned with Gacy. Like the others, Tim was raped and abused before being strangled to death. Yet this time he was not buried in the cemetery underneath Gacy's home. The crawlspace was now full of up to thirty bodies; the smell in the confined space was unimaginable; the stench of decaying bodies emanating through the floorboards of Gacy's house. So now Gacy had to find another graveyard. Tim's body was wrapped in a tarp and thrown into the Des Plaines River from one of the bridges along Highway I55.

The next victim was also thrown into the Des Plaines River. Nineteen-year-old Frank Landingin, a part-time male prostitute, argued with his girlfriend on the night of 3 November 1978. The argument continued into the early hours of the next morning and by 2 a.m. on 4 November 1978 Frank stormed out of the house and headed into the night and into the clutches of John Gacy. He was taken back to the house of horrors and raped and tortured for several hours before finally being strangled by Gacy.

The penultimate victim was 20-year-old James Mazzara who met his death in November 1978. The young man had been out looking for a new place to rent when he found himself on the doorstep of Gacy's home. He was ushered inside the house and shown around. Soon the scene turned ugly and James found himself bound and gagged. The killer raped the young man several times during which James was choked to death on his own underpants that had been shoved down his throat.

Robert Piest was a handsome young man with the long flowing hair. The evening he disappeared was Monday 11 December 1978. Robert was working at the Nisson Pharmacy in Des Plaines when John Gacy walked into the store. He had come to discuss with the owner a refitting of the pharmacy. The boy, with his mother waiting outside to pick him after his shift, went to see Gacy before he left. Gacy told the boy to get into the car to discuss a job and then leaned over towards the young man and clamped a cloth with chloroform on it over Rob's mouth. He had later tied a rope around the young boy's throat and twisted it twice to kill him.[87]

Being the last person to see Rob alive, Gacy was the prime suspect from the beginning and after he invited police into his home to look around, the stench of death told them there was something going on. One officer went down into the crawlspace and dug around in the soft earth where he quickly found a decomposed foot. Before he was arrested, Gacy confided in his business associate Ronald Rhode. He told the man, 'Ron, I've been a bad boy, I killed thirty people, give or take a few'.[88]

Within two days,[89] officers charged Gacy with murder, unaware of how many counts would be part of the final tally. However, Gacy was ready for them with an insanity defence. He began talking about 'Bad Jack' who hated homosexuals as well as other personas.

On 22 December 1978, Gacy was furious when he learnt that the officers were pulling apart his immaculate house to get to the crawlspace. He asked for a pen and paper and drew them a map of where the bodies were buried, so they would not destroy his home. The map was accurate, and though it did not prevent the officers from completely removing the floor from Gacy's house, it did give the prosecution an exact map to overlay to pinpoint the locations of the bodies recovered, that then cemented Gacy's guilt at trial.

In total twenty-eight bodies were removed from the crawlspace of Gacy's home. The body of John Butkovich was dug up from under the garage concrete floor and Rick Johnson's body was discovered under the laundry room. Three others, Tim O'Rourke, James Mazarra and Robert Piest were recovered from the waters of the Des Plaines River.

The trial of John Gacy opened in the Cook County Court on 6 February 1980. By 12 March 1980 the trial had come to its conclusion and after two hours the seven men and five women of the jury handed their decision to the judge. Gacy was found guilty of all thirty-three murders and the following day he was sentence to death by lethal injection. While in prison, Gacy gave numerous interviews. In one, he was disgusted that that the media grouped him in with other serial killers, saying, 'Whether it's Berkowitz, whether it's Bundy, whether it's Williams, Wayne Williams down in Atlanta, or Charlie Manson, God I hate that when they put they put me in the same club as them'.[90]

At midnight on 11 May 1994 Gacy became the 100th person to be executed in Illinois, his final words were 'Kiss my Ass'. At 12.58 a.m. he was pronounced dead.

Thomas Piper

'I struck her with the club two or three times and she fell where the blood was found'

On May 23 1875, 5-year-old Mabel Young went to her Sunday School at Warren Avenue Baptist Church in Boston, Massachusetts and met with her aunt, Mrs Hobbs. After ten minutes of chatting with other parents, Mabel's aunt was ready to leave, but her niece was nowhere to be seen. A frantic search of the area did not locate the young girl and Mrs Hobbs began to panic.

A scream from the belfry of the church saw several people rushing to the source. On the first floor of the tower a large pool of blood was found. Nearby lay a blood-stained cricket bat. Into the belfry, through a trap door the low moans of a small child in pain could be heard. In the corner of the room lay Mabel Young; her clothes were soaked with blood, her skull severely fractured above the left ear, such that the doctor would later recall being able to feel her brain through the wound. Mabel was carried down from the tower, where Doctor Coiling treated her at a nearby house. Unfortunately Mabel Young died at 8 p.m. the next day. She never regained consciousness and so could not tell her aunt the identity of her attacker. That did not stop suspicion being aimed squarely at one of the parishioners.

Thomas Piper, a bachelor in his twenties, a sexton at the church and known alcoholic, was quickly arrested for the murder of Mabel Young. The local community was shocked at the arrest but the police had good cause.

On 5 December 1873, less than two years before the murder of Mabel, Piper was arrested for a murderous attack on Bridget Landregan; her skull had also been fractured. Hours later a woman named Sullivan was found barely alive in a ditch with severe wounds to her head; she recovered after treatment but was unable to identify her attacker. Lack of evidence in the case resulted in Piper being released, but the authorities resolved to keep an eye on the suspect. So upon hearing of the MO in the Mabel Young case, officers instantly thought of Piper.

The police searched Piper's room and found bloodied clothing. At the station Piper was questioned and soon broke down and confessed to Mabel's murder. He told the arresting officers that he had, 'struck her with the club two or three times and she fell where the blood was found'.[91] Witnesses who saw Piper running from the church at the time of the murder backed up his confession. Other young girls at the Sunday school told of how Piper would make efforts to lure them to the belfry. In addition to the murder of Mabel Young, Piper confessed to the murder of three other women including Bridget Landregan and also to attacks on Ms Sullivan and the January 1874 attack on Mary Tynan, who died in a lunatic asylum after suffering brain damage caused by Piper's attack.

For his crimes Piper was executed on the gallows in 1876.

Mariusz Trynkiewicz

'When I get out into the wild, I will kill again, it's stronger than me'

Mariusz Trynkiewicz was born in Piotrkow, Poland, on 10 April 1962. As an adult, Trynkiewicz became a teacher and while completing his military service he sexually abused his first victim. Thirteen-year-old Robert was abducted on 29 December 1986. The man took the boy to his home where, for three hours, he was tied to an iron bar and assaulted before being released. Several days later another boy, 14-year-old Paul was abducted and again taken to Trynkiewicz's home where he was assaulted for three hours. The boy was released and he went to police who arrested Trynkiewicz. Trynkiewicz was returned to his military unit, where he was sentenced to one-year's imprisonment for the attack by the military court. However, the sentence was suspended for two years. When he abducted and raped another child, 12-year-old Simon he was again sentenced and sent to prison for one and a half years.[92]

In April 1988, while given a four-month leave from his prison term to look after his ill mother, he again attacked several children. Over the Easter break, Trynkiewicz lured two 11-year-old boys, Robert and Martin, to his home where they are both assaulted. In June, another boy, 15-year-old Robert, was attacked and released before the man unsuccessfully tried to abduct two twelve-year-old boys, Konrad and Thomas. The boys had heard rumours about the 'pervert teacher'[93] and had run away. By the end of June, Trynkiewicz had abducted and raped two more boys, 10-year-olds Mariusz and Jack.

Trynkiewicz was particular with the types of boys he abducted. He preferred to grab those who were naive and did not understand what he wanted with them and were happy to pose naked for the man. As a teacher he was an excellent judge of character of those whom he believed he could lure back to his apartment.

On 4 July 1988 he lured 13-year-old Wojciech to his apartment. He made the boy write a postcard to his mother saying he was going to go away. The man then raped the boy before strangling him to death. In the cover of darkness that evening Trynkiewicz buried the boy's body in the woods.

On 29 July, he lured another three boys to his home with the promise of BB guns and toys.[94] Twelve-year-old cousins Arthur and Christopher and 11-year-old neighbour Thomas were raped and then stabbed to death when they begged to leave. One of the boys was stabbed eighteen times. He again took the bodies to the woods where he set them on fire before burying the charred remains wrapped in pieces of curtains.

During their investigations into the missing boys, Mariusz Trynkiewicz was stopped and questioned by police for acting suspiciously. He confessed to the murders and took police back to his home where they found blood and items belonging to the boys. The killer then took police to the boys' bodies that were wrapped in curtains that matched those still hanging in the man's apartment.

Trynkiewicz was found guilty of the murders of the four young boys and sentenced to death.[95] However, his sentence was soon commuted to life imprisonment in 1989 after Poland abolished the death penalty. In Poland, a life sentence is a 25-year sentence, after which the prisoner is to be released. In February 2014, Trynkiewicz was released from prison.

Not only did the public cry for his return to prison, but his mother also feared for her life following his release.[96]

Enriqueta Marti

'Come, pretty come, I have candy for you'

Born in Sant Feliu de Llobreat, Spain, in 1868, Enriqueta Marti worked as a maid to several wealthy families in France before turning to prostitution.[97] At the age of twenty-seven she married a painter but due to her extramarital affairs the relationship failed.

In February 1912, after kidnapping her last victim Teresita Guitart Congost, police searched the city[98] and a neighbour of Marti's told police of the many children she had seen going in and out of Marti's home. Most of the children were enticed to her home with the Grimm-like offer of 'Come, pretty come, I have candy for you'.[99]

When police arrived to question her they not only found the missing girl, Teresita, but also another victim, who had been kidnapped by the killer at birth. The young girl Angelita told police her tale of watching other children being murdered and that she had been forced to eat the flesh from their bodies by the 'witch'.

Angelita told police about many of the victims she had seen murdered during her time confined to the woman's home. She saw the woman she called 'step-mother' murder a 5-year-old boy on the kitchen table one evening. Enriqueta Marti was arrested in March 1912 for the murders of more than a dozen children.

At trial it was claimed that Enriqueta would dress as a beggar woman during the day and abduct children from the streets of Barcelona to be sold into prostitution. If she could not sell the victims she would kill them.

She would then boil the bodies to make 'love potions', that she sold at a local market.[100]

Though police suspect she was responsible for hundreds of victims over a 20-year period police were only able to find evidence of twelve bodies.

While in prison Marti attempted suicide, but survived. When the public heard about her attempt to die before she was to be executed, a gang of prison inmates lynched her on 12 May 1913. However her death has been officially attributed to illness.[101]

Killings by those who are often active and supported in their community breaches the trust that we have in those around us. It is an innate part of the human psyche to size up and 'profile' those around us. The horrific private actions of known strangers like Gacy and Fish, who presented themselves as successful businessmen, show that sometimes our ability to assess those around us is flawed. This is not because of our own flaws, but because we do not expect evil deviants—those who murder and abuse our children—to be likeable and pleasant. We want to have them as we imagine them, as snarling monsters.

The next group of killers, the thrill killers, often seemed as unlikely to kill as the known strangers. Many of them were friendly and personable. But they all have a compulsion to kill, just for the thrill.

THE THRILL KILLER

The Thrill Killer is a term used to define the 'grey area' between the categories of serial killer and mass murderer that is not covered by the 'spree' killer (someone who kills several people in a short period of time). The key difference between the thrill killer and the broader serial killer is that in the former there is no functional need to kill. Their actions are based on the high of the kill itself, similar to the feeling an extreme sports enthusiast may experience.

The thrill killer murders his/her victims for the death alone; there is usually neither prolonged attack nor sexual interference. The killer seeks the adrenalin rush from the hunt and kill. The thrill killer is sometimes able to abstain from killing for long periods of time. The killer is fully aware of his actions and often becomes more professional and more successful over time as he continues to refine the method of murder. Many thrill killers attempt to commit the perfect crime and assume they will not be caught.

The lack of a solid motive (be it sexual, robbery etc.) means that the thrill killer can be harder to catch and often is only caught after they make an error.

Marcel Barbeault

'I wanted to be a soldier. I loved everything related to the military'

Marcel Barbeault was born on 10 August 1941 in Laincourt, France. He was the son of working-class parents who raised a child that, on the surface, seemed to be a well-adjusted young boy. Like many boys in France, with the Algerian War raging, as a nineteen year old he enlisted in the army in 1960 and spent two years of the war as a stretcher runner. He had tried out as a parachutist, but due to dizzy spells he was unable to join.

When Barbeault returned from the war he married a local girl Josiane and the couple had two children[102] and built themselves a home while Barbeault worked in a menial job that required very little technical skill.[103]

However, with what he had seen in the war and following a succession of deaths in Barbeault's family during the late 1960s and early 1970s, the man became irrational and began a murderous campaign that saw the deaths of eight young women in seven years in the French province of Nogent-sur-Oise.

He had an obsession with war and acted out life as though he were a soldier fighting against unseen enemy lines. He claimed that he 'wanted to be a soldier. [he] loved everything related to the military'.[104]

Like serial killer Ted Bundy, Marcel Barbeault preferred a particular type of victim. All of his female victims had brown hair set in a similar style. At night he would stalk his victims, shooting them in the dark. His ability to hide in the shadows and avoid detection gave rise to a nickname of the 'Shadow Killer' because of his preference for the night-time assaults.

Barbeault's first victim survived the attack when the 'big and fat'[105] man pounced on the night of 10 January 1969. The young woman was shot at close range by Barbeault but was not killed; she was taken to the hospital but was unable to give police a description of her attacker who struck in the dark of night.

The second potential victim was just as lucky when Barbeault struck four days later. Just before dawn on 14 January 1969, Barbeault shot his victim in the stomach. Although she suffered extensive blood loss, she managed to get help. However, again the victim was unable to help police when she was unable to give them a description of the shooter.

The third victim was not as lucky. Forty-nine-year-old Therese Adam arrived home on the evening of 23 January 1969 when Barbeault snuck up behind her. He bashed her on the back of the neck. Therese fell to the ground where Barbeault shot her dead with one bullet fired into her throat. Therese was found the next morning by neighbours.

After striking three times in less than a fortnight the killer went into hiding, returning to his family life for ten months before he decided to kill again.

During the evening of 16 November 1969, Suzanne Merienne was home with her 19-year-old daughter Micheline when Barbeault broke into their house. The killer, soaked from the wet weather outside, held a gun to the woman's face and demanded that they all head outside into the wet evening. Barbeault marched the women to the nearby railway tracks where he shot dead 44-year-old Merienne with a single shot fired at her temple. When Micheline saw her mother collapse to the ground, she made her escape. In the dark rainy night Micheline was able to run away. She made her way to the local police constabulary where she gave them a description of her mother's killer.

A composite drawing of the killer was released and a countrywide search began while Barbeault returned to his wife and children and his normal life without incident and without being a suspect.

Three years later, during the night of 6 February 1973 Barbeault shot his next victim, 29-year-old Annick Delisle.[106] She was found the following day with her clothes in disarray that suggested the killer had also assaulted the woman's dead body.

Barbeault murdered again on 28 May 1973 when he shot a young couple, 25-year-old Eugene Stephan and 23-year-old Mauricette Van Hyfte who had been walking during the balmy evening.

The killer stopped killing again for another seven months before shooting dead 29-year-old Josette Routier on 8 January 1974. Once she was dead he stripped the woman's body naked. In November the next year Barbeault shot and stripped another young woman, 29-year-old Julia Goncalves who had been walking in Hebert Park. Then again on 6 January 1976 he shot another victim. This time he also stole 20-year old Francoise Jakubowska's underwear and stabbed her body. The killer's crimes were escalating in their violence and sexual elements. However the times between murders were stretching further apart. The man was highly controlled in his killings. However Barbeault was never to kill again.

In December 1976, following an anonymous tip Barbeault was arrested. A search of his home yielded the gun, bullets and knife used in the murders. The killer claimed he was innocent, stating that he had found the items in a local cemetery.

Barbeault was found guilty of five of the eight murders and sentenced to life imprisonment. The killer appealed his sentence but was again found guilty and given a twenty-year sentence in 1982.

Klaus Gossman

'They were themselves to blame if I had to shoot them'

Born in Germany during the height of the Second World War, Klaus Gossman claimed that he saw his father shot dead by an enemy soldier. The shy, quiet boy[107] from that moment on became obsessed with guns and violence, though still also yearned to become a priest. He became a bully and physically assaulted anyone he chose, often at random.[108]

By the time he was nineteen his obsession had become deadly and he decided to bring death to those around him. He was dubbed the 'Midday Murderer' as he murdered most of his victims at precisely midday, as the clocks of Nuremberg sounded the hour to hide the sound of his gunfire.

In 1960, as a teenage theology student, Gossman murdered his first victims. At midday as he left the University of Nuremberg's library he spotted a couple and demanded money. When they did not hand over their belongings he shot them both dead, using the clock's hourly chimes to cover the sounds of his gunfire. He casually walked away, leaving the couple to die where they lay.[109] That evening, after completing his studies for the day, he wrote an in-depth diary entry describing his emotions and feelings and the enjoyment of the killings.

In 1962, two years after the murder of the young couple, Gossman struck again. Choosing a bank as the scene of the gun attack, Gossman entered the bank armed with a gun at midday. He robbed the bank then shot the manager as he left.

A few months later, on 30 November 1962 Gossman killed his fourth victim, another bank employee. Again at midday he robbed the bank before shooting dead an employee chosen at random.[110]

On 29 March 1963, the killer decided he needed more guns. Gossman walked into a German gun store and shot dead the owner and the owner's adult son, before taking as many weapons as he could carry. Again, after the murder he added an entry to his journal.

The final murder occurred in April 1965 after Gossman went AWOL following his enlistment in the army. Gossman attempted to steal the handbag of a woman in a shop. When the woman attempted to fight back, Gossman shot her dead. The killer was quickly subdued by other shoppers, injuring two who tried to arrest him. They held the killer until police arrived.

Once in custody the killer quickly confessed to the murders, claiming that 'they were themselves to blame if [he] had to shoot them'.[111] He said the killings were out of necessity. They could either they hand over everything they had or he would shoot them. He enjoyed walking around alone and knew he would not be caught. He did not feel like a criminal. His obsession with guns gave him a sense of security.[112]

Gossman's mental state was examined at trial where experts believed that he could not differentiate reality from his world of make-believe. 'What people do in a dream, he did in reality'.[113] Gossman was sentenced to life imprisonment for seven murders. The diaries that the killer had maintained were used as evidence against him. The diaries also contained a fantasy plan to kidnap and murder popular German actress Elke Sommer. Her name had also been etched onto the side of the killer's gun.

Richard Marquette

'I wish I could live it all over again'

On 21 June 1961, the FBI increased their Ten Most Wanted Criminals list to Eleven Most Wanted when they needed to capture 26-year-old Richard Laurence Marquette who had murdered a woman in Oregon.

Born on 12 December 1934, Richard Laurence Marquette was withdrawn and shy as a child but usually pleasant to those who talked to him. According to his mother, 'he never could get enough love. He seemed very jealous of other children'.[114] He was also known to have violent temper tantrums that his mother and the school authorities were loathe to punish as they found it would often make matters worse. He would 'blow up and scream' if anyone attempted to punish him.[115] He was also the product of a broken home, with his mother bringing home a string of boyfriends who cared little for the young boy.[116]

Marquette's violent spree commenced in June 1956 when he raped his first victim. The woman survived the attacked and went to police. However she later dropped the charges and Marquette was free to embark on a brutal spree that involved assault and murder.

In August 1957, Marquette was sentenced to eighteen months in prison for the brutal assault of an attendant and the attempted robbery of a service station in Portland. However the prison sentence did little to deter the man and after his release Marquette struck again. On 5 June 1961, 24-year-old Joan Caudle disappeared while out shopping. She had stopped by a bar where Marquette had chatted with her before inviting her to his home, though her family claimed this was highly unlikely to have happened. Pieces of her dismembered body were found three days later in various places around Portland. Investigators identified Marquette as the last person to be seen with her and he was placed on the FBI's list.

Marquette was arrested in Santa Maria, California after he was recognised from the wanted posters. Marquette confessed to strangling and dismembering Joan after she declined his sexual advances. He told police that he had wished that he could 'live it all over again'.[117] Additional pieces of her body were found in a duffel bag in Marquette's refrigerator.[118] While awaiting trial he took police to the location of the woman's missing head.[119] Six months later Marquette received a life sentence for the murder and thanked the court after the sentence was read out.

After serving twelve years for the murder, Marquette was released on parole and by April 1975 he had killed again. Betty Wilson became Marquette's second victim. The 40-year-old plumber's apprentice chatted to Betty at a bar before inviting her to his home. There she suffered the same fate as Joan Rae Caudle. She was dismembered after her murder in her hometown of Salem, Oregon. Her head, breasts and genitals had been removed. All police were able to find were her arms, legs and torso. [120]

Marquette was quickly arrested and again the killer confessed to the murder. He also confessed to the murder of a third victim that he dismembered shortly after his release from prison in 1974 and took police to her grave where they recovered two legs, a torso and one arm.[121] Her identity could not be established as the victim's head was missing, therefore the killer was never charged with her killing. Marquette was again sentenced to another life sentence. He remains in Oregon State Penitentiary.

Gennady Mikhasevich

'When I saw her for the first time I had an idea to strangle her'

Gennady Mikhasevich was born in 1947 in Polotsk, Byelorussia, in the former USSR and went on to kill an unknown number of people during the 1970s and 1980s. Like serial killer Andrei Chikatilo who murdered fifty-two victims during the same time, several innocent men were tried, convicted and executed for the killer's crimes.

Mikhasevich drove around Polotsk wearing his volunteer policeman uniform and offered his victims a lift home. Once he had his victims in his car he drove to a secluded place where they were strangled with his scarf. At some of the murders the killer left hand written notes that were signed 'Patriot of Vitebsk'.

His first murder occurred on 14 May 1971. His victim, a young woman by the name of Lyudmila Andaralova, was walking home in the dark when Mikhasevich came upon her. He offered to help her with her two large suitcases and she happily accepted. When the pair walked further down the road towards an apple orchard the man pounced. He later claimed that he had no desire to kill until he saw the victim. He then said, 'When I saw her for the first time I had an idea to strangle her'.[122]

On 29 October 1971, a victim was lucky to escape. In Vitebsk the killer attacked a young woman. He asked her the time and when she went to look at her watch he wrapped a rope around her throat and pulled it tight. She fought back and was able to get away.[123] The next victim was not so lucky. That same day, Mikhasevich grabbed another woman. She was strangled and dumped in a forest near New Ruba. The victim was never identified.[124]

On 15 April 1972, he strangled and killed another woman, followed by another on 30 July 1972. Both victims had been strangled with ropes made of rye. Another victim was strangled on 11 April 1973 and dumped on the outskirts of Vitebsk. The killer then stopped murdering.

After a hiatus of almost two years, he struck twice in 1975. The first victim was strangled on 17 May. The killer claimed that the young woman was the youngest of all of his victims. He then killed a 25-year-old woman on September 28.[125]

Marrying in early 1976, Mikhasevich stopped killing, but only briefly. By 28 April 1976 he had killed another woman. His next victim was strangled on 2 July, followed by another three weeks later. Mikhasevich's next victim was raped and strangled in Vetrino on 1 November, before he again stopped killing.

On 26 August 1978 the killer strangled another victim, before taking another break. Over a year later, on 9 September 1979, he killed another victim in Polotsk. Then in October of the following year he killed another woman in Ropno. On 15 July, following a shorter break, he killed again.

After the July murder, Mikhasevich changed the way he killed. Rather than attacking women on the side of the road, he commenced abducting them. He picked up and killed two more victims, one on 12 September and the other 23 October. Both victims were raped repeatedly before being strangled and dumped.

He began killing in a spree. Without the concerns of someone coming past, he began abducting victims more fervently. Five victims were taken within a month in July/August 1982. He then killed twelve more victims between 1983 and 1985, sometimes killing two woman on the same day. He began leaving notes with the victims, often leaving hand-written, taunting letters inside the mouths of his victims for police to find.

As part of his work as a volunteer police officer, he would question the suspects who were arrested for his crimes and have them charged with the murders. In total, four men were found guilty of Mikhasevich's crimes, yet the murders did not stop and the 'patriot of Vitebsk' continued to leave notes at subsequent scenes. Police soon found that a small red hatchback car was seen at a number of the scenes and so local red car owners were asked to provide handwriting samples. After going through dozens of samples police discovered that Mikhasevich's handwriting matched the killer's.

Mikhasevich was arrested and interrogated until he confessed to the murders of more than two-dozen people. However the police believed that he may have killed many more. Mikhasevich took police to the place where he hid the personal effects of many of his victims, including items belonging to victims who had not been identified. Mikhasevich was found guilty of the murders and sentenced to death. His execution, by a single shot to the back of his head, occurred during the late 1980s.

Ivan Milat

'Stop, or I'll shoot you'

On 27 December 1944, Ivan Robert Marko Milat was born to his Croatian-born father, Stephen, and his Australian-born mother, Margaret. He was the fourth child in an extremely large family of fourteen siblings. The large family lived in a small, yellow, three-bedroom weatherboard house in Guildford on the outskirts of Sydney.

While at school, Ivan played football well but performed poorly academically, so he left school and quickly got a job in road and construction work. He held jobs all over Sydney.

Ivan met his wife in the late seventies. They married and bought a house in Mount Druitt but they divorced during the eighties. Milat went on to have a few relationships, though nothing serious.

Milat was charged with the rape of two young backpackers in 1971 but he fled to New Zealand and he was rearrested in 1974 when he arrived back in Australia. However the victims refused to testify and the charges were dropped. Prior to the rape charge, Milat had several criminal convictions for car theft and had spent some time in jail and boys' homes for the offences. But it was in the final week of 1989 that Milat turned to murder.

On 29 December 1989, Deborah Everist and James Gibson told friends they were going to hitchhike together along the Hume Highway to Albury on the New South Wales–Victoria border. It was the last time they were seen alive. Their bodies were found in Belanglo Forest in October 1993, along with the bodies of the five other known victims. By then what was left was little more than skeletal remains. Deborah had been stabbed and struck in the head and jaw.[126] James had been stabbed to death.

A little over a year after the couple disappeared, German backpacker Simone Schmidl, aged twenty, left Sydney on 20 January 1991 to travel to Victoria. She also did not arrive, having been picked up by Milat. The skeletal remains of Simone were recovered on 1 November 1993. The scene was only one and a half kilometres from where the remains of Deborah and James were discovered. Simone's body was lying beside a large fallen log. She had been buried in a shallow grave with leaf mulch as a covering. Her body was covered with horrific stab wounds.

On 25 January 1990, five days after Simone was last seen, Englishman Paul Onions was offered a lift by Milat, but unlike the others Paul was able to escape when Milat tried to tie him up before entering the forest's dirt road. The man jumped from the car when Milat produced a gun and ropes. He zigzagged across the highway as Milat called out after him, 'Stop or I'll shoot'.[127] Though Paul went to police, his statement was lost and Milat was able to continue killing.

German backpackers, 21-year-old Gabor Neugebauer and his girlfriend Anja Habschied, twenty, were Milat's next victims. The couple had been travelling around Australia when Milat picked them up while travelling the highway south from Sydney on 26 December 1991. Three days after the discovery of Simone's body, the remains of Anja Habschied and Gabor Neugebauer were recovered.[128] Gabor had been shot six times in the head. Three shots had been fired into the left side of his skull and a further three to the rear of his skull. Gabor had also been strangled. Inside the young man's mouth a piece of cloth was found. Another piece of material was found around his face, suggesting it had been tied as a gag. Anja had had her head severed from her body in one violent blow. They had both been bound with tape.[129]

British backpackers Caroline Clarke and Joanne Walters left a Kings Cross hostel on 16 April 1992. They were seen several times along their travels, before being picked up by Milat. Their bodies were the first to be found in the forest on 19 September 1992. Joanne Walters' body was found wedged under a rock ledge, her body only partially covered by a thin layer of leaf matter. Joanne had been gagged by a cloth and two more pieces of her clothing covered her face. Her body had suffered multiple stab wounds in what could only be called a frenzied attack. The wounds covered the top half of both her front and back torso. Forensic evidence later revealed that Joanne had also been sexually assaulted by her killer.[130]

The following day, the body of Caroline Clarke was discovered in a shallow grave. Caroline's head had been covered before her death and she had been shot ten times in the head. She had also been stabbed in the lower back, rendering her paralysed. Though it was unclear, evidence did suggest that Caroline may have also been sexually assaulted.[131]

In the early hours of Sunday 22 May 1994 Ivan Milat was arrested on charges of armed robbery and possession of firearms. Though police refused to say whether they had a suspect for the 'Backpacker Murders', the media knew something was important about Ivan Milat. Within a few days, Ivan Milat was charged with the seven brutal murders and one attempted murder of Paul Onions. The arrest was after months of intense investigation of a mountain of information, mainly given to police by one of the Milat brothers.

Simultaneously, heavily armed police swooped on several more properties belonging to Milat family members. Items seized including equipment owned by the dead backpackers.

After one of the biggest trials in New South Wales history Ivan Milat was found guilty of all seven murders as well as the attempted murder of Paul Onions. He was sentenced to life imprisonment with the recommendation that he never be released.

Anatoly Onoprienko

'I am a robot, I don't feel anything'

Claiming that he had been hearing voices since the age of seven when his brother had sent him to an orphanage after his mother had died, Ukrainian Anatoly Onoprienko believed he was compelled him to kill.

Anatoly Onoprienko had worked as a sailor and had studied forestry at university before his killing spree. He was known to authorities for various petty crimes and was on an outpatient program of a local psychiatric hospital department.

Onoprienko began his murderous campaign in 1989 in a spree where he and accomplice Serhiy Rogozin robbed and killed nine people. Onoprienko's first victims were a young couple, standing by their car on a motorway: 'I just shot them. It's not that it gave me pleasure, but I felt this urge. From then on, it was almost like some game'.[132] Though he felt a compulsion to kill he believed that he got no thrill from it. 'Corpses are ugly, they stink and send out bad vibes. Once I killed five people and then sat in the car with their bodies for two hours not knowing what to do with them. The smell was unbearable'.[133]

Onoprienko continued his rampage alone from late 1995. In the next six months he murdered forty-three people. By March 1996, eight entire families had been brutally murdered in their homes and a manhunt was launched across western Ukraine. Many of Onoprienko's victims lived in remote villages near the border of Poland.[134]

In his later confession he spoke of confronting a young girl who was huddled on her bed, praying. She had seen him kill both her parents. 'Seconds before I smashed her head, I ordered her to show me where they kept their money', he said. 'She looked at me with an angry, defiant stare and said, "No, I won't." That strength was incredible but did nothing'.[135] He shot her dead.

He dramatically blew the doors off homes on the edges of villages and gunned down adults before beating to death their children. He stole money, jewellery, stereo equipment and other items before burning down the houses, leaving little evidence behind.

On 2 January 1996, he murdered a family of four before robbing them and burning down their house in the Ukraine. After fleeing the scene he saw a man beside the road; he shot him dead before continuing on his rampage.[136]

On 6 January 1996, the killer shot dead four car drivers while travelling along the highway between Dnieprovskaya and Berdyansk. On 17 January 1996, Anatoly Onoprienko broke into the Pilat family home and shot all five members of the family dead. He robbed the house and set it alight. Two people additional people who came to the Pilats aid were also shot dead.

On 30 January 1996, Onoprienko broke into a home and shot dead a young mother, her two sons and a male friend before setting the house on fire.

Anatoly Onoprienko committed his most brutal murder on 19 February 1996. He broke into the home of the Dubchak family. He shot the husband and son to death and killed the wife and daughter by tearing their skin from their bodies with a claw hammer. Eight days later, on 27 February 1996, the Bodnarehtik family were murdered by Onoprienko. The killer shot dead the parents and then hacked the two daughters to death with an axe. The Novosad Family was then shot dead by Onoprienko on 22 March 1996. He set the house on fire after looting it.

On 7 April 1996, Pyotr Onoprienko called Ukraine police after evicting his cousin Anatoly from his house. A few weeks earlier the man had discovered that Anatoly had hidden several guns under the house. As Onoprienko left the house he told Pyotr that he would come back and kill his family.

Police were now in pursuit of the violent killer. They used a tactic of blockading the area trying to capture the killer. However Onoprienko easily slipped through the police trap.

On 16 April 1996, 37-year-old Anatoly Onoprienko was arrested at his girlfriend's house in Zhitomir, Western Ukraine.[137] His arrest ended a reign of terror in which he was reported to have murdered at least forty people. The dramatic manhunt involved more than five thousand police and military personnel. When he was arrested, Onoprienko had in his possession a 12-gauge shotgun that was linked to bullets found at one of the murder scenes. He also was in possession of jewellery and electrical equipment belonging to several of his victims. Once in custody he confessed to everything he had done. He told police that he watched the killings as if he were a predator watching a sheep.[138]

At his trial in November 1998, Onoprienko stated he felt like a robot driven for years by a dark force, and argued that he should not be tried until authorities determine the source of the force.[139] Hundreds of spectators watched the trial and many villagers throughout the Ukraine wanted their own revenge. 'Let us tear him apart', shouted a pensioner at the back of the court just before the hearing started, her voice trembling with emotion, 'he does not deserve to be shot. He needs to die a slow and agonizing death'.[140]

At his trial Onoprienko was silent. The court asked him if he would like to make a statement to which he replied with a shrug of his shoulders.

Onoprienko's co-defendant Sergei Rogozin, accused of helping in the first nine murders, did speak and proclaimed his innocence.

Onoprienko pleaded insanity. His police interviews were peppered with rantings about conspiracies against him by the CIA and Interpol, unknown powers and future revelations. However psychiatrists ruled him fit to stand trial.

Onoprienko was found guilty and sentenced to death, but was not executed due to the Ukraine's pledge as a member of the Council of Europe to suspend capital punishment. After his trial Onoprienko said, 'Naturally, I would prefer the death penalty. I have absolutely no interest in relations with people … I have betrayed them'. Onoprienko insisted he should be executed, claiming: 'If I am ever let out, I will start killing again'. 'But this time it will be worse, 10 times worse. The urge is there'.[141]

Carl Panzram

'Right there and then I began to learn about man's inhumanity to man'

Carl Panzram was born on 28 June 1891 to Prussian migrant parents in Minnesota, whom he described as poor and ignorant.[142] As a child, Panzram was always in trouble and police knew his name from quite early on. When he was eight he was convicted for drunk and disorderly conduct. Then again three years later, when a string of burglaries landed him in reform school, he retaliated by burning the place down. He left the institution at age thirteen and headed home, filled with criminal knowledge that he would use for the rest of his lifetime. He claimed that it was during his incarceration at the Minnesota Training School that he learned, 'right there and then … about man's inhumanity to man'.[143] He learned 'how to steal, lie, hate, burn and kill'. He went home to his mother who was grieving over the drowning death of her favourite son and ignored Panzram's homecoming. So the teenager pursued a transient life, catching trains across the country like many others. It was during that time that he was gang raped by four hobos on one occasion. He later said, 'I cried, I begged and pleaded for mercy, pity and sympathy, but nothing I could say or do could stop them from their propose'. He left that boxcar a sadder, sicker but wiser boy. 'I had learned that a rectum could be used for other proposes than crepitating'.[144]

For a brief stint Panzram joined the army. He claimed he was drunk when he enlisted and remained so for most of his tour, which culminated in a court martial and three years at Leavenworth Prison.

In 1911, after his release from prison, Panzram, with an accomplice, attacked a railroader. The men robbed him of 35 dollars, bound his arms and legs, and stuffed a sock in his mouth. 'I figured that as I had such a good chance as that, I would commit a little sodomy on him … He is still there, unless the buzzards and coyotes have finished the last of him long ago'.[145]

At one point during his trips Panzram claimed he killed a young boy, Henry McMahon[146] in July 1922. In his own words he explained what happened: 'I sat down to think things over a bit. While I was sitting there, a little kid about eleven or twelve years old came bumming around. He was looking for something. He found it too. I took him out to a gravel pit about one quarter mile envoy. I left him there, but first committed sodomy on him and then killed him. His brains were coming out of his ears when I left him, and he will never be any deader'.[147]

Travelling around the world—South America, Europe, Africa and the US—Panzram left a trail of corpses in his wake. With proceeds from one of his many robberies Panzram bought a yacht, named the John O'Leary, a name he would adopt himself, and lured ten sailors aboard with the promise of free bootleg liquor. However, after the sailors drank themselves into oblivion, Panzram raped them, slit their throats and dumped them all at sea. Later, in West Africa, he hired eight native guides under the guise of hunting crocodiles. Instead, he killed the hired hands, sodomised their corpses and fed them to the hungry reptiles 'for sport'.

When he returned to the United States in 1928, Panzram was arrested for a string of burglaries and sentenced to twenty years in prison. Once incarcerated, Panzram vowed he'd 'kill the first man that crosses me', and did. Robert Warnke,[148] a civilian laundry man murdered by Panzram who took an iron bar and smashed the man's skull in. According to the killer, he had reported Panzram for a minor infraction the week before.

He was sentenced to death for the murder and was sent to Death Row, where he befriended jailer, Henry Lesser, who listened to Panzram's story (and later published it). During his final prison stretch in the late 1920s, Carl Panzram confessed to twenty-one murders, 'In my lifetime I have murdered twenty-one human beings, I have committed thousands of burglaries, robberies, larcenies, arsons and last but not least I have committed sodomy on more than 100 male human beings. For all these things I am not in the least bit sorry'.[149]

Even when human rights organisations tried to have his life spared, Panzram would retort,

'I prefer to die that way, and if I have a soul that soul should burn in Hell for a million years, still I prefer that to a lingering, agonizing death in some prison dungeon or a padded cell in a mad house ... The only thanks you or your land will ever get from me is that I wish you all had one neck and that I had my hands on it ... I have no desire to reform myself. My only desire is to reform people who try to reform me, and I believe that the only way to reform people is to kill them. I don't believe in man, God or Devil. I hate the whole damned human race including myself'.[150]

He had hoped to kill 'another twenty-two'.[151] Finally, he got his wish and was due to be hanged on 5 September 1930. Bitter to the end, Panzram went to his maker with a curse on his lips: 'Hurry up you Hoosier bastard', he snarled at the executioner preparing the noose. 'I could hang a dozen men while you're fooling around'.

Eusebius Pieydagnelle

'The smell of fresh blood . . . the bloody lumps all this fascinated me'

During 1871, Frenchman Eusebius Pieydagnelle stabbed to death six people and during each murder he claimed to experience a 'blissful orgasm'. His on-scene confession in court went on to describe how, when growing up in Vinuville, the butcher's shop opposite gave him great excitement, he claimed 'the smell of fresh blood ... the bloody lumps all this fascinated me and I began to envy the butcher's assistant'.[152]

Against his father's wishes, a man who according to Pieydagnelle was held in high esteem,[153] wanted more for his son, Pieydagnelle became an apprentice at the shop and revelled in the blood that he began to drink. He took to slaughtering the animals with intense pleasure, but soon it was not enough. He commenced drinking their blood as well.[154]

Pieydagnelle's father refused to accept his son becoming a butcher and had him removed from the apprenticeship. Pieydagnelle became severely depressed; he needed to have the sensation of fresh blood on his skin. So, not being able to slaughter animals, the man turned to human victims. He claimed that he was now a 'blood thirsty monster'.[155]

His first victim was a 15-year-old girl whom he said he could not resist. He had seen her sleeping at a table inside a homestead. He grabbed a knife and stabbed her to death on 14 June 1860. He would go prowling about at night in a scene that would later be copied by Jack the Ripper. On 19 October 1860 he killed a 19-year-old man. He had offered to peel an apple for him, but instead stabbed the young man to death.

His third victim was the police commissioner, who he killed on 6 March 1861. He stabbed the man to death like he had done to the previous victims. On 7 November he killed a pastor and then on 12 March 1863, he killed another man, Martin Wagner.[156]

He stabbed to death all of his victims, finding intense pleasure in the scent of their blood. His sixth and final victim was the butcher shop owner, Mr Crist Oval.

At his trial in 1871, Piaydagnelle requested to be sentenced to death as he wanted to die. He begged the court, saying 'I want to die . . hurry to get to the end'.[157] But he would not commit the sin of suicide. The request was granted.

The thrill killer is often left in the ether between the 'true' serial killer and the mass murderer, but still remains separate from the spree killer. The thrill killer may leave an extended period of time between kills, greater than that of the spree killer.

The thrill killer usually has no functional need to kill, except for the pure enjoyment of killing. Sexual assault may or may not be a part of the killer's campaign. The thrill killer usually does not kill in close proximity, preferring to shoot or kill their victims from a distance. The thrill that the killer experiences is also often the motive for killer children. Children who murder are often themselves victims of violence and may use their own experience to torture or kill others.

KILLER KIDS

Killer children such as 15-year-old Jesse Pomeroy and 17-year-old William Heirens are examples of the heightened escalation in murders exhibited in children who kill. Young killers are often more brutal and cruel than their adult counterparts as they lack empathy and cannot understand the pain felt by another, even at their own hand. Their crimes are usually indirectly sexually motivated. The killer child knows they want to experience sexual pleasure but their actions are misdirected, often resulting in murders of victims much younger than themselves.

Mary Bell

'I'd like to see Martin in his coffin'

Mary Bell, one of the world's youngest serial killers, was born in Newcastle, England on 26 May 1957. She grew up in a rough neighbourhood where families lived among abandoned and boarded-up houses. An author who attended her trial described her as 'the epitome of a battered child, that throughout her life, Mary's cries for help had been ignored by teachers and relatives'.[158]

At her birth, Mary's mother rejected her, telling doctors to 'take that pig away from me',[159] before feeding the baby barbiturates to keep her quiet and dumping her at an adoption agency after Mary had fallen on her head from a top-story window.[160] She was taken home by her mother's family, but still the small child received no love or attention, growing up to be a 'disturbed, emotionally wooden, cunning psychopath'.[161]

In the decaying slums of Newcastle upon Tyne on 25 May 1968, three boys, Walter Long, Freddie Myhill and John Souther, searching for scrap timber, discovered the body of 4-year-old Martin Brown inside one of the abandoned buildings. Upon hearing the boys' tale, two workers rushed to the scene but failed in their attempts to resuscitate the boy. Nearby, watching the scene unfold stood 11-year-old Mary Bell with a second girl, her neighbour 13-year-old Norma Bell (no relation). The girls walked towards Martin's aunt Rita Finlay's house and told her of the accident, claiming there was blood all over him, which was not true.

An ambulance quickly arrived on the scene, but was unable to revive Martin. With no obvious signs of trauma, it was assumed that Martin had been poisoned because several empty pill bottles were found at the scene. A post-mortem found that this was not the case. The child had been strangled, however whoever had killed him was not strong enough to leave any telltale bruises. Police suspected that a child may have been the culprit.[162]

While prepared for her son's funeral, Mrs Brown answered a knock at the door to find Mary Bell asking, 'I'd like to see Marin in his coffin'.[163]

When a 3-year-old boy fell from the roof of a disused air raid shelter on May 11, it was also deemed an accident and suspiciously, both Bell girls were witnesses.

On 27 May 1957, the day after Martin's death, teachers at the Woodlands Crescent Nursery School arrived to find that vandals had broken into the school. Amongst the damage, several notes were found:

I murder so that I may come back

Bas Fuch off we murder, watch out Fanny and Faggot

You are mice Y Because we murdered Martain Go
Brown you Bete Look out there are Murders about
by Fanny and auld Faggot you Screws

And finally:

We did murder Martain Brown Fuckof you
Bastard.[164]

On 1 June 1968, another break-in at the school occurred, but this time a silent alarm was triggered. The police were waiting for the culprits upon their exit, and were shocked to find that the vandals were Mary Bell and Norma Bell. When questioned they denied responsibility for the previous break-in.

About 3.30 p.m. on 31 July 1968, 3-year-old Brian Howe vanished from sight. He was last seen playing with Mary Bell and Norma Bell. According to Brian's mother, Mary had often taken the small child for a walk with the promise of sweets. She again had decided to lure him away with the promise of lollies, but instead she took him to a 'rat-infested vacant lot called the "Tin Lizzie"'.[165] Throughout the afternoon and evening concerned relatives and neighbours searched the local area for Brian. At 11.10 p.m. the search came to an abrupt end when the little boy's body was found wedged between concrete slabs. Brian's body was covered with bruises and he had scratches on his throat; there was also blood and saliva on his lips.[166]

At the post-mortem, Dr Tomlinson concluded that Brian's death was caused by manual strangulation, probably caused by a child due to the small amount of force used. Questioned on 1 August, Mary Bell was vague in her answers to police concerning the death of Brian Howe. The next day when questioned further Bell suddenly recalled that she has seen an older boy 'attacking' Brian.

Norma Bell told a different story and as a result, on 4 August, Mary broke down and confessed that she had taken Norma to the body of Brian and shown her how it was done by squeezing Norma's throat. In addition, Norma Bell admitted that Mary had stabbed Brian with a pair of scissors (a fact missed during the original post mortem).

When the small child's body was being brought out of the church at the funeral, Marry Bell was standing amongst the crowd that had gathered. Detective Chief Inspector James Dobson looked over at the young girl: 'I was watching her and it was when I saw her there that I knew I dare not risk another day. She stood there laughing—laughing and rubbing her hands'.[167]

On 7 August, both girls were arrested and charged with the murder of Brian Howe, Mary Bell's reply, 'that's all right by me'.[168]

The trial began on 5 December 1968 at Newcastle Assizes, with both pre-teen girls pleading not guilty. The trial lasted for twelve days with Mary Bell continually pinning the blame on her 'partner' and the 'older boy' for Brian's murder. An 8-year-old girl, Pauline Watson, was called as a witness and explained how Mary had also tried to strangle her.[169]

In the end, it was three pieces of evidence that proved her guilt. Fibre evidence lifted from the bodies of both Martin and Brian was identical to clothes owned by Bell.

Secondly, a handwriting expert testified that the notes were written by Bell (with some words written by Norma Bell). The third piece of crucial evidence was the admission of the use of scissors to cut Brian after death.

On 17 December, after three hours and twetnty-five minutes of deliberation, the jury returned a verdict of guilty of the manslaughter of both Martin and Brown on grounds of diminished responsibility due to her tender age. The judge's summation of the case stated that Mary 'had killed solely for the pleasure and excitement of murder. This girl is dangerous and therefore steps must be taken to protect other people'.[170] She was sentenced to detention at Her Majesty's pleasure. Norma Bell was cleared of all charges. However, finding a suitable detention centre for the child proved difficult with most facilities refusing to take her because of the 'very great risk Mary presents to other children'.[171]

While in detention, Bell accused a male teacher of sexually abusing her. There was an investigation that almost destroyed the man's career before it was discovered that the accusations were a plot by the killer to frame the teacher so she could go to a different reform school.[172]

In September 1977, 20-year-old Bell escaped from Moor Court Open Prison with another inmate, Annette Priest[173] but was captured three days later. Fellow prison inmates who were interviewed about the killer on the run claimed that Bell's 'mind was still a bit dodgy … she is definitely a psychopath. I have seen the things she has done. Mary used to go everywhere to kill a cat. Mary is very sick and she shouldn't be let out yet'.[174]

She was caught in a car with two men two days later and arrested.[175] Bell was interviewed by the press after her capture and claimed that she lost her virginity while on the run. After serving twelve years in custody Bell was released from Askham Grange Open Prison having been granted a new identity.

In 1984, she gave birth to a daughter, who became a ward of the court with 'Bell' listed as her carer. The media challenged Bell's anonymity in May 2002 after the injunction preventing her name being released ended when her daughter reached eighteen. Journalists had tracked Bell to her house on the south coast on England after the publication of the biography *Cries Unheard* that Bell had published with author Gitta Sereny.

However, in September 2002, a permanent injunction was ordered preventing 'Bell's' new name and identity from ever being published.

Jummai Hassan

'We attend meetings at a church where instructions are given to us as to which parts of the human body to take'

In July 2001 a 13-year-old girl was arrested in northeast Nigeria for ritual-linked killings of fifty-one people, including her father, whom she said had been obstructive.[176] According to her confession, she had been killing since she was seven as part of a blood cult in Lagos that stole body parts for voodoo rituals.[177] She claimed that the murders were ordered by the leader of the cult, Emanuel. She told police, 'He is our initiator. We do what he says, my spirit is away … we attend meetings at a church where instructions are given to us as to which parts of the human body to take'.[178]

Jummai Hassan, a pupil at the army college Maimalari Government

Secondary School, was arrested on 17 July in Maiduguri, the capital of Borno State over the disappearance of a 2-year-old boy, Ibro Joseph.[179] She took police to the child's grave where the body was exhumed. No obvious cause of death was found.[180]

She was charged with the murder of another boy, a five year old in Pimpomari Housing estate in Maiduguri,[181] as well the attempted murder of a teenage girl by throwing her into a large ditch and an arson attack on a neighbour's home.[182]

The last known information is that the girl was to face trial for forty-seven murders in December 2001. She was to face life imprisonment or execution if she was found guilty. No further information is available.

William Heirens

'For heavens Sake catch me before I kill more cannot control myself'

On 15 November 1928, William George Heirens was born to Margaret and George Heirens in Rogers Park, Chicago. He was the eldest son of the couple and was born after a very traumatic pregnancy and delivery. The pregnancy was almost terminated after ten weeks, however Margaret Heirens carried the baby to term. He was delivered by forceps after a long 62-hour labour.

The boy was an average boy growing up during the Depression. The family struggled financially but they got by.

The moment everything changed was on 13 June 1942, when Heirens, aged just thirteen held up a local store with a gun.

The boy was arrested and soon confessed to a dozen burglaries, He was sent to a Catholic reformatory for boys, in Gibault, Terre Haute,

Indiana. He escaped and soon found himself back in front of a judge for breaking and entering charges.

He was sent to a different Catholic school and thrived. He remained there until January 1945. After he finished, he applied and was accepted as an underage student at the University of Chicago. Being an on-campus student gave him the opportunity to slip out at night, breaking into homes and stealing what he wanted. The sixteen year old would break into apartment-building basements in search of laundry washing lines, looking for lingerie. He liked to steal ladies' underwear and put them on. For the burglar, breaking into a home would produce an orgasm.

On 5 June 1945, while on his way to his summer job, Heirens decided he 'needed' to break into a house. After failing twice to gain entry to homes, at 10.30 a.m. Heirens' third attempt was successful. He walked straight into an apartment-building lobby in Kenmore Avenue, Chicago and took the lift to the top floor, trying every door on every floor until he found an open door on the fifth floor.

Little did the boy know but the owner, 43-year-old Josephine Ross, was sleeping in her bed, a bull terrier on the floor beside the bed. When Heirens entered the bedroom the dog began to bark and startled the sleeping woman, who screamed. Heirens pounced on the woman as he retrieved a knife from his pocket and stabbed her in the throat and chest as she attempted to fight off the sixteen year old. He beat the woman before strangling her with her own stockings.

Once Josephine was dead, Heirens carried her body to the bathroom and cleaned off the drying blood, before returning the woman's dead body to the bed.

Heirens, cleaned the apartment to remove traces of his fingerprints and kicked and bashed the dog, which had tried to protect its owner, before leaving the scene. He took with him several rings and a fur coat.

At lunchtime, Josephine's daughter returned and found her mother dead on the bed, the dog injured and cowering in a corner. Police were called and assumed that the woman had disturbed a burglar in her house.

On the night of 1 October 1945, William Heirens broke into the home of Veronica Hudzinski. The 19-year-old woman was at home in her North Winthrop Ave, Chicago, when she was startled by Heirens breaking in through a window.

Heirens grabbed the gun from his pocket and aimed it at the woman, who recoiled in fear. The seventeen year old fired two shots at Veronica. She fell to the ground, both bullets entering her shoulder. She survived the attack.

The boy dropped the gun at the scene and ran home to his dormitory room at the University of Chicago.

After the shock of the shooting attack of Veronica Hudzinski only four days earlier, William Heirens again decided to break into another home. Late in the night of 5 October 1945 he broke into the Chicago apartment of Evelyn Peterson. The woman was alone, asleep in her bed when the attacker bashed her over the head with a metal bar. The woman was knocked unconscious and tied up, never seeing Heirens. The sight of the woman bound aroused Heirens and he ejaculated over Evelyn's body before escaping with money from her purse.

The woman regained consciousness after the attack, escaped from her binds and headed to the phone, intent on calling the police, but instead answered a knock at her door. Standing there was Heirens. He told her he had heard something and would go down to the foyer and call for help. Heirens had the building manager call a doctor for Evelyn. He then disappeared.

It was a little over six months after Heirens had killed Josephine Ross when he decided to murder again.

On 10 December 1945, Heirens broke into the apartment of 30-year-old Frances Brown in Pine Crest, Chicago. As he climbed through the window the woman screamed and Heirens attempted to silence her by pistol-whipping her with his gun. The woman continued to fight her attacker until he fired the gun at her. He shot her twice and she fell to the ground in a pool of blood. The killer grabbed his knife, and to ensure that Frances was dead, he stabbed his knife into the left side of her neck. It was such a brutal wound that the knife pierced through to the other side of her neck.

Once she was dead, the killer stripped the pyjamas from Frances and dragged her body to the bath. He attempted to wash the blood from her face and head, but tired of trying to hold the woman. So he left her kneeling beside the bath, her head immersed in the bathwater and her pyjamas wrapped around her throat, concealing the knife embedded in her neck.

Before leaving the apartment, Heirens took a lipstick from the woman's handbag and wrote on the wall:

'For heavens Sake catch me before I kill more cannot control myself'.[183]

After getting drunk William Heirens decided he did not want to go back to his dorm room at the University of Chicago, instead he went in search of a home to break into. The young man caught a train and fell asleep as it travelled through the night. The killer woke up just after midnight on 6 January 1946, as the train pulled into Thorndale. Heirens decided to try his hand at breaking into one of the wealthy homes; his fetish for ladies' satin underwear driving his lust.

Heirens stole a ladder he found leaning on the side of one of the mansions, as he knew in his drunken state he would not be able to climb into the high windows of the larger houses.

At 5943 Kenmore Avenue, Thorndale, the young killer spotted a window slightly ajar. He pushed the ladder up the windowsill and clambered up the ladder.

Inside the darkened bedroom, he saw the silhouette of a young girl. Six-year-old Suzanne Degnan was asleep in her bed when 17-year-old Heirens climbed through her window. He shone his torch around the room, when suddenly Suzanne sat up in bed and started talking in her sleep. The noise startled Heirens and he pounced on the young girl. He threw her to the ground and strangled her until she stopped breathing.[184]

Once the girl was dead, the teenage shoved his handkerchief deep into her throat to make sure she would not wake up. As he sobered, Heirens tried to decide on his next course of action. He dumped Suzanne's body in an alleyway outside of her home and went looking for an open basement window. He found one in a nearby street and returned to get the girl's body. Once inside the basement, Heirens placed the girl's body into one of the laundry tubs. With the water running over the corpse, he took his knife and proceeded to dissect the girl's little body.[185]

He cut the body in half, before removing the head, arms and legs. Once the body was in smaller pieces he wrapped it up with rope and pieces of cloth that he found in the basement. He then took each piece and secreted it into manholes in nearby streets, hoping the sewers would take the pieces away.[186]

His last task was to return to the basement and clean it, to eradicate any evidence that would incriminate him. As he was about to leave the basement, he felt a rumpled piece of paper in his pocket and decided that he should write a ransom note for the young girl.

It read:

Gel $20,000 Reddy and WaiTe FoR word

Do NoT NoTiFy FBI oR Police

Bills iN 5s and 10s

On the reverse side it read:

BuRn This FUR heR SAFTy

He coated the note in grease in an attempt to remove any possible fingerprints.[187] He took the note back to the girl's home and threw it into the window of her bedroom. He then threw the knife away and burnt his coat after finding blood on the sleeve.

The next morning as Heirens made his way to lectures, James Degnan discovered his youngest daughter missing. The police were called immediately and a search of Suzanne's room produced the ransom letter. The Degnans began recording messages to be played on the radio, begging for the safe return of their youngest daughter.

By that evening, the first pieces of Suzanne's body were found in a manhole. A search was made of all the surrounding manholes and, with the exception of her arms, most of the young girl's body was found. Coal soot in her her hair directed the police search to nearby basements where coal was delivered for apartment-building furnaces. The crime scene was found, despite Heirens attempts to clean it up. Suspicion instantly fell on the building's janitor, but he was released later when his hand-print did not match one found at the scene.[188]

On 26 June 1946. Heirens decided to break into another home; his compulsion and sexual energy from the burglaries was a driving force and his undoing.

He broke into the Peras' apartment in Wayne Manor Building in

Chicago in the middle of the afternoon. Mrs Pera was home and bumped into the burglar as he made his way silently around the house, secreting items into a bag as he went. Mrs Pera screamed and Heirens ran from the building. He was chased by several of the building's tenants but the young man was too fast and able to get away from them.

Still with the stolen loot, Heirens climbed onto the balcony of the Willetts' home and bashed loudly on the door, Frances Willetts, a policeman's wife, opened it. The panting young man told the woman a story about being chased by hooligans and asked if he could have a drink while hiding out on her balcony. The woman was suspicious of the boy's story and so while inside she called the police, who ask her to keep the boy there as long as she could. They had received calls about the burglary in Mrs Pera's apartment and it appeared that Mrs Willetts had found the thief .

Two police officers arrived at the Willetts home and when Heirens saw them he opened fire. But his gun misfired twice and they were able to return fire. The boy attempted to jump from the balcony but was grabbed by one of the officers and a vicious struggle ensued,[189] knocking over the officers. As one of the officers struggled to keep hold of Heirens, a third officer arrived, grabbed a concrete flowerpot and struck the boy over the head, knocking him unconscious and fracturing his skull.[190]

Heirens was taken to hospital, while police searched his dorm room looking for evidence of any further burglaries; they found enough to charge him with twenty-two counts of burglary.

The seventeen year old's fingerprints were also taken while he was in hospital and compared to fingerprints from other open cases. A match was found. A palm print and fingerprint lifted from the ransom letter for 6-year-old Suzanne Degnan matched Heirens'.

They had found the little girl's brutal murderer. Yet his mother was incredulous at the accusations. She believed that he could have been responsible for the spate of burglaries saying, 'I thought the other trouble was possible, but not this', when she was asked about her son's violent background.[191] Neighbours were also shocked by the boy's arrest. They said that William and his brother were 'fine boys, courteous and likeable'.[192]

While he remained in hospital, Heirens tried to convince police he was still severely injured, pretending to be in a stupefied state, refusing to answer their questions.

One doctor suggested the use of Truth Serum, sodium pentothal. It did not work. Instead, Heirens used the guise to blame an imaginary other person called George for the murders.[193] Psychiatrists were called to examine the boy to see if he was suffering from schizophrenia. He was found to be mentally sane.

On 9 July 1946, after spending almost three weeks in hospital feigning injuries at the hands of police, 17-year-old William Heirens was charged with three counts of murder, four counts of attempted murder and twenty-two counts of burglary.

On 26 July 1946, William Heirens formally confessed to three murders. He confessed to the 5 June 1945 stabbing murder of 43-year-old Josephine Ross, the shooting murder of 30-year-old Frances Brown on 10 December 1945 and the brutal slaying and dismemberment of 6-year-old Suzanne Degnan on 6 January 1946.[194]

To supplement his confession, police had fingerprint identification from the ransom letter he wrote for Suzanne's murder. Also, his handwriting and spelling matched that of the lipstick message and ransom letter. Days later during a plea-bargain, Heirens recanted his confession, saying it was coerced from him using the sodium pentothal.[195]

After confessing and recanting his confession again at the end of July, William Heirens once again confessed on 6 August 1946 to the murders of three people. This time he offered to take police to the crime scenes to show them how he murdered each victim.

At trial William Heirens was sentences to three consecutive life terms for the murders and an additional life term for the four attempted murders and twenty-two counts of robbery.

On 5 March 2012 at the age of eighty-three, William Heirens died at the University of Illinois Medical Centre after being transferred from the Dixon Correctional centre a week earlier.

Harold Jones

'The arrival of the men from Scotland Yard fascinated me. I had only read of them before. Now I saw them in the flesh and I beat them'

On 5 February 1921, 8-year-old Freda Burnell was sent on an errand by her father to the local oil and seed store in Abertillery to buy chicken feed.[196] When she did not arrive home, her father Fred Burnell went to the store to look for her. Behind the counter 15-year-old Harold Jones admitted that the young girl had come in, he had served her and then she had left. Freda's father returned home hoping that she would soon return safely.

The next day Freda was found dead in a lane near the store. The post-mortem revealed that Freda had been strangled after receiving a blow to the head with an axe. Her killer had also attempted to rape her. A search of the area uncovered blood and signs of a scuffle in a barn. The barn was part of the store's business and so authorities again asked Jones what he knew. He denied knowledge of the bloodstains and denied having been near the barn the previous day. With the FBI now involved in the case and despite the lack of evidence linking Jones to the crime, he was arrested for Freda's murder.[197]

At trial, held in Monmouth, Jones pleaded not guilty. The jury believed his version of events and gave a verdict of not guilty on 23 June 1921, after deliberating for ninety minutes.[198] Jones was released to great fanfare. He felt superior to those who had arrested him. He later said, 'The arrival of the men from Scotland Yard fascinated me. I had only read of them before. Now I saw them in the flesh and I beat them'.[199]

Two weeks after the teen's release, on 18 July 1921, 11-year-old Florence Little was last seen playing by herself outside the house of Harold Jones with the teen's younger sister. When questioned, Jones confirmed that he had seen the girl outside his house but denied knowledge of her whereabouts. A routine search of nearby houses was conducted and Jones joined in on the search for the little girl.[200] However, the search ended when a trail of blood was found inside the Jones' house. Authorities followed the trail into the attic that was only accessible through a narrow trapdoor, where the semi-naked body of Florence Little was found with her throat cut. Jones confessed to Florence's murder, as well as the murder of Freda Burnell. Given Jones' young age he was sentenced to be held at his Majesty's pleasure.[201] While in prison, many articles emerged featuring the chilling psychopathy of the child killer:

'He can banish what to others would be of the greatest concern like flicking dust from a sleeve. He permitted nothing to worry him, and was a fatalist of the most pronounced order. His cunning and calm though, is perhaps better shown in the second case, when the mother of the murdered girl called at Jones' house to ask if the girl was there. Harold Jones had just placed the bleeding body of his victim in the attic, and calmly told her mother she had been, but had gone out with his own sister; and then as an afterthought, he asked how the woman's little boy who had been unwell, was doing. His hands were literally still dripping with the young blood of this woman's little girl'.[202]

Jones was released from prison in December 1941. He married and had a child. The family moved around several times and Jones used numerous false names to hide his horrific past. Jones died in 1971.[203] Following his death, several suggestions have been made that, as an adult, Jones was a suspect in the unsolved Jack the Stripper murders of up to eight women between 1964 and 1965.[204]

Robert Nixon

'The woman sat up and screamed. Hicks hit her over the head with a brick and I ran out'

Known as the 'Brick Moron', teenager Robert Nixon used a brick to beat to death a cocktail waitress in Chicago in 1936. After fleeing Chicago, Nixon next appeared in Los Angeles where he broke into several homes. Those who tried to protect their houses were beaten to death with his favourite weapon, a house brick. At least five people died from being bludgeoned to death by Nixon between 1936 and 1938.

Robert Nixon was born in 1919 in Tallulah, Louisiana. An African-American, he was often described in the media as dim-witted and one even juxtaposed the young teenager as an ape, heightening despicable racial stereotypes.

Twenty-five-year-old Alda Deery, a vaudeville actress, was assaulted and beaten by Nixon on 25 September 1936. When her hotel roommate arrived the following morning she found the woman's stockings tied around her neck.[205] Florence Thompson Castle was also beaten to death with a brick by Nixon in a hotel room. He wrote 'black Legion' in lipstick on the dressing table mirror.[206] On 4 April 1937, Edna Worden and her 12-year-old daughter Marguerite were also bludgeoned to death in Los Angeles.[207]

On 16 August 1937, Virginia Austin was attacked at the same hotel as Alda. The woman had been beaten with a brick by Nixon before being sexually assaulted. Student nurse Anna Kuchta was raped and then bludgeoned to death in a hospital room in Chicago on 21 August 1937.[208]

On 29 May 1938, Florence Johnson was beaten to death with a brick inside her home. Nixon and Earl Hicks were both arrested for the murder. Taken to the scene both blamed the other for the killing. Nixon said, 'the woman sat up and screamed. Hicks hit her over the head with a brick and I ran out', while Hicks claimed, 'I was standing at the doorway … when the woman screamed. I saw him strike her several times with both hands. He was holding the brick in his right hand and I saw him strike her with that hand at least twice'.[209]

Nixon was arrested after he left fingerprints on a brick found at the Worden murder scene.[210] At trial, the husband of Florence Johnson leaped at the killer and punched him in the face while he was on the stand, leaving the teenager with a bleeding lip.[211] For the murders of five of his victims, Nixon was found guilty after a jury deliberated for seventy-five minutes.[212] He was sentenced to death and executed in the electric chair on 15 June 1939.

Jesse Pomeroy

'I can't help it'

Jesse Harding Pomeroy was born on 29 November 1859 in South Boston, and was well known around the neighbourhood due to his physical features. The boy had a milky eye almost devoid of pigment that would later help victims identify him. He also had a cleft palate and hair-lip. The boy was tormented by his peers and spent most of his earliest years alone or with his mother, who would take him to see his father at the abattoir where he worked. The young boy had watched hundreds of sheep and cows being slaughtered.[213] His life was not a happy one and soon the boy was full of hatred and sexual desire even at the age of eleven. He began taking smaller children into the woods where he would strip them and attack them. Eventually the attacks became fatal.

On 26 December 1871, three-year-old Billy Paine was found hanging from the rafters in a disused farmhouse in Chelsea. The young boy survived the attack but had been severely beaten and covered in welts. His attacker was 12-year-old Jesse Pomeroy.

On 21 February 1872, Jesse Pomeroy attacked his second victim. This time, 7-year-old Tracy Hayden was coerced into joining Pomeroy in a disused farmhouse. The little boy was beaten badly around the face, he was stripped and Pomeroy beat the child severely with a stick. Tracy was found later by a passer-by. The little boy survived the attack.

Eight-year-old Robert Maier from Chelsea was asked by 13-year-old Jesse Pomeroy if he would like to go and see a circus. The boy agreed and followed Pomeroy to a disused outhouse. The little boy was stripped naked, tied up and whipped. Pomeroy masturbated as he beat the young boy, then absconded. Robert was later found and taken home. Robert was Pomeroy's third victim and it was obvious the attacks were getting more brutal and sexually explicit.

Jesse Pomeroy attacked another child on 22 July 1872. He asked 7-year-old Johnny Balch if he would like to earn some money by doing an errand for a rich man. The little boy happily accepted and followed Pomeroy to the outhouse at Powder Horn Hill, Chelsea. Once inside, Pomeroy stripped the boy naked, tied him up, hung him from a rafter and beat him until he was almost dead. The boy barely survived the attack. A 500-dollar reward was offered to find the culprit of the four attacks on small children over the past eight months, without success.

With Jesse and his brother Harry in tow, Ruth Pomeroy moved from Chelsea to South Boston on 2 August 1872. Jesse was the major suspect in the brutal attacks on the young children in Chelsea, so his mother thought it best if they leave the area. Soon after the Pomeroys moved, the attacks began in South Boston.

Seven-year-old George Pratt was spirited away by thirteen-year-old Jesse Pomeroy in South Boston on 17 August 1872. The boy was offered twenty-five cents if he went on an errand. The boy was taken to an area near the Boston River where he was stripped of all of his clothes and beaten with the buckle end of a belt. Pomeroy kicked the young boy to the ground and gouged long strips of skin from the child's chest with his fingernails. As the boy screamed in agony, Pomeroy bit into little George's cheek, taking a large bite from it. He then stabbed the boy in the chest and genitals with a large sewing needle before biting the child's face again. Somehow George survived the attack and was found a few hours later, in severe shock and bleeding profusely.

On 5 September 1872, 6-year-old Harry Austin was lured to a railway bridge in South Boston by Pomeroy, where he was stripped and severely beaten. Pomeroy stabbed the boy in both of his armpits and between the child's shoulder blades. He then took his knife and attempted to cut off the little boy's penis. He failed in his bid, but left the boy with permanent injuries.

Only a week after the previous attack, Pomeroy attacked 7-year-old Joseph Kennedy on a vacant houseboat in South Boston Bay on 11 September 1872. He bashed the child's head against a wall before stripping the young child and beating him, breaking the child's nose and knocking several teeth from the boy's mouth. Pomeroy also used his knife on the little boy. Joseph was cut on his face, his legs and his back. As a final injury, Pomeroy splashed salt water all over the boy's wounds. Joseph survived the attack and was able to tell his parents that he had been attacked by a boy 'with a bad eye'.[214]

Five-year-old Robert Gould was Pomeroy's next victim on 17 September 1872. The boy was tied to a telegraph pole and stripped. Pomeroy attempted to scalp the young boy but was disturbed by a passing railway worker who came to the boy's rescue. Pomeroy escaped.

Thirteen-year-old Jesse Pomeroy was positively identified by many of his victims due to his milky eye and was charged with the attacks of nine young children and sentenced to six years at House of Reformation at Westborough on 21 September 1872.

In less than two years Jesse Pomeroy was released into his mother's care on 6 February 1874.

On 18 March 1874, 10-year-old Katie Curran went to the local store run by the Pomeroy family to buy a new notebook. She was served by 15-year-old Jesse Pomeroy and was never seen alive again.

A handyman found her body in the basement of the store four months later on 18 July, but by then Pomeroy would have killed again.

After going to church on 22 April 1874, 4-year-old Horace Millen remained in his church clothes when he went to buy some bread for his mother at a local bakery. On the way, he encountered Pomeroy. The boy was taken to Savin Hill Beach where he was stabbed eighteen times in the chest. The little boy's throat was cut so deeply his head was almost severed from his body. His eyes were gouged out and his testicles partially removed. The young boy had put up a good struggle and his hands had been cut to pieces in the attack. However he could not survive the injuries inflicted upon his tiny body. Two brothers found the mutilated body later that same afternoon.[215]

On 23 April 1874, the day after the brutal murder of 4-year-old Horace Millen, Jesse Pomeroy was arrested for the murder. The police tried to get a confession out of the fifteen year old but he refused to talk. So, after several hours of unsuccessful questioning, the police took Pomeroy to see the body of Horace lying in the funeral home. The 15-year-old was shaken enough to confess to the boy's murder. He was asked to explain why he had done such heinous things to the child. Pomeroy bowed his head and said, 'I can't help it'.[216]

Five days after confessing to the murder of Horace Milieu, Jesse Pomeroy was found guilty of murder in a Boston Coroner's Court on 28 April 1874.

While Pomeroy was in custody, the burnt and mutilated body of 10-year-old Katie Curran was uncovered in the basement of the store on Broadway, Boston on 18 July 1874. She had been stabbed and had her chest and vagina cut open,.

When confronted with the discovery, Pomeroy confessed to the murder of Katie. At court, he read out his confession: 'I opened my mother's store in the morning at half past nine. The Curran girl came in for papers. I told her there was a store down stairs. She went down to about the middle of the cellar … I followed her, put my left arm about her neck, my hand over her mouth and with my knife, cut her throat, holding my knife in my right hand. I then dragged her behind the water closet …'[217] Jesse Pomeroy was found guilty of the murder of Katie Curran in a Boston Coroner's court on July 30, 1874 and sent to trial in December. The trial of 15-year-old Pomeroy for the murders of 10-year-old Katie Curran and 4-year-old Horace Millen opened on 10 December 1874. It lasted a little over two months and resulted in Pomeroy being sentenced to death for the murders.

The sentence was later commuted to life with hard labour, but that too was taken away when the killer was found to have made tools to aid with escape attempts, in total he tried to escape twelve times.[218] Pomeroy commenced his sentence on 1 September 1876, and it was forty-one years before he was even allowed to sit with other prisoners to eat his meals.[219] He had requested the end to his isolation, claiming, 'I am not asking to be pardoned, I am asking for more liberties ... the privilege of seeing my fellow men and talking with them'.[220]

After fifty-five years in Sing Sing, with forty of them spent in segregation, Jesse Pomeroy was moved on 1 August 1929 to a prison farm, a halfway place to his release before he was due to be set free on 29 September 1932 when he was seventy-two years of age. Jesse Pomeroy died on 2 October 1932, just short of his seventy-third birthday.

Unlike their adult counterparts, killer children are often far more brutal because of their lack of empathy. Their relatively lacking-life experience means that they often do not understand the pain of others and therefore, where an adult might refrain from further torture due to the cries of their victims, a killer child may lack that empathetic ability. The same can be said for those who poison family members and other victims. Poisoners will often watch with malice as their victims writhe in pain begging for their lives.

POISONERS

Today, killers are generally loathe to use poisons as a tool for serial murder for two reasons: the change in laws making poisons increasingly difficult to purchase; and the advancements in forensic science and the ability to detect the smallest trace amount of most toxins in post-mortem examinations.

From the late 1800s through to the early twentieth century, however, poisons were often used by killers wishing to dispatch of cheating or wealthy spouses or children, often revelling in the agony the victim suffered.

Another type of serial-killer poisoners are product-tampering poisoners, such as the still unsolved 'Tylenol Killer' case in Chicago in 1982, where seven people died after consuming Tylenol laced with cyanide. Regardless of scientific advancements and the risks involved, some mass murderers have continued to use poisons and toxins in widespread murders, such as the subway attack in Tokyo in 1995 and the infamous Jonestown cyanide-laced drink mass suicide twenty-five years ago, where detection was not of concern to those who masterminded the killings.

Dr H. H. Holmes

'Where others' hearts were touched with pity, mine filled with cruelty and where in others the feeling was to save life, I revelled in the thought of destroying'

Herman Webster Mudgett was born in Gilmanton, New Hampshire on 16 May 1860.[221] In his prison memoirs he wrote: 'I was born with the devil in me … I was born with the Evil One standing as my sponsor beside the bed where I was ushered into this world. He has been with me ever since'.[222]

This is how the man the world would come to know as Dr H. H. Holmes began life. His life was full of evil and death from the beginning. His father was an abusive man and his mother was a tiny, submissive woman. Mrs Mudgett would do everything her husband commanded and this was the way that Holmes would always expect women to behave.

School life was good to Mudgett, with his natural intelligence, charm and handsome looks he was able to influence most people and dreamed of a life as a doctor. By puberty, Mudgett had developed a hobby of killing and dismembering stray animals. He was fascinated with anatomy and would often conduct experiments on his prey.

He left school at sixteen and married Clara Lovering at the age of eighteen in 1878 and soon enrolled in medical school. As a poor student, Mudgett also worked as a security guard to pay his school tuition fees.[223]

Yet his hopes of becoming a doctor were soon dashed when he was expelled at twenty-four from the University of Michigan Medical School after he was discovered stealing cadavers.

In 1886, Mudgett moved to the upper-class area of Inglewood, Illinois, changing his name to the better sounding Dr Henry Howard Holmes.

The newly dubbed Dr Holmes walked into Dr E Holton's chemist holding the advertisement that had been placed in the window asking for a pharmacist. Holmes introduced himself to Mrs Holton, the druggist's wife. She explained to Holmes that her husband was terminally ill and she was struggling to keep the store running. She would do the prescriptions she knew and for the others she would wearily traipse upstairs to ask her husband.

Dr Holmes saw his opportunity. He took a prescription from Mrs Holton and promptly dispensed it for her. Mrs Holton hired Holmes on the spot. Holmes, with his dapper persona, brought in more customers than the little chemist had before and it thrived with Holmes as the pharmacist and Mrs Holton assisting. Then the inevitable happened and Dr Holton passed away.

Mrs Holton could not bear to leave the premises. She felt that her husband was always close by if she stayed. Dr Holmes came up with an idea. He offered to buy the Pharmacy from her, giving her a monthly salary so she could stay. The idea sounded great and the two entered into an agreement.

However Holmes defaulted on his payments pretty soon and the two ended up in court over the matter. But before the case was concluded Mrs Holton disappeared. According to Dr Holmes, she could not bear the pain of being in the place her husband had died and had moved to California. Mrs Holton was never seen or heard from again.

With the profits from the pharmacy, Holmes began the construction of his 'castle' across the street from the drug store. During the construction of the three-story building, Holmes routinely hired and fired hundreds of contractors, claiming their work was not up to his standard.

He also refused to pay them any money, and when he was taken to court over non-payment he sought continuance after continuance until the other party gave up in frustration.

The real reason behind Holmes' constant firings were so none of the contractors would get an idea of the purpose of the building, with its secret rooms, staircases that went nowhere and hidden passageways. The castle was a rabbit warren with hundreds of rooms. The cellars had vast furnaces, torture chambers, acid baths and everything a demented mind could want.[224] He did not want builders to ask questions about the sealable rooms with gas jets or the room with an enormous kiln with a cast-iron door; the large vats in the floor that would be filled with quicklime or acid; the secret chutes that led to rooms of torture and his favourite; the basement with its dissection table and surgical tools and implements. Once the building was complete, Holmes moved the pharmacy into the first floor. In 1887, while still married to his first wife, Holmes married Myrta Belknap. The marriage was not a happy one, with Myrta not able to stand Holmes' ways, and she would often berate him in front of customers, causing the good doctor great embarrassment in the neighbourhood. To stop her interfering, Holmes sent her, pregnant, to his parents, where she remained. The couple never bothered to get a divorce. Holmes was always interested in making money. He regularly devised new 'get rich quick' schemes to make money. Once he tapped into the town water supply and sold it mixed with a little vanilla essence as a cure-all tonic he named Linden Grove Mineral Water. The authorities quickly stepped in and Holmes stopped selling the water—but he was not punished for the scam.

The local medical schools also knew they could rely on Dr Holmes to supply them with fresh cadavers. If he was ever short of cash he would murder a customer and sell the body for 25–50 dollars each.

In 1890, at the tender age of thirty, Dr Holmes was quite prosperous. His new chemist on the bottom level of the castle was attracting more and more business with its polished-wood panelling, frescoes and arched ceiling—it was the epitome of class.

Next to the pharmacy Holmes opened a jewellery store, a restaurant and a barber, as well as a business manufacturing soap in Chicago. With so many business dealings, Holmes needed a manager to help him. Ned Conner was a job-to-job drifter who dragged his wife Julia and daughter Pearl with him to each job he held. When he saw the advertisement for a manager, he applied for it and got the job. He thought his problems were over—the job paid well and seemed permanent. Conner introduced Holmes to his wife and daughter. Holmes was instantly stunned by the Julia's beauty: a 6-feet-tall, red-haired, green-eyed woman. Holmes instantly fired his current cashier and hired Julia.

Julia could not believe her luck. She rang and invited her 18-year-old sister to visit her in Chicago. Gertie was as beautiful as her sister and quickly caught Dr Holmes' eye. He showered the young woman in gifts and affection. Holmes even told Gertie he would divorce his wife to be with her. Gertie was shocked by his proposal and hastily left Chicago. Holmes rebounded quickly from Gertie's rejection by returning his attentions to Julia. After drinking heavily one night, Ned was confronted by his friends who told him of his wife's dalliances with Holmes. Ned stormed home to speak to his wife.

He told Julia that Holmes did not love her, that she was only his second choice since Gertie had rejected him. Julia made further accusations at Ned until the couple decided to separate. Ned stayed in another room in the castle for a while before moving out permanently. On his departure he told Julia he wanted a divorce.

Julia was deeply in love with Holmes and subsequently became pregnant with his child—a fact that Holmes did not like. The doctor told his lover that he would only marry her if she aborted the pregnancy. Being a mother to Pearl already and feeling the unborn child inside her, Julia could not bear the prospect and continually put the procedure off.

After further insistence by Holmes, Julia agreed that he could perform the procedure. Holmes put Pearl to bed and then carried the hysterical Julia down to his makeshift operating theatre in his basement. Neither Julia nor Pearl were ever seen alive again.

Dr Holmes had one of his lackeys clean off Julia's dismembered body and removed all the flesh, leaving only the bones. Julia's skeleton was sold to a medical school for 200 dollars. According to Holmes, he felt nothing when he killed his victims. He later said in his confession: 'Where others' hearts were touched with pity, mine filled with cruelty, and where in others the feeling was to save life, I revelled in the thought of destroying'.[225]

In May 1894, Holmes hired Minnie Williams as a typist, but soon the pair became romantically involved. Several months later, Minnie's sister Etta also joined them, living together at the Plaza Hotel in Chicago. Holmes was aware that the girls were heirs to a 50,000 dollar fortune. Holmes claimed that Minnie had become jealous of the attention that Holmes had begun showing Etta and she struck her sister and killed her.[226] He claimed to have then dumped the body in a lake. Minnie disappeared as well.

Benjamin Pitezel, another of Holmes' lackeys who hung off his every word and did everything asked of him, soon gave his life for Holmes. The two men came up with an insurance scam where they could share in ten thousand dollars. The plan was that Pitezel would take out a life-insurance policy for 10,000 dollars with Holmes as the beneficiary. Pitezel would then disappear to Philadelphia. Holmes would get a corpse, disfigure it, then with the help of Pitezel's children he would have the body identified as Pitezel and claim the 10,000 dollars.

The plan worked brilliantly and Holmes claimed the money. However, Holmes was fearful when the police became interested in him. He torched the castle and fled Chicago with one of the Pitezel daughters. Mrs Carrie Pitezel followed behind, presumably to meet up with Benjamin in Philadelphia. What Mrs Pitezel did not know was that Holmes had murdered Benjamin while he was in a drunken stupor. The killer 'poured chloroform and lighter fluid all over his body, then lit it'.[227]

In the burnt-out remains of the castle, authorities found the remains of dozens of skeletons.[228] A press conference was held in which police reported that 'He killed women and girls in there; how many we have no idea. He may have killed a score … WE know he shipped out boxes and trunks that may have contained bodies'.[229] A warrant was issued for Holmes and he was arrested in Boston in 1894 and extradited to Philadelphia, where several people came forward with the names of missing persons. The brother of Peter Verrett went to police claiming that his brother had gone to Holmes' castle to be cured of a drinking problem. The man, an heir to large fortune, was never seen alive again. Verrett's brother hoped Peter may have been amongst the remains.[230] The bodies of Minnie and Anna Williams were found and identified in the basement due to two large hair samples left behind after lime had been used to turn the bodies into dust. Another body was also located, that of Emeline Cigrand.[231]

While in prison, Holmes shared a cell with Marion Hedgepeth. Hedgepeth would continually boast about his escapades. To get even,

Holmes told Hedgepeth about the murder of Pitezel for the insurance money, and that Pitezel was not the first he had killed. Hedgepeth told the authorities.

Holmes was charged with the murder of Benjamin Pitezel and confessed. He told the police how he had burned the man alive despite 'the victim's cries for mercy and his prayers, all of which upon me had no effect'.[232]

At the castle, the police began the tally. It was suspected that as many of the fifty guests who stayed at the castle during the 1893 Chicago World Fair fell victim to Dr Holmes. Also at least one hundred typists and secretaries were murdered there. One after another would fall victim to the doctor's charms and murderous lust by responding to the never-ending advertisements placed by Holmes.

Three of the Pitezel children were also located. Alice and Nellie had been stuffed into a trunk and gassed with chloroform.[233] Their brother Howard had been poisoned, burned, dismembered then buried. Police found the bodies when a trap door in the kitchen that led down the stairs to the cellar was opened.[234]

On 28 October 1895, Holmes pleaded not guilty to the murder of Benjamin Pitezel and sent to trial. At his trial on 4 November 1895, Holmes was convicted of first-degree murder and sentenced to death. He remained wanted in Chicago for the murders of Julia Connor and her daughter Gertrude, who died sometime between August and November 1892.[235]

Holmes enjoyed the notoriety he gained from the trial. He gave many reporters access for interviews and began writing his own memoirs. He signed a statement claiming responsibility for the murders of a further twenty-seven people, adding to his infamy.

As he was brought to the gallows on 7 May 1896 at Moyamensing

Prison, he recanted most of his statements, regarding the murder of Minnie Williams exclaimed, 'As God is my witness, I was responsible for the death of only two women. I didn't kill Minnie Williams. Anna killed her …'[236] Following his death, Mudgett's grandson sent a letter to *The Michigan Daily*. In it, the writer claimed that he wanted to clear his grandfather's name by giving a reason for the murders. The letter stated that Mudgett was a poor student at the medical school and when fees rose, he had no choice but to rob people to make money to complete his school … 'from then on the fate of [his] grandfather was sealed'.[237]

K. D. Kempamma

'Mallika had brought her to Mysore on the pretext of performing a puja'

Forty-five-year-old K. D. Kempamma, also known as Cyanide Mallika amongst a half dozen other aliases, murdered at least six victims with cyanide between 1999 and 2007. The killer met her victims in the temples of Bangalore and would entice them to her home with offer of work or various other duties. She had deserted her own family before the killings commenced.

Kampamma's first victim was a 30-year-old woman whom she poisoned on 19 October 1999.[238] Another victim named Nagaveni was abducted and killed in Doddaballapur on 18 December 2007. The housewife was praying at the temple when the killer struck up a conversation. Nagaveni told Kampamma that she had been praying for a child. Kampamma told the woman that if she accompanied her to her home, she would give her potions to help with her prayers. The woman was given water laced with cyanide.[239]

Another victim was Muniyamma, who was abducted from the Siddalingeshwara Temple in Kunigal Taluk in 2010, she had brought her to Mysore on the pretext of performing a puja,[240] a religious ceremony.. Her last victim, 50-year-old Pillamma, a sculptor, was enticed away from the temple by Kempamma who asked that she accompany her to Vaidyanathapura to create sculptures of the temple there.[241] Once there, to bless them, she would offer her victims a glass of water, stating it was holy water. The victim would drink the cyanide-laced concoction. Cyanide Mallika also strangled some of her victims.

She was captured on 31 December 2007 when she tried to sell pieces of jewellery belonging to her last victim, Pillamma.[242] It was only after her arrest that neighbours told the media that they had been complaining to police about the smell emanating from her home.

In 2010, she was found guilty of the murder of Muniyamma and sentenced to death. Two years later she was given another death sentence for the murder of Nagaveni. However, both sentences were reduced to life imprisonment. In October 2013, the serial killer was sentenced again to life imprisonment for the murder of Pillamma in 2007 and fined five thousand rupees.

In jail, Mallika was assaulted by eight other women prisoners.[243]

Madame Popova

'I never murdered a woman'

In March 1909, Russian police arrested a woman named Madame Popova for a suspected poison attack. However, her confession surprised everyone. Madame Popova gave details of the poison murders of over three hundred husbands over thirty years in St Petersburg.[244] She claimed that unhappy wives would contact her about their unwanted husbands, whom she would eliminate using poison for a small fee.

The wives would pay Popova half the money before the murder. The killer would then strike up a friendship with the husband before offering him a drink or a meal laced with poison. After the murder had been committed, the wife would pay the rest of the fee charged by Popova.[245] She claimed that she had obliged in the killing of so many men to free unhappy wives from their tyrant husbands. In her confession, she said that she was 'justified in her work for the only persons she killed were men who had abused their wives and that she had saved the women from further misery'.[246] She was adamant to point out that she had never 'murdered a woman'.[247]

The arrest came after one client felt remorse for her husband after his death. When news of the crimes were published a lynch mob attempted to seize her and burn her at the stake, but the mob was held back by police and soldiers who drew their guns.[248] For her crimes Madame Popova was executed by firing squad.

The Gonzalez Valenzuela Sisters

'The food didn't agree with them'

Sisters, Maria de Jesus Gonzales, Eva Gonzalez Valenzuela and Delfina Gonzalez Valenzuela of Mexico murdered at least ninety-one people between 1955 and 1964.[249]

The sisters owned a profitable brothel in Guanajuato, Mexico, where they offered a good time for any gentleman who came looking for a girl for the night. However, if a prostitute working at the bordello did not satisfy them, she was disposed of by poison or prolonged beatings by the killer madams.

To keep up a steady stream of prostitutes, the women would procure young girls through the classified advertisements, or abduct them from the streets. Yet it all came to a halt when Josefina Guierez, one of the prostitutes working at the brothel, was arrested by police for the attempted kidnapping of a potential victim while attempt to recruit new girls for the brothel.

In an attempt to lessen her own charges Josefina told police about the numerous women and wealthy customers who had disappeared from the brothel. Soon, the sisters were arrested, along with nine other people[250] and police commenced the excavation of a pocket of land near the brothel. Several other sites in Leon, San Francisco and Guadalajara were also excavated. At the first excavation, police unearthed fifteen bodies of teenaged girls, as well as two babies, but knew that the body count could go higher.[251] In total the bodies of eighty women, eleven men and a handful of babies were found buried around the bordello's outskirts.

When police raided the brothel, one girl, Maria Trinidad Hernandez Martinez, explained to them that she had been told that she was to be murdered the following weekend.[252] The fifteen year old had been abducted and forced into prostitution two years earlier. Two weeks before the arrests, she had become recalcitrant and had been moved to the ranch at Leon where most of the murders took place. She had seen three murders during her two weeks at the ranch.[253]

When the women were questioned about the killings, the response was 'the food didn't agree with them'.[254] Two of the sisters, 56-year-old Delfina and 39-year-old Maria, were found guilty of the murders of at least eighty girls. They were given the maximum sentence of forty years in prison. They were also fined 67 209 dollars that was to be paid to the families of their victims.[255] Delfina died in prison, while Maria served out her entire sentence before being released. She spent the rest of her life in fear that people would attack her. Eva was also sentenced to prison for her part in the crimes and died of cancer while incarcerated.

Graham Young

'I started experimenting at home, putting one and sometimes three grains in the prepared foods which my mother, father and sister ate'

Graham Frederick Young was born on 7 September 1947 at Neasby Hospital in North London. His mother, Margaret, unfortunately died at Christmas that same year leaving Graham's father, Fred, to look after the 3-month-old baby as well as his 8-year-old sister, Winifred. The Young's extended family helped out, and Winifred lived at her grandmother's house and Graham with his aunt Winnie.

Fred visited his children daily and took them out at weekends. Fred remarried, and as the years passed Graham grew to despise his stepmother, Molly, whom he referred to as the 'outsider' and told friends that he hated her.

In his early school years, Young's hobby was reading. He always had his nose in a book from the local library. At nine years old, Young developed the first signs of an interest in chemistry and gathered some small bottles of acid and ether. His interests expanded and his reading material stretched into black magic and the Nazi movement. He began to wear a swastika that he refused to take off. Young's parents realised that his seemingly innocent hobby was now turning into an obsession. Young experimented with mice and his acid and took part in imaginary sacrifices.

Into his pre-teens, Young chose science, particularly chemistry, as his specialist subject. He excelled in the lessons, such that he was given free reign, allowing his mice experiments to continue. Young's drawings would also leak a potential clue to his state of mind. His main topic of art was death. On one occasion Fred and Molly found a drawing of coffins marked with 'mum' and 'dad'.

In April 1961, 13-year-old Young visited Geoffrey Reis' chemist, where he asked for 25 grams of antimony. When asked his age, Young replied that he was seventeen, the minimum legal age needed to purchase the poison. Unsure about the honesty of the boy's answer the shopkeeper questioned him as to why he wanted the poison. Young's knowledge of chemistry ensured that he was able to demonstrate a number of experiments for which he could use the chemical. Impressed with his knowledge and Young's false age of seventeen, he sold the chemical to the boy. Young signed the poison register using the name of M. E. Evans and also provided a false address.

Having been able to convince the chemist to sell him the poison and armed with a small amount of pocket money and an additional five shillings from a part-time job cleaning floors, Young was able to regularly return to the chemist for additional bottles of antimony. Weeks later, Young got into a fight with a school friend, Chris Williams. Young was jealous that Chris was spending more time with other people than with him. Chris easily won the fight over his much smaller opposition, after which Young threatened to kill Chris.

On the following Monday at school, Chris was suddenly overwhelmed with nausea and was sent home after he began vomiting. Every following Monday Chris was violently ill but no one could understand why. Young was persuading his friend to eat lunch with him, having prepared some sandwiches for the pair of them. The Williams family took Chris to the family doctor and then onto Willesden Hospital, where he was diagnosed as having a migraine. Nobody suspected poison.

Young's stepmother Molly found a bottle in his room marked

poison. She let Fred know of her find and in turn Young was banned from keeping such items in the house. When the chemist who sold Young the antimony was informed of Young's age, Young simply changed his source of the poison to chemist Edgar Davies. He used the same method as he had with the previous chemist, by giving a false name, age and address.

In early 1961, Molly and Fred both suffered violent illnesses, followed soon after by Young's sister Winifred. The family believed that they had been infected by a bug, but then suspicion was aimed at the boy and his chemistry set.

They theorised that he had innocently used teacups to mix his chemicals and had failed to clean them out properly. Fred disciplined his son about playing with his chemistry set in the house. Suspicion moved on to other possibilities when the illnesses continued. The home's water was tested for contamination without result. The family couldn't explain the spate of illnesses affecting them, yet it continued throughout the year.

In November 1961, Winifred became so ill that she was taken to hospital for treatment before being released. On 21 April 1962, Molly Young felt worse than she had done over the past year, but there was still no real explanation why. As the day went on, Molly could no longer do her regular chores and stayed at home. After lunch, Fred came home to see his son staring from the window at this wife rolling in agony in the garden. Fred immediately took her to Willesden Hospital. The doctors insisted that she stay overnight for observation. That evening Molly was discharged home where she soon died.

Because of the sudden nature of her death, doctors insisted that a post-mortem be carried out. Doctor Donald Teare completed his report and indicated that death was due to a 'prolapse of a bone at the top of the spinal column'.[256] The cause of this was linked to a crash that Molly had been involved in the previous year. No further investigation took place.

At Young's suggestion, to which his father agreed, Molly was cremated on 26 April. All evidence of the crime was destroyed.

A few days after Molly's death, Fred again fell ill. He vomited several times and suffered intense stomach pains. Winifred insisted that her father see a doctor. The doctor could not find anything specifically wrong with Fred, but suggested he go to hospital for further tests. Fred was about to leave the doctor's surgery when he collapsed in the office. An ambulance arrived and took Fred to Willesden Hospital.

Fred's suspicion lay directly on his son, who visited him in hospital but never said a word to his father. Instead, he was more interested in learning of the symptoms of the illness from the doctors and nurses. After a short stay at the hospital, Fred improved in health and was discharged. The doctors were still unaware of the cause, when only days later the symptoms returned. Winifred took charge of the situation and called an ambulance to take Fred back to the hospital. Initial tests indicated that he had been poisoned with either arsenic or antimony; however, it was yet to be confirmed.

The family instantly blamed Young. The following day, antimony was proven to be the cause of Fred's illness and doctors told Fred that his liver was permanently damaged, explaining that as little as one more dose of the poison would have killed him. During Fred's recovery at the hospital Aunt Winnie looked after the children, but was given strict instructions by Fred that his son was not to visit him under any circumstances.

At the school, the science teacher Mr Hughes heard of the sad news concerning the Young family. His own suspicions grew about Graham Young. One evening after lessons, Mr Hughes searched Young's desk and discovered several small bottles of poison and a notebook containing notes on several poisons and famous poisoners. Mr Hughes recalled the mystery of Chris Williams' illnesses and, making the link, went to talk to the headmaster who agreed with his suspicions. The pair decided to visit the family doctor, Dr Willis, who suggested that it was too early to point the finger at Young, but did suggest that an evaluation by a psychiatrist would help in the matter.

The interview took place on 20 May. The psychiatrist was acting the part of a careers officer to get Young to discuss his chemistry ambitions. Young proudly talked about his experiments involving poisons and his knowledge of them. He told the fake careers advisor that he had 'started experimenting at home, putting one and sometimes three grains in the prepared foods which my mother, father and sister ate'.[257]

After the meeting, all notes were given to Detective Inspector Edward Crabbe. The following day DI Crabbe visited the family home, searched Young's bedroom and discovered various types of poisons including thallium, digitalis and antimony.

Crabbe briefly spoke to Aunt Winnie and told her that he would be arresting her nephew for malicious administration of poison. As Young returned from school that day, he was greeted by the detective and instructed to empty his pockets. They yielded nothing. Then he was asked to remove his shoes; still nothing. Finally, Young was asked to remove his shirt. A small vial of Antimony fell to the floor along with two other bottles that further testing would identify as containing thallium. Young was arrested and taken to Harlseden police station.

At the station Young initially denied everything, before giving a full confession to his activities the following day. He even confirmed where he had hidden additional bottles of poison. With this evidence, Graham Young was charged on 22 May with poisoning Fred Young, Winifred Young and Chris Williams. No charges were brought against Young concerning the death of his stepmother, Molly.

Young appeared at the Old Bailey on 6 July 1962, where he pleaded guilty on all three counts. In court, a prepared statement was read out on behalf of Young that outlined the methods he used to poison his family and school friend Chris. He also admitted to regularly giving his stepmother doses of antimony.

The prosecutor Mr E. J. P. Cussens brought up the subject of Molly Young. He reiterated that her death had been due to natural causes and not an intake of poison. However, a consultant psychiatrist, Dr Donald Blair, believed that antimony may have led to the condition that affected her spinal column, which, in turn, led to her death. Dr Christopher Fysh, a senior medical officer, gave the court his medical opinion of the defendant: 'Young is not suffering from a mental illness but from a psychopathic disorder, in my opinion he requires care in a maximum security hospital'. Fysh suggested Broadmoor Hospital.

Jean Southworth, acting for the defence, asked Fysh if Young had the killer instinct. Fysh replied that Young was 'prepared to take the risk of killing'. The judge handed down his sentence and under Section 66 of the 1959 Mental Health Act, Young was committed to Broadmoor with an instruction that he was not to be released for a period of fifteen years without the express permission of the home secretary.

Young's time in the hospital was spent away from his father. Despite a few visits in the early months after his sentencing, Fred hardly saw his son. Aunt Winnie was Young's most regular visitor. Young would shy away from group contact while in Broadmoor, preferring to be on his own. His interest in Nazism continued and he made his own swastika that he proudly wore on a chain around his neck. As time went on, the staff at Broadmoor became more and more confident in Young. At one point they even placed him in charge of making coffee for the staff. Almost inevitably, several cups of bitter-tasting coffee were found. Bleach had somehow found its way into the pot.

After his third year at Broadmoor, Young wanted to leave. The only option available to him was to petition the annual review tribunal to look into his case. His family attended the review and Fred asserted that his son 'should never be released'. The review resulted in the petition's rejection. Several months later, a packet of sugar soap disappeared from the cleaning room. A full tea urn was analysed just as rounds were about to begin. It contained the missing soap, which would have caused severe stomach burns to any who would have drunk from it.

It was never proven that Young was responsible for the incident, though suspicion lay heavily on the teenager. After the incident, Young recognised that another option for release lay open to him. Young became the model patient, using good behaviour as his route to early release.

In June 1970, the subject of Young's future was again discussed at the hospital. The doctors believed that he was 'no longer obsessed with poisons, violence and mischief', and no longer a danger to others. The senior psychiatrist at the hospital, Dr Edgar Udwin, suggested that to help facilitate Young's development, a stay at a family member's home for a few days would do him some good. Given that Fred would immediately refuse, they decided to approach his sister.

Winifred was unsure, but eventually decided to give her brother a chance and therefore on 21 November 1970, Young was granted leave for a week long stay at Winifred's house, where she now lived with her husband Dennis Shannon and their newborn child. The couple, on Dr Udwin's advice, gave Young a free reign of the house, including the kitchen. At the end of the week Young returned to the hospital. Dr Udwin was pleased to receive a good report on his patient's behaviour. The Shannon's even suggested that they would enjoy a second visit, maybe over the Christmas holiday. The request was approved and again the visit went well, Young was showing no signs of his previous obsessions and spent the time indulging in new-found happiness.

Backed up by the good reports from Young's sister and by his own observations, Dr Udwin believed that Young was ready for release. In early 1971, he petitioned the Home Secretary for release. Following the ruling from Young's 1962 trial, the request was approved and Young was given a release date of February 1971. After hearing of his upcoming release, Young privately let other patients and some nurses know of his resentment at having been kept 'locked up'. Young once admitted to a nurse that he intended to kill one person for every year he spent in the hospital. However, the concerns the nurse had about Young's release fell on deaf ears. Young was released from care on 4 February 1971. No one told Fred. It wasn't until a month after his son's release that a Broadmoor official finally let Fred know.

Young gained a place at a government training centre in Slough. On February 8 1971, he began a course in storekeeping, quickly making friends with another trainee at the centre, 34-year-old Trevor Sparkes. The two would regularly drink together, discussing various topics. A week after meeting, Trevor confided in Young about some abdominal pains he was suffering from, confessing that his doctor couldn't help.

In the short time he had known Trevor, Young had persuaded his friend that he was knowledgeable in the field of medicine and offered him a glass of wine, convincing Trevor that it would help. For four days Trevor vomited violently and suffered pains across his whole body. He spent a further four days in the sickbay of the training centre until the pains subsided and he was able to return to work. He still believed that Young was helping him and so continued to take his advice, drinking the wine he was offered. The pains continued and he visited his doctor as well as Queen Elizabeth II Hospital in Welwyn, but doctors were baffled by the symptoms.

In April 1971, Young applied for the job of storeman at John

Hadland Ltd in Bovingdon, Hertfordshire. Prior to his interview at the firm, Young travelled to London and visited John Bell and Croydon chemists. There, he attempted to purchase antimony potassium nitrate. Young employed the same method he used years earlier, but the request was turned down. The chemist rightly informed Young that despite his impressive knowledge he did not have the written authority to purchase such substances. One week later, on 24 April, Young returned to the chemist with a letter headed 'Bradford College London', which gave authority for Mr M. E. Evans to purchase antimony for experimental purposes. The chemist, Albert Kearne, handed Young the bottle and recorded his signature in the poison register. Meanwhile, Young's interview at Hadland's had gone well, such that he was offered the job. Young agreed to start on 10 May 1971.

At Hadland's, the storeroom workers found Young to be quiet and unpredictable; he would be talkative one minute and then ignore everyone the next. Young would spend his breaks sitting reading his favourite topics of Nazism and war. Despite this, whenever topics of chemistry came up, Young would suddenly brighten up and become talkative. Young's manager in the storeroom was 58-year-old Bob Egle. Bob was a war veteran and Young enjoyed listening to his stories of the battlefields in France.

The store's team would regularly help Young out with favours: rides to and from work, the occasional cigarette etc. Young would repay their kindness by fetching their cups of tea from the trolley. On 3 June 1971, Bob Egle fell ill and went home for the day, not returning until the following Monday when his diarrhoea attacks had ended.

The day after Bob returned to work, on 8 June, storeman Ron Hewitt also began suffering from diarrhoea and stomach pains. The symptoms continued for three weeks. Bob Egle took another two weeks off work with abdominal pains and returned on 28 June. But on his second day back, he once again fell ill and was sent home. Bob couldn't sleep; he complained of numbness in his hands and feet; his back caused him pain and his headache just wouldn't go away.

Bob's wife, Dorothy, called a doctor who diagnosed Peripheral Neuropathy. An ambulance was immediately called. Bob was taken to the West Herts Hospital in Hemel Hempstead, but the pain continued to get worse. He was transferred to St Albans City hospital into the intensive care unit but his condition did not improve. Bob's body was by now almost completely paralysed and his heart stopped twice. On each occasion the staff at the hospital was successful in reviving him. But on 7 July 1971, Bob Egle died.[258] A post-mortem on the body was performed two days later. The cause of death was put down to Bronchopneumonia in conjunction with polyneuritis.[259] After Bob's death, Young was placed in charge of the storeroom for a probationary period and the illnesses at Hadland's continued.

In September, Fred Biggs began to feel stabbing pains in his stomach and also suffered periods of severe vomiting. Fred returned to work on 20 September, the same day that Peter Buck fell ill with the same symptoms, returning to work the following day.

On 8 October, David Tilson was next to succumb to the mystery illness sweeping through the storeroom. After drinking a cup of tea with Young, David began to feel nauseous, but continued to work before going home for the weekend. The pins and needles David felt in his arms and legs were slowly getting worse. By Sunday his limbs were numb and he visited his doctor who prescribed rest.

On Tuesday 12 October, David returned to work, although the pain in his legs would not go away.

On the Friday afternoon, Jethro Batt gave Young a ride home. As they drove, Young described how easy it was to poison somebody and get away with it. The next day, Jethro was violently ill after having a mouthful of coffee made by Young. Over the weekend, Jethro's legs went from numb to painful, then the pain moved to his stomach.

David Tilson felt just as bad. His chest and stomach were painful and he was struggling to breathe. His doctor sent him to St Albans City Hospital for observation. Then his hair started to fall out. Jethro remained at home but he was in immense pain, unable to move easily. On 5 November, he was admitted to West Herts Hospital and, as with David Tilson, he too was going bald. David was released from hospital on 28 October, but four days later he was readmitted. In the storeroom at Hadland's only one member of the staff was unaffected by the illness: Graham Young.

Fred Biggs continued to suffer stomach pains and vomiting, which was affecting everyone in the company stores, bar Young. Fred returned to work to help out with the annual stocktaking. The following day however, he once again was overcome with the same symptoms, but this time the pains were more intense. On 4 November, Fred was admitted to West Herts Hospital, where Jethro Batt would join him the following day. Young was now under suspicion by the staff at Hadland's. Rumours spread through the company.

When Young overheard Diana Smart call him a germ carrier, the next day she was off work after suffering attacks of vomiting.[260] Fred Biggs continued to deteriorate during his time in the hospital. Several doctors reviewed his case, but could find nothing that would cause the symptoms, however they did believe Fred was suffering from some form of nervous complaint. On 11 November, Fred was transferred to Whittington hospital where his condition worsened still. The skin on his face and scrotum began to peel away. He was virtually paralysed. Fred was transferred again, this time to the National Hospital for Nervous Diseases. At 7 a.m. on 19 November, Fred died.

Panic set in at Hadland's; several employees wanted to quit. Doctors visited the factory but couldn't find anything that could have caused the massive outbreak. The factory owner John Hadland returned from abroad and called in the local doctor, Dr Anderson, to talk to the staff. Dr Anderson admitted to the staff that there were three possibilities, radiation, a virus or perhaps some form of metallic poisoning. Of the three options he believed that it was a, as yet unidentified, virus working its way through the factory. One of the staff had other ideas. From the back of the room, Graham Young spoke out, pointing out that metallic poisoning was clearly causing the symptoms.[261]

Dr Anderson had privately believed that metallic poisoning could not yet be dismissed and became suspicious of Young's statements. Dr Anderson spoke to John Hadland about his suspicions and John Hadland decided to secretly act. He spoke directly to Detective Chief Inspector John Kirkpatrick of Hemel Hempstead police. He detailed the illnesses and Dr Anderson's suspicions, but would not name Young as a suspect.

DCI Kirkpatrick visited Hadland's to begin an investigation. One of the first things he noticed was that the illnesses began shortly after they employed Young. He spoke to Detective Chief Superintendent Ronald Harvey for his opinion on the case. Despite his experience Harvey did not have an answer, but he was able to speak to a forensic expert who, upon hearing the symptoms, immediately gave a diagnosis of thallium poisoning. Kirkpatrick made a request that the employees at Hadland's have their backgrounds checked. Graham Young was instantly placed to the top of the list. Scotland Yard spoke to John Hadland and Godfrey Foster, the managing director, to tell them of Young's poisonous past. Officers were immediately sent out to arrest Young on suspicion of murder.

Officers visited Young's flat at 29 Maynard Road, Hemel Hempstead, but the owners didn't know where he was. They checked with his sister,

Winifred. She gave the officers the address at which her brother was on holiday with his father and aunt in Sheerness. Fred Young answered the door to the arresting officers and almost instantly knew why they were there. As the handcuffs were 'snapped' onto Young's wrists, Aunt Winnie asked of her nephew 'What have you done now?'

Detective Sergeant Robert Livingstone returned to Young's flat on Maynard Road to search his room. Amongst all the Nazi paraphernalia, he found a collection of bottles marked 'poison' and several drawings of men with no hair. During questioning at Hemel Hempstead police station, Young boasted of how he got away with poisoning his stepmother Molly. He then suggested that doctors were failing with David Tilson and Jethro Batt by not treating them correctly.

Kirkpatrick spotted the mistake and was able to trap Young. He asked Young what poison he had used. Young, however, refused to answer the question but gave Kirkpatrick the antidote for it. As the interview wore on, Young could not resist boasting of his work. Eventually, using Young's arrogance against him, Detective Chief Superintendent Ron Harvey was able to gain a confession from Young. He admitted using thallium on Bob Egle, Fred Biggs, David Tilson and Jethro Batt, in addition to using antimony potassium nitrate on Peter Buck, Diana Smart, Ron Hewitt and Trevor Sparkes.

The following day, 22 November, the police were hoping for further evidence of poisoning to corroborate Young's confession. The body of Fred Biggs was to undergo a post-mortem performed by Professor Hugh Molesworth-Johnson. The initial observations concluded that the symptoms of Thallium poisoning were present. However traces of the metal could not be found. Fred's internal organs were sent away for more detailed analysis, Despite lack of real evidence in his hand, Ronald Harvey returned to the police station and charged Young with the murder of Fred Biggs. Young made a court appearance on 23 November to be remanded in custody awaiting trial.

Evidence of Bob Egle's murder was next on the agenda. Bob had been cremated after his death, but his ashes were buried in Gillingham cemetery. After gaining authority, Bob's ashes were exhumed and sent for testing. The results of both Bob Egle and Fred Biggs' post-mortems came through on the same day. In both cases thallium poisoning was confirmed as the cause of death. Young was now additionally charged on 3 December 1971 with the murder of Bob Egle. These charges were quickly followed with charges of attempted murder on David Filson and Jethro Batt and charges of grievous bodily harm on Diana Smart, Peter Buck, Ronald Hewitt and Trevor Sparkes. Young was then transferred to Brixton Prison.

After a delay, the trial of Graham Frederick Young began on 19 July 1972 in the St Albans courtroom of Mr Justice Eveleigh. With Sir Arthur Irvine QC acting as his defence, Young entered a plea of not guilty on all counts. After all police evidence and other witnesses had been presented, Young made an appearance at the stand. His evidence took two days and consisted mainly of prosecutor John Leonard QC verbally squaring off with the defendant.

Young's intelligence however shone through. He was able to fend off the prosecutors' questions with arrogant ease, giving confident answers to all points raised. Summing up in the case barely took an hour before the jury were given final instructions and asked to begin their deliberations. Less than one hour later, they returned.

Young was found not guilty of the charges of grievous bodily harm against Peter Buck and Trevor Sparkes, but guilty of the murders of Bob Egle and Fred Biggs. He was also found guilty of the attempted murders of Jethro Batt and David Filson and guilty of grievous bodily harm against Ronald Hewitt and Diana Smart.

Sir Arthur Irvine called for common sense in sentencing, reminding the court that the crimes were unlikely to have been committed had Young not been released from Broadmoor early. He further suggested that a custodial sentence was inappropriate and that Young should be returned to Broadmoor to continue treatment. However, Young was sentenced to life imprisonment for the two counts of murder and two counts of attempted murder.

In addition, Mr Justice Eveleigh sentenced Young to five years for each count of grievous bodily harm. Young was taken from the courtroom and transferred to Wormwood Scrubs then Parkhurst Maximum Security Prison on the Isle of Wight to serve his sentence.

Young made the headlines of the national press again in August 1990. This time however, the media were reporting his death. Graham Young had died alone in his cell less than a month before his forty-third birthday from a heart attack.

Anna Zwanziger

'I had my fun, the people who tormented me so, had to vomit'

Anna Margaretha Zwanziger was born Anna Schonleben in Nuremberg on 7 August, 1760. By 1765 she was an orphan and moved for the next five years between different family members. At the age of ten she was sponsored by a wealthy guardian and received a decent education.

At the age of fifteen she married a drunken 30-year-old lawyer called Zwanziger. Her guardian had arranged the marriage. The couple had two children together, but it was far from a happy marriage. Anna became a prostitute at one point to support the family, as her husband had become unable to work due to his alcoholism.

Anna however, still had standards. She maintained to only have had judges and men in powerful positions as her clients and lovers. She left her husband at one stage to be with a lover but Zwanziger persuaded her to come back. Zwanziger had a hold over Anna. When they finally divorced, they remarried the next day.

In 1796 Zwanziger died, leaving 33-year-old Anna to look after the two children alone. She attempted to open her own store but failed. She felt back into prostitution but again became pregnant and had to stop. The baby was sent for adoption but died at an orphanage.

It was around that time that Anna began to show signs of ageing beyond her years. Her mental stability also began to waiver; she went into house service but would ignore the wishes of her employers. She felt she was above doing menial work, but needed the money. Over the next two decades she continued to do housekeeping. But the last two years of her freedom saw her became an embittered woman who believed she should be the mistress of the house and not the maid. She poisoned several women to try to get their husbands to marry her. Little did she know she was suffering delusions and was not desirable.

Anna Zwanziger had made herself a reputation as an expert knitter and housekeeper, when she was visited by Justice Wolfgang Glaser at her house in Pegnitz, Baireuth, Bavaria. He asked the now fifty-year-old woman if she would become his housekeeper. Justice Glaser went on to explain that he had recently separated from his wife and needed someone to tend his home.

On 5 March 1808, Anna became the Judge's housekeeper. However, the appointment appeared to have been unnecessary when Frau Glaser returned home to be with her husband once again. The reunion was short-lived. Though Frau Glaser was a strong and healthy woman, she became suddenly ill on her return on 22 July.

She suffered violent vomiting bouts, diarrhoea, pain and nausea. Five weeks later Frau Glaser was still writhing pain when she died on 26 August 1808.

A month later on 25 September, Anna left the Glaser's service and went to keep house for Justice Grohmann in Sanspaared. The 38-year-old man suffered poor health and spent a lot of time in bed. Anna doted on the man and he soon became well, only to be stricken once more.

In spring 1809, Grohmann was inflicted with diarrhoea, vomiting and severe abdominal pain. The illness lasted eleven days and he died on 8 May 1809. Grohmann's death was attributed to natural causes due to his long-term health issues. Anna was inconsolable after the man's death.

Frau Gebhard, wife of Justice Gebhard, had heard of Anna's fine skills as a 'perfect housekeeper'[262] and quickly took her on after Grohmann's death. Frau Gebhard was pregnant and needed help during her confinement. On 13 May 1809, the baby was born and both mother and daughter were well.

Yet three days later Frau Gebhard became extremely unwell. She began vomiting profusely. She was completely bedridden. On 20 May 1809, Frau Gebhard died from the illness. Her last words to Zwanziger were, 'For God's sake, you have given me poison'.[263] However, due to Frau Gebhard's long-term ill health, no one in authority took much notice of her accusation and her death was ruled to be due to natural causes.

By now, people were beginning to suspect that it was more than mere coincidence that Anna's employers kept expiring. However nobody talked about their suspicions. So Anna continued her employment as a housekeeper to Bavarian Judge Gebhard.

On 25 August 1809 Justice Gebhard dined with two guests, Mr Beck and Mr Alberti. After dinner the two guests were both stricken with a similar illness to that of Gebhard's wife. A messenger who had come to the house and stayed for a glass of wine also suffered from the gastrointestinal illness. A porter, Johnny Krause, had stopped for a glass of port and only had a small sip. He noticed white sediment and had heard the gossip about Anna and chose not to drink any more from the snifter.

Yet there had been enough poison in the small mouthful to cause him to become violently ill. Others in the household were also sick. One of the kitchen maids, Barbara Waldmann, became ill after a cup of coffee made by Anna. Yet again no action was taken as no one had seen Anna put poison in any of the vessels. It was all still conjecture.

On 1 September 1909, Gebhard entertained five friends for an evening with games of skittles. All of them, including Gebhard, became ill after drinking beer.

At the urging of his ill guests Gebhard dismissed Anna from his service the next day. However, on 3 September 1809 Anna decided to do some last-minute chores before leaving her employment. She took the saltbox from the kitchen cellar and filled it with salt from the barrel in Gebhard's room. Barbara the kitchen maid saw Anna do it. The job was actually Barbara's and she found it unusual that Anna would do it.

She then gave Barbara and another maid a cup of coffee, and the 5-month-old Gebhard baby some milk and a cookie. All of it was laced with poison.

After Anna had left all three of them became ill. The household knew now for sure that Anna was responsible and Barbara remembered the salt barrel. The police were called and the salt was tested. It contained a high level of arsenic.

Anna was arrested shortly after and when she was searched, two more packets of arsenic were found in her possession. Police then began investigating the deaths of Anna's other employers. Frau Glaser's body was exhumed and arsenic was found in her body.

Anna confessed to all of her crimes, claiming, '[I] had my fun, the people who tormented me, had to vomit'.[264] She showed no remorse for any of the murders except that of Grohmann, who she claimed was 'my best friend, my everything'.[265] Zwanziger was sentenced to death for the murders and was beheaded on 17 September 1811.[266]

As shown in this chapter, poisoning is no longer a popular weapon of choice for the serial killer. Poisonings through conventional means using toxins such as arsenic and antimony are almost unheard of. Today, with poisons such as those no longer available at the local chemist, poisoners turn to such overdosing on toxins such as illegal or legal narcotics to kill their victims, which do not give off the telltale signs of traditional poisons.

Poisoners are one of the most patient type of serial killer. They are willing to stand by and watch their victims die slow and agonising deaths. Their victims are usually relatives, but some killers like H. H. Holmes gassed many of his victims or dispensed of them using the drugs from the drug store he ran.

At opposite end of the patience scale are the mass child killers in the next chapter. Where poisoners can wait years to watch a victim die, Child killers are rampant, taking as many of two and three victims a day to satisfy their sexual blood lust.

MASS CHILD KILLERS

S erial killers who target children often get away with the murders due to the fact that the killers are strangers to the victims, leaving no possible link between killer and victim. In many lower socio-economic countries where children are often left to fend for themselves as street beggars, their disappearances are often not noticed, giving predators free reign to kill indiscriminately until they are caught.

This chapter on mass child killers focuses on murderers who killed a large number of child victims, mainly boys, until they were caught. Had they not been caught, the numbers could have been frighteningly higher. Most of the victims are sexually assaulted before being murdered, but the frenzied spree provides evidence that in most cases the murder was part of the sexual thrill.

Manuel Bermudez

'I was forced to kill them, so they could not recognise me later, but I am sorry'

Known as the 'Sugarcane Monster', 42-year-old ice cream seller Manuel Octavio Bermudez from Columbia, confessed to the murders of thirty-four boys. The boys had been raped before being killed, their bodies found in the sugarcane fields of Valle de Cauca, Palmira during a killing spree from 1999 to 2003.

The body of 10-year-old Andres Felipe Serna was found in a Palmira sugarcane field on 6 April 1999. Bermudez had bound his hands and feet together before raping the boy. He then smashed in the boy's skull before putting him in a sack and dumping his body.

Bermudez abducted his second victim. The child's body was found on 20 September 1999 and again the killer had dumped the remains in the same regional sugarcane field. Ten-year-old Daniel Valencia was raped and beaten before being dumped.

The next child abducted by Bermudez was found on 5 May 2000. The 11-year-old boy's beaten and sodomised body was found in a sugarcane field. Bermudez was charged with aggravated assault and sentenced to five years and four months in prison. The killer promptly escaped and began raping and killing boys once again by the end of 2001, when another 11-year-old boy's body was found in the sugarcane fields of Palmira. Javier Fernandez has been abducted and raped by Bermudez before being killed.

On 12 January 2002, Bermudez murdered another child. The eleven year old, Jose Sinisterra, was raped, killed and dumped in Palmira.

On Valentine's Day 2002 another body was discovered. The identified boy was approximately twelve years old. Like the others, he had been sodomised, beaten and dumped in the sugarcane fields.

In Hacienda another body was found on 9 April 2002. The remains were those of a 12-year-old boy. More than three months passed before another body was found. In late July 2002 the remains of 12-year-old Edwin Perez were found in Tulua. On 3 December 2002, another of Bermudez's victims were uncovered. The defiled body of 9-year-old Miguel Arce was found in Palmira; he had been missing for two weeks.

A fortnight after the discovery of Miguel's body, another one was found. The body of 12-year-old Candelo Hurtado was found in Palmira. Bodies continued to be located, yet police were no closer to catching the killer. Nine-year-old Carlos Morcillo's body was found in Palmira in January 2003 two weeks after he had gone missing. Two weeks later the body of 9-year-old Cascajal Torres was found.

In April 2003, the abused and beaten body of 12-year-old Jose Figueroa was found in Yotoco. In May 2003 the body of a 12-year-old boy was found in Padera. The child was not identified due to the length of time between being murdered and the discovery of his body. The body of 13-year-old Jorge Rodrigeuz was also found that same month in the town of Meadow.[267]

On 11 June 2003, 12-year-old Luis Galvis was the final victim to be found. Bermudez was the last person to be seen with Luis and was identified by witnesses. The killer was quickly arrested by police and a search of his home uncovered numerous pairs of boy's underpants and lengths of rope similar to those found with the victims. Bermudez confessed to the murder and took authorities directly to Luis' body.

Bermudez stated in his confession that he had to kill the boys as they would recognise him and tell police of his sexual advances. He confessed, stating that 'yes I raped and killed children,[268] ... I was forced to kill them, so they could not recognise me later, but I am sorry'.[269] He also confessed to mutilating his victims as well as sodomising them. It was found that at the time of the murders he was on the run after escaping from a prison where he was serving a five-year sentence for rape. He was found guilty of the murders and sentenced to forty years imprisonment.

Francisco das Chagas de Brito

'My lawyer is God . . . I'm not crazy head . . . One day the truth comes . . . I never killed anybody'

Francisco das Chagas de Brito claimed a voice spoke to him, and over fifteen years he was responsible for the rape, torture and murder of at least forty-two boys. Born in Maranhao, Brazil in 1965, he murdered his victims who were mostly orphans and beggars that had willingly gone with the killer when he offered them fruit-picking work. Once he had his victims alone he would strangle them, before raping and mutilating them.

Chagas snuck into a home one evening and abducted a sleeping four year old from his bed. Daniel Ribeiro was taken into the local woods where he was tortured and raped before being strangled until unconscious. Then, like he had done to other victims, Chagas mutilated the unconscious boy by cutting off his penis, testicles, fingers and ears. When a search team was assembled the following day Chagas joined in to help look for the missing boy.

He collected the blood of many of his victims and used it to consecrate the ground where he would leave them wrapped in palm leaves. Other victims were dumped in waterways.

His final victim was 14-year-old Jonnathan Vieira. The boy was taken on 6 December 2003. The boy had told his family he had been asked by

Chagas to go into the wood to pick berries. When the boy did not return, Chagas became the prime suspect.

Jonnathan was already dead. The killer had raped him before cutting off the boy's penis. When police went to arrest the man, a search of his home unearthed the parts of forty-two boys, including Daniel Ribeiro and Jonnathan Vieira.

Following Chagas' arrest he confessed to seventeen murders. He quoted the Bible verse of Isaiah when given a reason for the slaughter: 'Prepare slaughter for his children for the iniquity of their fathers; that they do not rise, nor possess the land, nor fill the face of the world with cities'. His first trial for the death of a 15-year-old victim saw him receive a twenty-year sentence. In 2009, the killer was put on trial for the murders of another two of his victims, where he claimed not to remember killing any of the victims.[270] He was found guilty and given an additional 36-year sentence. He was tried for another murder at the end of 2009 and more time was added to his sentence. He has spoken to many media outlets since his incarceration protesting his innocence, claiming, 'My lawyer is God … I'm not crazy head … One day the truth comes … I never killed anybody'.

Luis Garavito

'I ask you to pardon me for all I have done and I will confess. Yes, I killed them—and many others'

Luis Alfedo Garavito is one of the world's most prolific serial killers. Between 1992 and 1999 he brutally murdered at least 172 children and documented each murder in a carefully maintained diary. His male victims were mostly street children and were aged between seven and sixteen years of age when they were abducted. Each victim was tortured and raped before being decapitated. Forty-one of the bodies were discovered in a ravine in Risaralda, Colombia in November 1998.[271] Many of the victims had had their intestines pulled from their bodies and tied around trees.[272]

Born on 25 January 1957, Garavito was the eldest of seven brothers born to a subservient mother and a violent and cruel-tempered father in Genova, Colombia. As a boy, Garavito claimed he was often at the receiving end of physical and emotional abuse at the hands of his father. He was also sexually abused by two men as a young boy. To block out the pain of his childhood, Garavito commenced drinking and was a chronic alcoholic with a violent and sexually explosive temper by the time of his arrest.

Working as a street vendor in Pereira, Garavito committed his first murder in 1992. He murdered the street urchins who hung around his market stall after giving them money and food to entice them away as he travelled across the country. Garavito used a number of disguises during the abductions, including dressing and acting like a cripple, a priest, a street beggar, a charity worker and a monk, among others.[273]

Due to the transient nature of his victims, no one noticed their disappearance and Colombian authorities were unaware that a serial killer was operating in the city until 1997 when the bodies of thirty-six boys were discovered. Garavito had been seen with several of the victims and police soon tried to find the killer.

Garavito was arrested in October 1999 after being caught attempting to rape a small boy. When police questioned him about the bodies, he produced his notepad and confessed to 140 of the murders. He told police bluntly, 'I ask you to pardon me for all I have done and I will confess. Yes, I killed them—and many others'.[274] Relying on the killer's confession, the police in Columbia searched through almost sixty villages and found the remains of a further 114 victims. The killer, known as 'La Bestia' (The Beast) in the media, confessed to 139 murders of the 172 that he was charged with. He was sentenced to 1853 years imprisonment, however Colombian law states that no criminal can be imprisoned for longer than thirty years. That meant, with the decrease in sentencing for his cooperation in locating the bodies, he was to serve a sentence of no more than twenty-two years.

Javed Iqbal

'I have sexually assaulted and killed one hundred children, all boys, and erased their bodies in acid-filled containers'

According to psychologists who extensively interviewed the man after his arrest, the Pakistani killer was born into luxury and used his wealth to pursue his penchant for violent sodomy on boys. Witnesses would later describe how he always surrounded by young boys, and he earned the eerily accurate title of 'boy hunter'.[275] He would initiate friendships with boys via children's pen-pal magazines.

In once case the killer took one of the victims' mothers as a wife as an attempt to conceal the abuse of her son. The marriage was also an attempt to avoid an arranged marriage that his family had organised. Iqbal claimed that he had married his wife because of his love for her son.[276]

For years the man's abuse of children went unnoticed until 1990 when one boy complained to his father that he had been sodomised by Iqbal. When police arrived to arrest him, he had already fled and his father and two sons were arrested and tortured in an attempt to flush out the predator. Eight days after the incarceration of his family, police arrested one of Iqbal's abused 'boys'.[277] The arrest scared the man who gave himself up to procure the boy's release. It prevented the boy from telling police of the abuse he had suffered at the hands of Iqbal.

He was later again arrested for sodomy charges and served a six-month sentence. However, the brief incarceration did little to stop him abusing hundreds of victims on his release, resulting in further charges and his eventual expulsion from the city of Shadbagh.

Following the death of his wealthy father in 1993, Iqbal, one of six siblings, inherited a substantial sum of money that he used to further his sadistic abuse of local boys. He built a large house with a pool, as well as several luxury cars that enticed many boys to the man's doorstep. The abuse of his victims continued until September 1998 when two of the boys rose up against him and his accomplice. Iqbal was left with critical head injuries. On release from hospital after months and spiralling medical costs, Iqbal found himself destitute and his mother dead. Iqbal also found himself under arrest, again for sodomy. His plea of innocence fell on deaf ears with the authorities and he was incarcerated.

According to the killer's diary confessions, he began his six-month murderous campaign in June 1999 after his release from prison. He would sometimes murder two or more boys in one day. 'I did it to avenge an attempt on my life by my boys, the death of my mother and injustice in society'.[278] As he commenced his war against the authorities, he kept meticulous notes, savouring in full detail the extent of the sadistic means he would use on his victims.

'I have sexually assaulted and killed one hundred children, all boys, and erased their bodies in acid-filled containers. In terms of expense, including the acid, it cost me 120 rupees to erase each victim'.[279] So taunted Javed Iqbal in a letter he sent to police and the media in Lahore, Pakistan in December 1999. It was the final letter after his murderous campaign where the killer taunted the city with parcels sent to a local newspaper that included diaries, photographs and evidence documenting the sexually motivated murders he had committed. In the confessional letter, he wrote that he was to commit suicide by jumping into the Ravi River. Police searched the river to no avail and instead headed to the man's home.

When police arrived at the man's rundown flat they found the bodies of three young boys melting away in a large acid vat and piles of clothing from his victims littering the home. Pinned to the walls were detailed notes of what he and his accomplices had done to each of his victims before killing them and putting them in the acid vats.

Yet police found no sign of the man. The killer and his accomplices had fled the apartment before investigators arrived. The suggestion of suicide had been a ruse to send police looking in the opposite direction as they escaped.

Days after the final shocking confession had arrived at police headquarters, four of the killer's accomplices, 17-year-old Sajid Ahmad, 16-year-old Mamad Nadeem and 13-year-olds Mamad Sabir and Ishaq Billa were arrested after trying to cash a forged traveller's cheque in nearby Sohawa. The accomplices were interrogated by police in an attempt to find Iqbal. On 8 December 1999, Billa leapt from the third floor window of the Ravi Road police station. The boy died on impact. Even with his accomplices in custody, father of two Javed Iqbal remained on the run.

The man's diaries described at length the various ways that he had been able to abduct so many young boys. According to one entry, his accomplices would entice young boys, many of them homeless runaways that hung around the Data Sahib shrine, to his home under the noses of the Ravi Road police station. Once inside the man's blood-filled apartment, the boys would be subjected to hours of torture and sexual abuse before being murdered.

Twelve-year-old Imran Satar disappeared in October 1999. The young boy had gone for a walk one afternoon and never returned. His clothing was found in Iqbal's home. The clothing of 12-year-old Muhammed

Ahmed was also found. He had gone missing six weeks before Iqbal's final letter. A photo of the boy found in the apartment included the details of the boy's death as well as the number 39. Muhammed was the thirty-ninth victim of the hundred boys Iqbal and his accomplices murdered.

For a month, police searched for Iqbal without success until the killer decided to give himself up on Thursday 30 December 1999. The short, middle-aged man walked into the office of *Jang*, an Urdu-language newspaper, with two satchels containing food. He told a journalist who was keen to hear his story, 'I have no regrets. I killed 100 children. I could have killed 500; this was not a problem ... but the pledge I had taken was 100 children, and I never wanted to violate this'.[280] Shortly afterwards, police arrested Pakistan's most wanted man.

With Iqbal and three of his accomplices in custody following the death of the fourth during interrogation, Pakistan's trial of the century began. Iqbal, a natural performer, played to the media as he pleaded his innocence in the face of his own handwritten notes. He even attempted to say that the gruesome discovery in his home was staged to highlight the plight of Pakistan's runaway children.[281] He then tried the defence that the confessions were made under duress fearing that should he not confess, that he too would meet the same fate as Billa.

On 16 March 2000, the man was found guilty of the murders of his one hundred victims. The killer's sentence was death. The judge outlined the exact nature of his execution: 'You will be strangled to death in front of the parents whose children you killed. And your body will then be cut into one hundred pieces and put in acid the same way you killed the children'.[282] Iqbal escaped the gruesome death by killing himself in his Kot Lakhpat prison cell on 9 October 2001. His accomplice, 20-year-old Sajid was dead beside him. Both men, who were in adjoining cells, had hung themselves.

Gilles de Rais

'He is nobody in the world which knows or which can understand all that I made in my life. He is nobody in the planet which can thus make'

Gilles de Rais was born Gilles Laval in 1406 in the 'Black Tower' at Champtoce, France to Marie d'Craon and Guy de Rais. When de Rais was eleven his uncle, Armaury d'Craon, was killed in battle at Agincourt, leaving him as one of two heirs to the vast wealth of his aunt Jeanne La Sage. The marriage between his parents, Marie d'Craon and Guy de Rais was a political union, culminating in the combined fortunes of three of France's wealthiest families,

Gilles' father Guy de Rais had changed his name from Laval to de Rais to help cement his inheritance from Jeanne la Sage as the last of the de Rais family. However, before la Sage died she decided to change her will and instead gave the money to Catherine de Maehecoul, Marie d'Craon family that resulted in the union of the two families.

Two years after Gilles was born, his parents had another son. The life of the de Rais boys was quite cold and distant. The privilege class preferred to treat their sons as adults from a very young age. They were raised mainly by nurses and teachers and rarely saw their parents.

The first time de Rais saw his parents was at the age of seven when he was introduced into French society. From the age of seven Gilles was tutored in the classic arts, humanities and Greek and Latin. He was also taught warfare and the ways of high-society court. Though he was a willing student, de Rais never got used to courtly behaviour and grew up rough and only semi-skilled.

In 1415, after the feast of Epiphany, Gilles' mother Marie died. The death was devastating to the young boy and within three years Gilles' father also died while boar hunting. The children were sent to live with a cousin but after contesting the will of their father, the two boys were given to maternal grandfather Jean d'Craon. D'Craon was the second richest man in France and spared nothing when attempting to gain further wealth. He was described by many as a ruthless and cunning man who taught the boys the art of warfare. By the age of fourteen, Gilles began his first campaign as a squire. He would practice his new skills of sword fighting, jousting and hand-to-hand armed combat for hours. But he yearned to fight in the real battles he had heard so much about.

Jeand'Craon encouraged the young man's ambition, telling him that by fighting in war, de Rais would be able to expand his own wealth and land holdings, he also arranged the marriage of Gilles to Jeanne Paynel, the daughter of the wealthy and powerful Lord de Jamye of Normandy. The marriage would make the d'Craons the most powerful family in France, if not in Western Europe. The French Parliament knew what power such a union could create and forbade the marriage until Jeanne was eighteen.

The decision angered D'C'raon and less than a year later he announced the betrothal ceremony of Gilles to Beatrice de Rohan, the niece of the Duke of Burgundy. The marriage however never eventuated.

Instead, Gilles de Rais married Catherine de Thonars on 30 November 1420, and became one of the richest noblemen in Europe. He lived extravagantly until his arrest.

On 8 May 1429, Joan of Arc and her captains, Gilles among them, fought the siege of Orleans on 17 July. The Dauphin was crowned King Charles VII, and one of his first acts was to name Gilles de Rais a Marshal of France. At the same time, Gilles formally allied himself with his cousin Georges de La Tremoille, a favourite of the new king.

Gilles' wealth and powers were immense, but the man was unable to deal with all that society had given him as Joan of Arc's chief of the militia.

Gilles spent money as fast as he earned it, bringing his wealthy family to the edge of bankruptcy many times.

Towards the beginning of 1432, Gilles de Rais withdrew from public life and spent his time studying science and the theories of alchemy after the war had finished. Yet the man was restless. He enjoyed the sport of war and the smell of blood and wanted more.

So he ventured out and murdered children, often sodomising the corpses as he went. He would also have servants murder victims as he watched on, re-enacting battle scenes de Rais had seen during the war. At other times he would wine and dine his victims before slaughtering them.

On 30 July 1440, Jean de Malestroit, Bishop of Nantes and Chancellor of Brittany, issued the first document in the proceedings against Gilles de Rais. Based on public innuendo only, it accused Gilles of murdering children and performing sodomy and other unnatural acts with them. He was also accused of evoking, sacrificing to, and entering into compacts with demons.

At his trial, Gilles was given a list of his crimes. According to the list, during a total of fourteen years he had seized at least 140 children, committed sodomy, murdered and dismembered them. He was also charged with conspiring with others in worshiping demons and studying the dark arts.

Gilles confessed to having once borrowed and read a book on alchemy and demon summoning and having practiced alchemy. Everything else he denied. There were many accusations based on hearsay and innuendo. Many historians have the number of kills by Gilles as high as 140–70, but these are highly sensationalistic.

The less than accurate charges included the children who disappeared during 1438. Three children disappeared in January, two in June, one in

September, one in October and one in November: a total of eight. In 1439, seventeen disappearances were reported: two in January, one in February, three in April, two in May, one in June, three in August, three in October and two in December. For 1440, the year of Gilles' trial, one child was stated to have disappeared in February, two in March, three in April and one in July. The children's ages range greatly, however the median age was ten.

After being interrogated for several weeks by the judge in one of his torture chambers, Gilles 'confessed' and was put to the stake and burned on 26 October 1440.

Child killers who murder on such a mass scale often hide their crimes amid poverty or civil war. They are able to abduct children that will not be missed, or who are from such poverty-stricken environments that concerns raised by families fall on deaf ears, with little investigation done to unearth the real reason behind the missing children. The large number of victims, who are almost always boys, continues until the perpetrator is captured. There has been no documented killer who stopped killing without arrest. All of the victims in these examples were sexually assaulted before or during the murder.

The sexually motivated murders by mass child killers are also seen in the murders committed by serial killer couples. The sexual motive is often the basis of the fatal couple killing teams.

KILLER COUPLES

Murder is a shocking crime. But to kill in the company of a lover or spouse, to most, defies explanation. This chapter examines the killers who, once they became a couple, became deadly. Most of the killers, with the exception of Fred West, did not kill before the deadly relationship emerged. In most cases, the male was the dominant figure in the relationship and was often responsible for the suggestion and procurement of the chosen victim to be raped and murdered.

Most of the murders were sexually motivated, often to increase the sexual pleasure of the male perpetrator. The women in the killer couples was often seen as subservient and willing to do anything to please their partner—even murder.

However, like with anything involving human nature, there are always exceptions to every rule, and there is evidence that suggests that women such as Rosemary West were equally excited and involved in the murders as their husbands.

With the examination of the cases in this chapter, one must ask the question, if these couples did not come together, would they have become killers on their own? The answer may never be known.

Paul Bernardo and Karla Homolka

'We raped a little girl . . . in my room. You . . . found her . . .
I was shocked. I gave you that. I let you do that because I love you.
Because you're the king' *Homolka*

'Obviously, looking back, I had a problem with sexuality.
It's hard to explain . . . I was enjoying myself'[283] *Bernardo*

Paul Bernardo was conceived illegitimately in Ontario, Canada, when his mother, Marilyn Bernardo, returned to the comfort of a previous boyfriend after problems in her marriage. Marilyn's husband, Kenneth Bernardo, was an abusive man who was known by neighbours to be a peeping tom. When Marilyn had found him fondling their baby daughter, she left him and sought out an ex-lover. However, she returned to live with her husband once again and Paul was born, believing Kenneth was his father. It was only years later, during a violent argument with his mother, that the teenage boy discovered the truth about his real father.

By the time he was at university, Paul had grown bored of normal sex and preferred to dominate submissive women, demanding anal sex and fellatio. He would also beat up his numerous girlfriends and urinated and defecated on them during sex.[284]

In October 1987, 23-year-old Paul Bernardo was working at a large Toronto accounting firm when he met Karla Homolka.

Karla Leanne Homolka was born on 4 May 1970 in Port Credit, Ontario. She was the eldest of three daughters born to Dorothy and Karel Homolka. The family lived in St Catherines, Ontario where Karla first became interested in working with animals. While still in high school she got a part-time job working at a veterinary clinic. After leaving school she started at another clinic as a full-time veterinary assistant.

Homolka was attending a vet conference in Toronto when she was spotted by Bernardo across a room. The seventeen year old was besotted by the attention from the older man. He was an attractive, successful businessman in her eyes and she soon told her friends she had met the man she was going to marry. The pair spent the first night together in a hotel room having rough, fervent sex for hours. The relationship was sexually charged from the very beginning and Bernardo gave Homolka a list of demands and instructions on how she should behave and dress and things he wanted her to do for and to him.

When Bernardo failed the exam to become an accountant he decided he could earn more money in other ways and soon began trafficking stolen goods across the American/Canadian border.

After a few years together Homolka made plans for a wedding to match the fairytale romance she was living, even as their sexual relationship grew more sadistic. Homolka started to encourage Bernardo's deviant behaviour: 'Karla, handcuffed, on her knees and begging for him, was scratching an itch. Paul asked her what she would think if he was a rapist. She would think it was cool. Their love deepened. He started raping women in earnest' as the unidentified Scarborough rapist[285]

From May 1987, Bernardo had savagely raped several women. He would often attack his victims from behind, grabbing them after they had stepped off a bus in a secluded area. He anally raped most his victims and forced them to perform fellatio before letting them go. One of the victims was able to get a look at her attacker and went to police with the description. Many of Bernardo's friends made jokes about how much the picture looked like him, but a few took it seriously enough to report him to the police. Police visited Bernardo and was asked to provide saliva, blood and sperm samples for DNA comparison. However, the samples were lost.[286]

By December 1990, Karla's parents were happy that their eldest daughter had found such a handsome successful young man; Karla's younger sister Tammy was also thrilled, yet she was to become the couple's first victim.

On 23 December 1990, Bernardo slipped a few sedatives into Tammy's drinks. He was frustrated that he wasn't his fiancé's first lover and so he wanted to take Tammy's virginity. Karla held a cloth soaked in halothane over her sister's nose and mouth. Tammy passed out from the drug quickly and Bernardo began the attack. Homolka filmed the abuse while she monitored Tammy's breathing. Homolka encouraged Bernardo to rape and sodomise her sister. Bernardo pushed Homolka's face towards her sister's vagina and told her to perform cunnilingus. Homolka refused several times before Bernardo became abusive, hitting her over the back of the head as he forced her closer to her sister's vagina. Tammy began to vomit and her head lolled forward blocking her airway. Karla redressed her sister and turned her upside down in an attempt to clear her airways. Unfortunately, Tammy fell into a coma. After hiding the videotapes, the couple called the paramedics and woke the family. The ambulance team attempted to revive the comatose girl without success. The family was questioned regarding any possibility that Tammy had taken anything besides alcohol—she had a huge purple stain around her mouth that suggested drug ingestion. Karla and Paul claimed that Tammy had only been drinking 'screwdrivers' but had drunk quite a few. In the end, Tammy's death was declared an accident and no toxicology tests were conducted. The purple stain was explained away as an acid burn from the vomiting.

One day, in January, Bernardo made a big announcement. He told Karla's parents that he was moving out and Karla was to go with him. The pair found a house in Port Dalhousie and moved in soon after Tammy's funeral. Paul continued to earn money by smuggling cigarettes and other merchandise across the border. The money was lucrative but Karla was concerned that it would bring unwanted attention from the police. Bernardo spent a lot of time away from their new home and continued raping women and girls he found walking home at night-time.

One evening, Homolka called Bernardo's mobile phone and told him she had a gift waiting for him. Bernardo arrived home and discovered a pretty teenage girl unconscious in their house. Karla had coerced Tammy's girlfriend Jane over and drugged her. She had thought that if she could find virginal victims for her fiancé then he may stay home and perhaps treat her better. Bernardo enjoyed his gift. He first made Homolka perform cunnilingus on their sleeping victim, and then raped the girl before sodomising her. But Karla's plan did not work; it did not stop him from going out and raping victims. He eventually became known as the Scarborough Rapist.

On Friday 14 June 1991, Leslie Mahaffy spent the evening with friends and ignored her parents 10 p.m. curfew. Her parents had asked her to be home early and to remain in a group. The Scarborough Rapist had been attacking victims more frequently and they were naturally concerned for their daughter's safety. But Leslie did not share their worry and 10 p.m. came and went. It was not until 2 a.m. that Leslie decided it was time to head home. When she arrived at her front door she found that her parents had locked her out, in an attempt to teach her a lesson. Bernardo spotted Leslie. He grabbed her at knifepoint as she walked by. He drove her to his house, where he forced her to strip naked as he filmed the terrified girl. He blindfolded the teenager and made her lie down. As he went to penetrate her vaginally he climaxed. Bernardo was furious at himself for ejaculating so quickly and took his anger out on the young woman, beating her savagely across her back and head. Karla heard the commotion in the lounge-room and went to see what Bernardo was doing. According to Homolka, 'We raped a little girl down here in my room. You went out and you found her. Got her. Brought her back to the house, brought her downstairs. I was shocked. I gave you that. I let you do that because I love you. Because you're the king'.[287] Bernardo was pleased that Homolka had woken up; he now had two women under his control. He grabbed the video camera and directed his fiancé to engage in various sexual positions with their captive. Bernardo then sodomised and raped Leslie before murdering her. Her remains where encased in concrete and thrown off a bridge on Lake Gibson.[288] The same day the girl's body was found, the couple were married.

On 30 November 1991, five months after Leslie's murder, 14-year-old Terri Anderson disappeared. The young girl's naked body was found in the waters of Port Dalhousie six months later on 23 May 1992, a month after the body of the killers' third victim was found. Though no charges were ever laid for the murder of Terri, many investigators believe that Bernardo and Homolka were to blame.[289]

Kristen French was abducted on 16 April 1992 and taken to the killer couple's home. For two days she was subjected to rape, sodomy and torture before the couple murdered her. Her body was found in a ditch near the Port Dalhousie lake two weeks later.[290]

By February of 1993, Bernardo, as the Scarborough Rapist, had raped dozens women and had murdered several teen girls, yet police were no closer to catching him. That was until Paul brutally beat Karla. She called the police and charged him with assault and battery. Using Karla as a punching bag proved to be Paul's fatal mistake. The physical abuse had been going on for years, but this time he blackened both her eyes, knocked out several teeth, and fractured several ribs. Homolka called the police who investigated the matter, taking the badly beaten woman to the hospital. Toronto detectives interviewed her at length as she began to tell them about the life she had led in the control of her sexually abusive husband. Piece by piece, the rapidly materialising jigsaw depicting Paul Bernardo as a serial killer were falling into place.

When Karla's favourite uncle arrived at the hospital she whispered to him that Paul was the Scarborough Rapist and he had killed Leslie Mahaffy and Kristen French. Bernardo was arrested on 10 February and charged with the Scarborough rapes and the murders of Leslie and Kristen. Karla became afraid of being pursued as an accomplice, so Karla made a deal where she would plead guilty to being an accomplice and received twelve years in penal servitude for each of the two victims in exchange for giving police the evidence they needed against Bernardo. Had the videotapes been viewed before the deal was made, a completely different outcome may have been achieved.

Twenty-five-year-old Homolka was convicted in 1993 of manslaughter and sentenced to twelve years in prison.[291] She was released from prison in July 2005. The Canadian government placed restrictions on her parole and she has been in the media many times since her release. Reports claim the woman, who helped murder at least two girls, is now a mother.

Thirty-one-year-old Bernardo, in the face of the evidence from his wife, pleaded not guilty. His defence was that both girls had died while he was out of the house. He claimed that Homolka was responsible for their murders.[292] However, he was found guilty of the murders and admitted to fourteen sexual assaults.[293] He was sentenced to two consecutive life terms[294] in prison, under a 'dangerous offender' classification, meaning he is to never be released. He has since been questioned about several other disappearances but he has refused to admit to any further murders.

The St Catherines home once owned by Bernardo and Homolka was torn down following the sentencing of the killers.[295]

David and Catherine Birnie

'The most macabre and sadistic crime in the history of Australia' *David*

'I'm not proud of what has been said about me but I have to live with that . . . why this happened I can only hope that the doctors can help me to find out' *Catherine*

David Birnie was born in 1951 in Wattle Grove, Australia, to alcoholic parents. He was the eldest of five children. After ten years of the children being repeatedly removed from their parents due to neglect, all five Birnie children were sent to different foster homes. Some of them lost contact forever. Later, Birnie contemplated what the rest of his siblings must have thought of him as one of the country's worst killers. He felt as though he were an embarrassment.

Catherine was born Catherine Margaret Harrison[296] and never knew her mother, who died when she was less than two years old. Catherine moved to South Africa where she was systematically abused by her father for two years before being rescued by her grandmother who took the toddler back home to Perth. However, life with her grandmother was also hard. She forbade other children from coming into the house and therefore most of Catherine's free time was spent alone, where she continued to go unloved and sink further into a morose existence. When Catherine's grandmother suffered a severe epileptic fit, she was deemed no longer fit to look after the young girl and Catherine was shipped off to another relative. This time Catherine moved in with her aunt and uncle in the Perth suburb of Lathlain.

Life for Catherine was extremely dull and she rarely smiled. Her upbringing was rather strict. Yet in a neighbour she found what she yearned for. When David Birnie came into her life she found a kindred spirit. The fast talking, intelligent David swept her off her feet and showed her the wild side of life and her own personality. Yet the relationship was short-lived as both teenagers were moved away by their families and soon lost contact.

David grew up as a scrawny boy; he was short and thin and often picked on at school. David left school at around fourteen and went to work as an apprentice jockey, a job perfect for his stature. He talked at length about his work with horses. He claimed that had he not been dismissed from the job due being suspected of stealing, he may never have gone on to commit the killing spree.[297]

In 1966, at the age of fifteen, Catherine and David met once again. This time David was wilder and drew Catherine deep into his world. He had quite an extensive juvenile criminal record for robbery and assault and an accomplice would suit him well. Catherine had also left school by this time and was working as a machinist in a window blind factory. But she was soon joining David in his criminal activities. By 1969, the 18-year-old couple found themselves in front of the magistrate in Perth Police Court several times, charged with breaking and entering and stealing. Both pleaded guilty to the charges and were remanded for sentencing. David received a prison term of nine months due to his previous extensive record for similar crimes. Catherine, who was pregnant with another man's child, was put on probation. The young lovers were not apart for long.

On 21 June 1970, David walked out of Karnet Gaol and found his way back to Catherine. Together, they committed a string of thefts that added another two and a half years to David's prison term. Catherine was sent to jail for six months and her newborn baby was taken from her by welfare authorities. After serving their prison terms, the couple went their separate ways again for a short time. David married and had a daughter. He settled down to family life. Believing she was rehabilitated and with the stipulation that she was not to see David Birnie, Catherine was released from prison and was granted custody of her child. She quickly found work as a live-in nanny for the respectable MacLaughlan family. Catherine fell pregnant to the son of her employers, Donald, and on her twenty-first birthday, 31 May 1972, the pair married. November saw the birth of 'little' Donny Jnr, and the couple seemed happy with their newfound family, a new experience for Catherine. However, the happy family would not last long. At the age of seven months, Donny was crushed by a friend's car and Catherine witnessed the accident.

Catherine and Donald made it through the terrible death together and had six more children. Donald was working as a council employee and though times could get a little tight, their family always had enough money to live on. However, after Donald injured his back he was no longer able to work and the couple, with their six children, were forced to live in a dilapidated government-provided house. The place was unkempt and the children ran wild most of the time. Catherine was exhausted and soon grew sick of life in poverty.

Around the same time, David appeared again on the scene and the two began an affair that would last two years, before Catherine finally rang her husband and told him she would not be returning. She left behind, in the Housing Commission house, her husband, her six children, her father and uncle. The couple was now destined to be together. They moved into a house in Willagee, Western Australia and Catherine changed her name by deed poll to Birnie. When questioned why the couple never married, David would explain that it 'just never came up'[298]. He believed that the relationship was always going to be volatile and by not being married it gave Catherine a way of escape should things become too difficult.[299] Nonetheless, the fire was now lit and David's sexual appetite was soon whetted. The couple would spend hours in bed having sex, often trying out new sexual positions or toys, between prison sentences for theft.

During one prison stint, David was reunited with his younger brother James; they were in fact cellmates at one time. James was in prison for the indecent assault of a 6-year-old girl. His defence had been that she had led him on. It was obvious that sexual deviancy ran in the Birnie family. According to James, David was heavily into kinky sex and had quite a huge pornographic collection. He wanted sex about six times a day, and would inject anaesthetic into his penis so he could last longer without ejaculating. When Catherine and David broke up for a short time in 1984, David forced James to submit to anal intercourse. In August 1986, James was allowed to have sex with Catherine as a twenty-first birthday present. The incestuous relationship would continue until David's final incarceration.

David Birnie was a brilliant conversationalist. He was a knowledgeable man on many subjects, from the Australian Constitution to Chaos Theory and the building of the pyramids; his erudition amazed and inspired Catherine. He was able to talk her into anything he wanted. Soon, David wanted to rape and murder and Catherine was easily talked into assisting.[300]

Sex for the couple became boring and so they began talking about abduction and rape for kicks. Catherine said she would love to watch David penetrate another woman who was gagged and tied up. She told him how she wanted to lick his penis as it went in and out of another woman's vagina. The talk didn't last long before action took over. David decided it was time to act, and with Catherine's devotion he knew he would get his wish. The first victim was happened upon almost by accident. According to David,[301] on 6 October 1986, he was working at a car-wreckers when 22-year-old student Mary Neilson asked him about the purchase of some tyres for her car. There was an instant flash. David knew that the pretty young woman standing in front of him would be a perfect victim. Looking around to make sure his boss was out of earshot, he explained to Mary that he could do her a better deal. He said he had some new tyres at home. He gave Mary the address in Willagee and told her to come after 5 p.m. Later that evening, Mary arrived on the doorstep of the Birnies' home. Though still unsure if he could go through with it, David decided it was time to act. The pretty young student with long brown wavy hair accepted the offer to enter the house, and as she did, David seized her. Mary was dragged to the bedroom where she was chained up and gagged to stop her screaming. David repeatedly raped the terrified young girl as Catherine stood and watched, encouraging her partner.

Catherine and David then drove their frightened victim out to the Gleneagles National Park where David raped Mary again before grabbing a rope from the car and using a tree branch to garrotte the young woman. He then dug a shallow grave and threw the woman's body into the hole. Before covering the woman in dirt, he stabbed her in the chest to make sure she was dead.

Within two weeks, David Birnie was on the hunt again. The couple realised that having people come to the house was an easy way to entrap victims. So they advertised for their next victims in the local classifieds: 'Urgent. Looking for a lonely young person. Prefer female 18 to 24 years, share single bedroom flat'. It is unknown if anyone answered the advertisement, however no victims were accosted this way. The next victim was found hitchhiking alone along the Stirling Highway. Susannah Candy was a young, free-spirited girl of only fifteen. She happily accepted the lift in a car by the friendly and seemingly harmless-looking couple. Susannah thought that, with a woman in the car, she would be safe. She was wrong. No sooner was Susannah in the car than she was tied up and driven back to the couple's house at knifepoint. David had been disappointed last time when they killed Mary so quickly. This time David knew he wanted to keep victim alive for longer. But he knew it was a risk. If someone had seen Susannah get into their car or enter their house, then they may be caught. To prevent this from happening, David forced Susannah to write reassuring letters to her parents, letting them she was okay. She was also made to ring them, reading a script written by Catherine.

Like Mary, Susannah was chained to the bed and raped and sodomised repeatedly by David over several days. Catherine also joined them in bed on occasions; she knew this would turn David on even more. Once David was finished with his sex slave he tried to manually strangle the fifteen year old. However, the young girl was too strong and fought to save her life. So the couple drugged her with sleeping pills. When Susannah fell into a comatose state, David gave Catherine rope and told her to prove her love for him and kill the girl. Catherine willingly pulled the rope tight around Susannah's throat until she had stopped breathing. They took the body out to Gleneagles Forest again and buried her adjacent to the gravesite of Mary Neilson.

On 1 November, 1986, 31-year old flight attendant Noelene Patterson became the Birnies' third victim. Noelene knew Catherine and

David quite well. In fact, the couple had helped Noelene a few weeks earlier wallpaper a room in her house. Noelene had been having a bad day when she had run out of petrol. Standing by her car, angry at her silly mistake, she was relieved to see Catherine and David pull up beside her. But Noelene's relief soon turned to horror when a knife was held to her throat. The Birnies took their sex slave home, chained her to the bed, gagged her and raped her repeatedly. Catherine was concerned this time. She knew that David had always liked Noelene and Catherine was worried the woman may come between them. After several days of continual rape, David did not want to dispose of Noelene. He kept putting it off. Noelene was kept prisoner for three days before Catherine held a knife to her own throat and said that David had to choose between the two of them. David forced sleeping pills down the victim's throat and strangled the unconscious woman as Catherine watched. Then the body was taken to the forest to join the others.

Only three days after Noelene's murder, another victim was abducted. On 4 November 1986, Denise Brown was picked up by the couple as she waited at a bus stop near the Stirling Highway turnoff. For some unknown reason, she accepted the lift from the friendly strangers rather than wait for her bus. A knife was thrust to her throat as she got comfortable in the car. She was the Birnies' slave now. Denise, like the others, was taken to the couple's house at Willagee, chained to the bed and repeatedly raped for two days. Like Susannah she was made to call her parents to let them know she was okay. Catherine decided that time was up for the young woman and so Denise was bundled back into the car and take to Gnangara Pine Plantation the next afternoon. The couple drove into the plantation and while waiting for darkness, David raped Denise again.

Catherine held a torch for light as David plunged a knife into Denise's neck while he continued to rape her. Denise survived the knife's cuts. She was still alive and making terrible gurgling noises. Catherine could not stand the sound and so returned to the car to get a bigger knife. David plunged the knife into the woman's chest. Denise stopped moving and so the pair dug a shallow grave and put Denise into it. As the killer couple tossed the earth over the woman's body, Denise sat up in the grave and began struggling for air. David grabbed the shovel he had been using to the dig the hole and swung it at the girl's skull, but again Denise fought to right herself. David then bashed the young woman's head in with an axe. Denise was finally dead. Catherine felt sick after the murder of Denise. She could no longer help David abduct girls. But David easily convinced Catherine that it would be better next time. Catherine conceded to David's plans, but she still felt that she could not go through with another murder like Denise's.

David did not give Catherine time to change her mind. He was now manic about murder and had such a lust for blood that the rampage had to continue.[302] The final victim was abducted only three days later. On 9 November 1986, David and Catherine abducted a seventeen-year-old young woman who was hitchhiking along Stirling Highway. She too was bound and gagged and driven back to the house. Inside the bedroom, the young woman was confined and subjected to a day of sex and violence. During the time she was held prisoner she was also made to ring her family and tell them she was okay. David told the young woman that if she told them anything that she would be 'murdered like the others'.

During the ordeal, David and Catherine left their prisoner alone and untied while they made a drug deal in another room of the house. The captive took the opportunity to escape. She hid her bag and cigarettes under the bed before she left as proof she had been there. She was a smart woman and had kept her wits about her during her entire ordeal. Consequently, the woman ran from the house, covering her body with the little clothing that still hung from her arms. She stumbled to nearby Fremantle Shopping Centre, where police were called.

Once at the police station, the young woman told the interviewing officers of her ordeal at the hands of the sex-crazed couple. The girl directed the police back to the house and told them they would find her bag and cigarettes, proof of her stay. Police arrived at the house to find no one home. So they lay in wait. Shortly afterwards, Catherine came home and was arrested. David was found at work as if nothing had happened and was also taken into custody.

Overnight, both Catherine and David were placed in separate rooms where they sat in silence. The police tried everything to make the couple talk to no avail. Police knew without their admissions they could only be charge with the abduction and rape of the young woman. Yet the police knew there were more victims and like David had told his captive, he had murdered them. Finally, in exhaustion one of the detectives said to David, 'It's getting dark, why don't you just show me where the bodies are, so we can dig them up'. David realised that the rampage of sex and violence was over. He would not be getting away with murder. He had known that this time would come.[303] He looked at the officers and said 'Okay, there is four of them'. Instantly the case took on huge momentum. With David's confession, Catherine also broke her silence and soon the couple, with a cavalcade of police cars, descended on Wanneroo Pine Plantation. After some initial problems finding the burial grounds, David pointed to the graves of Mary Nielson and Susannah Candy and police crime scene technicians began the arduous task of digging up the victims.

Catherine wanted to point out the next grave. With police watching, the hardened woman pointed to the grave of Noelene Patterson. With indignation for Noelene, a perceived threat to her love for David, Catherine spat on her grave. Denise Brown was also unearthed at another nearby plantation. On 12 November, the pair were charged with four counts of murder and one count of abduction and rape. No plea was entered.

At the hearing on 10 February 1987, Catherine and David pleaded guilty to all charges. According to David it was to save the families the tragedy of a trial in what he described in his confession as 'the most macabre and sadistic crime in the history of Australia',[304] a claim he continued to maintain until his death.[305] David was sentenced the same day. He was to be incarcerated for life, with the presiding judge Mr Justice Wallace saying, 'Each of these horrible crimes were premeditated, planned and carried out cruelly and relentlessly, over a comparatively short period ...[David] should not be let out of prison, ever'.[306] David's sentence was termed 'never to be released', a proposal that is given to Australia's worse criminals. A month later Catherine was sentenced to the same, however, she had a minimum term set and would eligible for parole in 2007. The judge said that Catherine lacked and remorse and 'each [murder] was premeditated, calculated and carried forward to its conclusion without mercy ...'[307] To date, she has been denied parole. In a letter to one of her children she tried to apologise, telling them that she was 'not proud of what has been said about me but I have to live with and the memories. As to why this happened I can only hope that the doctors can help me to find out'.[308]

Birnie also suffered a loss of his own. Catherine had begun her own parole proceedings and decided she stood a better chance if she severed all ties with David. After a number of unanswered letters, David realised that Catherine, after seventeen years in prison, had finally decided to end their relationship. The end of their relationship came as a bit of a shock to David, but he continued to wish Catherine well. There were no hard feelings and he knew that she had done it in the hope of a future out of prison. On 7 October, 2005, just a few hours after David was interviewed, he committed suicide.

At 4.30 a.m. on 7 October 2005, David Birnie was found hanging by a sheet in his cell in Casaurina Prison. He had been suffering quite severe depression at the time, and his health was failing, with numerous operations in the years preceding his death, his last comments were a line from the *Hitchhikers Guide to the Galaxy*, 'Funny, how just when you think life can't possibly get any worse, it suddenly does'.[309] It was a small glimpse into the killer's train of thought. He was buried in an unmarked pauper's grave after his death as no one claimed his body.

Douglas Clark and Carol Bundy

'It's fun to kill people and if I was allowed to run loose, I'd probably do it again ... I know it sounds pyscho, but it's kinda fun, like riding a roller coaster' *Bundy*

Carol Bundy was born Carol Mary Peters on 26 August 1942, to Charles and Gladys Peters in California. Carol was an unattractive and awkward child, unable to live up to her mother's expectations. At the age of eight, for some reason unknown to Carol, Gladys cut her off completely. Carol came home from school one day to find herself locked out of the house. Despite her tears and pleas to be allowed in, Gladys told her to go away because she wasn't her little girl anymore. It was only the intervention of her father that changed Gladys' mind. Carol was allowed to come home, but from that day onwards Carol's mother treated her as if she didn't exist

Carol learned at an early age to ignore the beatings inflicted on her by her mother. Once she sat and read a book while Gladys beat her severely around the face and body with a belt. By refusing to acknowledge the pain, she was able to remain in control of the situation.

Carol had already discovered the superior position of being the victim who forgave the weaknesses of her abuser, a position in which she would learn to thrive.

Though she preferred to paint a glowing picture of her father, the truth was far from her ideals. When her mother died suddenly, her father told Carol and her sister that they had to take their mother's place in the matrimonial bed.[310] During the years that the abuse continued, Carol took to running naked through the streets and used her sexual promiscuity to her own advantage, to feel the affection she craved, if only for a brief period of time.

The beatings from her father grew worse over time and he even attempted to kill the entire family, including his new wife. But Carol got the gun away from him after he had killed the family cat. The girls were shipped off to foster homes and grandparents before Charles went and got his daughters back.

To escape her father's clutches, at the age of seventeen Carol married a 54-year-old man, Leonard, but soon left him because he was a drunkard and tried to make her a prostitute.

Soon after she had left Leonard she met Richard Geis, a 32-year-old writer of pornography and science fiction. He had found her to be a convenient companion, with a pathetic eagerness to please. Believing her to be an intelligent and witty woman, Geis encouraged her to pursue her writing talents. She wrote a short story, which was published. That gave her the confidence to write a novel, but she stopped after writing only twelve pages.

In 1962, Carol's father Charles hung himself. Carol believed she was to blame for his death and the abuse she and her sister had endured. This victim role saw Carol abuse herself in sexual relationships. She moved between both female and male lovers, but soon returned to security with Richard.

However, when he found out she was sleeping with men for money he was furious, but decided to help her by sending her to nursing school. She graduated as valedictorian and began nursing in 1968. Life was beginning to settle down for Carol. Unfortunately, this was short lived.

She soon met Grant Bundy, a fellow nurse, and together they had two children, which did nothing to help the relationship. Grant was just like her father and beat and belittled her constantly until Carol took the kids and escaped to a shelter for women in January 1979.

After a short period she moved with her sons to Valerio Gardens apartment house in Van Nuys, a suburb in the San Fernando Valley. There she made friends with the managers of the complex, Jeanette and John 'Jack' Murray. Jack was a known 'lad'. His wife was well aware of his philandering, but saw no threat in the 38-year-old dumpy woman with extremely thick glasses. Jeanette was keen for her husband to help single mother Carol Bundy, who was down on her luck, by fixing small things in her apartment or driving her to appointments or the Social Security Office.

Jack, however, found Bundy to be a captive audience for his stories. She enjoyed hearing about his time in Vietnam and his old home in Australia. Bundy also let Jack know how the men in her life had treated her and he was sympathetic. She fell in love with the suave man and made sure she always had his favourite beer stocked in the fridge. Soon the two became lovers. Bundy was always calling Jack to her apartment to do odd jobs because her eyesight was failing. Sometimes Jack would call her to one of the vacant apartments for sex, or they would have sex in his van on the way to her appointments. However, sex consisted mainly of oral sex rather than intercourse.

Jack helped her to find out more about benefits and entitlements to which she had access and also suggested she seek a second opinion on her failing eyesight. Bundy found out her blindness could be reversed through surgery. She confused his help and sex with love and imagined a life with Jack, but he told her it would be years before he could leave Jeanette.

After the eye operation, Bundy could see again but her self-image was different to the fat and ugly woman she saw staring back at her from the mirror. Bundy knew that Jack felt something for her and any woman would be envious. She had also received 25,000 dollars from the sale of the home she had shared with her ex-husband. She spent some of it on furniture and other things for her and the children, but she also bought Jack a new VCR and desk for the office. To try to keep Jack for herself, she opened a joint account with him and deposited 13,000 dollars.

Jack told Bundy he couldn't leave Jeanette as she had been diagnosed with cancer so Bundy gladly handed over 10,000 dollars to Jack to help. When this didn't make his commitment any stronger, she attempted to make him jealous by having an affair with Jeanette's younger brother Warren.

When that failed to enhance Jack's commitment to her, she planned a romantic trip for the two of them to Las Vegas. But there he left her alone and only saw her when it was time to return home. Bundy had deliberately left her bag in Jack's car to try to split the married couple up, which caused an uproar between Jeanette and Bundy on their return home. Later, when Bundy brought up the subject of Jeanette's cancer, she was shocked to hear that she had never had cancer. The money had been used to pay off Jack's van.

Bundy offered Jeanette 1500 dollars to leave Jack, but the plan backfired when Jeanette told her husband and Jack told Bundy to get out of his life.[311]

She didn't want to believe this was happening to her and went to the Little Nashville Club, in the hope that Jack would be there. He was, looking adoringly into the eyes of his wife. Bundy knew it was over. But it was only the beginning for her new life.

Standing in the corner of the same club smiling at her was Doug Clark. The handsome blonde man came over to Bundy. The pair spent the evening dancing. Bundy had never met such a gentleman before. Clark promised to call her again and she looked forward to their next meeting.

Doug Clark was born on 10 May 1948 in Pennsylvania, where his father, Franklyn, was stationed in the navy. He was the third son of five children. The family moved often with the navy, including a time in India where they lived like royalty with servants and maids.

Later, Clark and his brother Walter were sent to Ecolat, the international school in Geneva attended by the children of UN diplomats, international celebrities and European and Middle-Eastern royalty. Unlike his brother Walt, who was popular and outgoing, Clark, though highly intelligent,[312] was considered sullen and arrogant and made few friends. He did not do well with his studies as he couldn't be bothered doing the work or completing assignments. Doug Clark claimed that he had developed his preference for kinky sex while living in Geneva.

Despite the fact that Clark's parents had been called to the school on a number of occasions because of his bad behaviour, they claimed that Clark had never shown any signs of behavioural problems as a child. After his expulsion, 16-year-old Clark was sent to Culver Military Academy in Indiana. Although rather intelligent, Clark was happy to scrape through his schooling with minimal effort.

Whether people wanted to hear it or not, Clark would often brag of outrageous sexual exploits with the town girls to anyone within earshot.

Like most teenage boys, Clark and his classmates were obsessed with teenage girls and the fantasy of sex, but for Clark it was much more than fantasy. He had a preference for deviance from an early age.[313] He was caught by his mother stealing and wearing her underwear. He would often bring girls to his room where he would record their moans and groans as he had kinky sex with them. He would then replay the tapes to his classmates, revelling in their obvious jealousy. It was a small step to sex using bondage gear and sex toys for the deviant teenager.

In 1967, at the age of nineteen, Clark graduated from Culver and went to live with his parents who were now retired and living in Yosemite. When he was drafted, he enlisted in the Air Force in radio intelligence to ensure that he would end up in the front line in the Vietnam War.

After an honourable discharge from the Air Force, Clark decided to move to Mexico. With 5000 dollars in his pocket, he headed south but stopped when he got to Van Nuys. In Van Nuys he moved in with his sister Carol Ann and her abusive husband.

At twenty-four he met 27-year-old Beverley in a North Hollywood bar. Beverley, blonde and heavy, saw herself as fat and ugly but found that Clark, with his big dreams and ambitions, would always try to boost her confidence. In 1972 the couple married.

However, their plans were not to succeed. Any time they got a little ahead with money, Clark would blow their savings, so their marriage began to waiver. As Beverly gained more and more weight during their marriage, Clark spent less and less time at home, preferring to go to bars.

In 1976, four years after they were married, Clark and Beverly separated and later divorced, although they remained close friends.

Clark began working at the Jergen's factory in 1979. His duties as stationary engineer required him to tend to the large boiler. He was lucky to get the job after the poor reference he had received from his previous job. In 1980 he set fire to his car outside the Jergen's factory while he was working night shift, in order to claim the insurance.

When he met Bundy he had found he had a talent for making unattractive and fat women feel good about themselves. This he used to his own advantage, getting free rent, food and sex.

So when Clark invited himself to Bundy's for dinner a few nights after their first. meeting. Bundy was a little apprehensive but glad he had called. That evening, with her children in bed, the two of them made love. Bundy recalls it was the most tender and beautiful feelings she had ever experienced; Clark had whispered to her how attractive she was and seemed to enjoy the entire experience.

It was time for Clark to begin his ruse. Bundy woke to find Clark staring at her, perplexed. He asked her if he could stay for a while as he was having problems with his landlady. She happily obliged, though she was still in love with Jack Murray.

When she moved to a two-bedroom apartment a few miles away. Jack helped her to move her things then came around for sex up to three times a week. While Bundy accepted this as genuine friendship, he used this as an opportunity to get her to buy him things he had needed.

But Bundy also had plans of her own, Jack and Clark hated each other immediately and Bundy played them against each other. Clark won out, when he proved to treat her better than Jack ever did. But Clark was also self-centred and spent a lot of time talking about himself. But Bundy did not seem to mind; their lovemaking made up for any other inadequacies Clark may have had.

After a while the couple began to discuss, in lurid detail, their sexual fantasies. Clark would describe how he wanted to get a girl and keep her bound as his sex slave,and Bundy would encourage his fantasies with her own about bondage and torture. Soon the fantasies went further and the couple would describe killing a woman. Clark reinforced his psychological grip on Bundy by making her say that she would kill to prove her love for him. He also had a 'consuming interest' in necrophilia.[314]

But Clark also liked his freedom and would leave and come back as he pleased. After a time, Bundy grew a little bored with his behaviour and answered an advertisement from a man looking for marriage. The man, Art Pollinger, was the antithesis of Jack and Clark. He was unattractive and overweight, but he was kind to Bundy and soon she told him of' the abuse she suffered from Jack and Clark. She also told Art about the cash deposit box she shared with Jack. Art got her to immediately go and close the account, only to find that Jack had already taken over 6000 dollars from it.

The relationship with Art soon failed. Bundy was a woman who was used to the emotional abuse and torment of the relationships she had been in. The care and love she received from Art did not satisfy her. She was soon back with Clark. Clark convinced Bundy to buy a big station wagon when she got her licence and he also convinced her to buy a gun for protection. The two of them went together and purchased two .25 calibre Raven automatics. Clark said they needed to use her name as he had been jailed for robbery years earlier. It was a lie, but to Bundy it made him more exciting.

Bundy was completely under Clark's spell and the man used it to his advantage. He even coerced a 12-year-old neighbourhood girl to come over to their home where she was raped. Even when Clark told her he no longer wanted to have sex with her she did not mind. Clark had recently started to suffer erectile problems anyway. She would often sit in the car while Clark had prostitutes attempt to stimulate him with oral sex, mostly without success.

Clark still came and went as he pleased, moving in with other girlfriends for a time before coming back to Bundy, who graciously took him back each time. In 1980, Bundy gave custody of her children over to their father and began looking for a new apartment closer to where Clark worked in the hope of winning him back permanently.

Soon the couple were cemented together in a frenzy of sex and murder. Clark had Bundy purchase two small calibre guns that they called their toys, for what was about to commence.[315]

On Wednesday 11 June 1980, Clark was cruising through the sunset strip in Los Angeles in his Blue Buick. A gun that was registered to Bundy was tucked down the side of the driver's seat. Clark spotted 16-year-old Cindy Chandler and her 15-year-old stepsister Gina Marano sitting on a bench by the roadside. The Buick pulled up to the kerbside next to them and after chatting to the girls briefly, Clark enticed them into his car. The two girls got in; Cindy in the front and Gina in the back.

Clark drove the car to a secluded parking lot and persuaded Cindy to perform oral sex on him. Unimpressed with her efforts, Clark pulled out his gun, pointed it at Gina in the back and fired. The bullet struck her in the head above her left ear. Cindy, hearing the gunshot looked up and was also shot in the head. However, the two girls were not yet dead, so Clark fired again hitting Gina in the heart and Cindy again in the head, killing them both. Clark drove the car back home with the girls inside and parked the Buick in the garage where he raped the girls' dead bodies for several hours.[316]

Later that night, Clark took pictures of the girls before driving to the Ventura Freeway Forest Lawn exit ramp where he dumped the bodies of Cindy and Gina down the embankment.

The next day, a highway worker found the bodies of Cindy and Gina. The scene was a short distance from where the body of Yolanda Washington was found on 18 October 1977 after being murdered by the Hillside Stranglers.

Clark could not stop talking to Carol Bundy about the murders . She called the police to tell them what her boyfriend had done, but after getting nowhere over the phone she soon gave up. Clark spent the next week trying to persuade Bundy to join him in his next murder hunt.

On 20 June, Clark's plan got underway. A prostitute by the name of Cathy was standing near Hughes Market on Highland Avenue in Hollywood, when Clark called her over to his car. He was craving oral sex and told Cathy to get into the front seat next to him. Bundy sat in the back with the gun hidden. The trio drove to a secluded area and after a few minutes Bundy got the gun ready, but couldn't shoot. Clark grabbed the gun and as Cathy looked up she was shot in the head. She was thrown into the backseat and Clark drove away until they came to a country lane near the Magic Mountain Amusement Park. There the couple dumped Cathy's naked body.

On 24 June 1980, Clark was again circling the Sunset Strip looking for prostitutes when he soon spotted two women on a corner. He paused and waited until the two drifted apart before deciding which one to take. Exxie Wilson was a 24-year-old prostitute who had arrived in Los Angeles earlier that week. Clark asked for oral sex and Exxie got into the car. Clark drove off to a secluded road and as Exxie began to fellate Clark, he pulled out his gun and fired it into the back of her head. Clark proceeded to drag her body out of the car to the waste ground nearby. He then returned to the car and picked up the 'kill bag' that he and Bundy had prepared earlier that day. The 'kill bag' contained items that Clark and Bundy felt they might need, including knives, paper towels, cleaning fluid and rubber gloves. With the dead Exxie now out of the car, Clark took his buck knife and hacked off her head, placed it in a plastic bag and put it in the boot of the car. Clark took the decapitated head home where, according to Bundy, she 'handled the head and played with it … Clark wanted the head made up. I applied cosmetics to the head',[317] before he again sexually assaulted the woman's dismembered head then put it in the freezer.

Clark became concerned that the second prostitute, who had been originally standing with Exxie on the corner, might remember him, so he went looking for her. Circling around the block, he found 24-year-old Karen Jones. As soon as she got into Clark's car he shot her in the back of the head and threw the body on the roadside near the Burbank studios where she was found at 3.08 a.m.

Two days later, on 26 June 1980, Clark and Bundy left their home to dispose of Exxie's head. Bundy had cleaned the head and placed it in a wooden box. After about half an hour of driving, Clark finally decided on the location: an alley near Hoffman Street. The next morning Jonathon Caravello found the wooden box, looked inside and discovered Exxie's head looking back at him.

Clark revealed to Bundy his other murder fantasies; he wanted to use a sniper rifle to shoot drivers on the freeway and he also wanted to raid a Mexican restaurant and kill everyone inside. Thankfully, the fantasies never came to fruition,

By July 1980, the pair argued constantly and Bundy blamed herself. On 29 July, she attempted suicide by injecting herself with 1250 units of insulin and 200 milligrams of Librium. She then telephoned her place of employment at Valley Medical Centre to tell them that she would not be going to work because she was committing suicide. Bundy then attempted to go for a drive but parked the car after only two blocks and fell unconscious. She woke the next day in St Josephs Hospital, having been found by Clark.

On 1 August she was released.

On 3 August 1980, Bundy went to see her ex-lover jack Murray at the club where he worked. When the pair were alone Bundy told Jack about the murders that she and Clark had committed. However Jack wasn't convinced the story was true, so Bundy left the club.

An hour later Jack left the club and found Bundy waiting for him outside. She asked him for a ride home and Jack agreed. On the way home Bundy retold the story of her and Clark's involvement in the Sunset Strip attacks, but again Jack was uninterested in what she had to say; he was more interested in having sex with his ex-lover.

Parking his van, Jack got in the windowless rear of his van and talked Bundy into having sex. He stripped off his trousers and motioned for Bundy to join him. Bundy moved to the rear of the van, pulled out a gun and shot the man in the back of the head. Bundy knelt down to check he was dead, but instead felt a strong pulse, so Bundy held the gun to the side of Jack's head and fired again.

Retrieving a knife from her purse, Bundy stabbed Jack in the back six times and once in the anus. She also slashed his buttocks to make it look like a sex attack. Concerned that the police would be able to trace the bullets that were still in Jack's head, Bundy coldly picked up the knife and proceeded to hack off her ex-lover's head. Bundy phoned Clark and told him what she had done. Clark insisted that she get home immediately. So Bundy returned to the club carrying Jack's head in a bag, got into her own car and drove back to Clark. Early the next morning, the head of Jack Murray was thrown into one of the garbage bins near Griffith Park.[318]

On 11 August, 1980, Bundy took the last of her pills in one handful and went to work. An hour after arriving she was overheard by a work colleague, Leanne Lane, telling one of the elderly patients about her lovers' involvement in the killings. Leanne ignored it, assuming that Bundy had made up the story.

A few minutes later, Bundy told the story to Leanne directly. She told her how Clark had shot two prostitutes while she was present and how she had killed Jack Murray. At the end of the story Bundy told Leanne that she was going home to surrender herself to authorities and left to get changed. Leanne, shocked by what she had heard, rushed to the administrator's office and dialled 911. Police officers reached the hospital quickly but Bundy had already left.

At home, Bundy tried to call various police departments, without much success. Eventually she reached Detective Kilgore at Northeast PD and gave enough details of the murders to convince the detective of her own involvement. She confessed, saying, 'It's fun to kill people and if I was allowed to run loose, I'd probably do it again'.[319] But Bundy refused to name Clark as the other killer.

Detective Kilgore told Bundy to stay where she was. He drove to the woman's house to escort her to the police station for further questioning. Before Bundy left the house with the police officer she deliberately led Detective Kilgore around her home and presented him with evidence that connected Clark with the murders. She then confessed to the murder of Jack Murray, saying, 'I want to make this perfectly clear, because Doug didn't do Jack. I did Jack. He was in no way involved with Jack Murray ...'[320]

At 11.30 a.m., as Clark left work to go on a lunch break, Detective Pida stepped forward to arrest him. Detective Pida and Detective Leroy Orozco interviewed Clark, but he refused to admit to any murder charges. However, he did admit to having unlawful sexual relations with the 12-year-old neighbour, an admission that lead to three counts of child molestation.

Detectives were now fully immersed in the hunt for evidence against Clark, with Bundy assisting where she could. The Buick was impounded and investigated and bullet holes were found in the front seats; accompanying bullets would also be found. Bloodstains were found on the rear seat and blood found on the front and rear mats matched the blood types of both Karen Jones and Gina Murano. On August 26, and again on August 28, detectives recovered two more bodies. Both were linked to the Sunset Strip murders. Bundy told detectives that Clark acted on his own in killing those victims. He had previously confessed, but at the time Bundy wasn't sure whether to believe him or not. She told police that he had bragged about forty-seven murders he had committed since the age of seventeen.[321]

Clark was charged with the multiple murders and pleaded not guilty, Bundy was charged with the murder of Jack Murray but pleaded not guilty by reason of insanity.

After two years of evidence gathering, the trial of Doug Clark facing six counts of murder began on 8 October 1982 in the court of Judge Ricardo Torres. Within five days Clark sacked his legal team and represented himself.

The prosecution's case against Clark ended after almost two months and 231 items of evidence. Then it was the defence's turn. Judge Toms was unimpressed with Clark's continual abuse of his privileges and revoked his right to defend himself. Therefore, Maxwell Keith was brought in to defend Clark. His first witness was Carol Bundy. After her testimony the trial broke for the Christmas break and returned with Clark taking the stand. Clark told the court that he was not guilty and that the deceased Jack Murray and Bundy were the real killers.

The jury left the courtroom to begin their deliberations on 23 January 1981. After five days of discussion they returned to the courtroom where they found Clark guilty on all six counts of first-degree murder.

After Clark's guilty verdict, the sentencing took place. Clark took the opportunity to plead for his life to the jury. The jury left the courtroom for their deliberations on 10 February 1983, and five days later they returned to give their verdict. On the six counts of murder Clark received a sentence of death. Judge Torres confirmed the sentence on 16 March, adding that the sentence would be carried out at San Quentin at a date to be confirmed. Clark demanded that he be put to death within 10 days. However, at the time of writing, Clark still sits on Death Row.

On 2 May 1983, Bundy changed her plea from not guilty by reason of insanity to one of guilty.[322] Seven years later, Bundy was found guilty and sentenced to two consecutive twenty-five year sentences by Judge Torres.

After months of heart and respiratory problems and complications with her diabetes, Bundy was admitted to hospital on 3 December 2003, where she died of heart failure at 11.20 a.m.

Martin and Marie Dumollard

'Oh unfortunately, but for me you would not have been here now'

Martin and Marie Dumollard owned a small cottage in the woods near the French town of Lyon. It was there between 1855 and May 1861 that the couple, posing as owners of a large chateau, lured at least seventy-eight young women from Lyon to their home. Seventy-one of the women were never seen alive again.[323] The victims were either buried in the grounds surrounding their cottage or thrown into the River Rhone.

On 25 February 1855, the body of a naked young servant girl, Marie Baday was found in the woods near Montiuel. The young victim had been stabbed to death before being dumped. She had once worked for another family but had left their employment when she had been offered a more lucrative position.[324] A friend of Marie's was able to give police a description of the man who had a limp and a scar. He had offered them both positions, but Marie's friend had declined. Another friend, Olympe

Alubert,[325] had accepted the position with Marie and when the employer had the victim alone, he had tried to put a rope around her throat. She was able to escape. Marie was not as lucky; she was later found buried. According to the medical examiner at the trial, she had been buried alive. He claimed that, 'her wounds were not mortal, nor even severe; that a clod of outer earth was grasped in her hand; and the teeth were set as if in agony'.[326]

In November 1858, Victorine Perrin had been attacked and robbed by the Dumollards. Victorine had fought back against her attackers and was able to stop the rope from being tied around her neck. She had screamed out in terror and a nearby farmer had come to her rescue as Martin made his own escape.[327]

One of the victims was a young servant girl who disappeared in December 1858. The victim had been taken into the forest where she was raped and attacked. The Dumollards then buried her alive.[328]

In February 1860, 18-year-old Louise Bussod accepted a servant position. She was never seen again. Her younger sisters told police that she had headed off with a lamp with a limp. After the Dumollards' arrest, her body was recovered. She again had been buried alive.[329]

The case broke when the Dumollards attempted to murder 27-year-old Marie Pichon on 25 May 1861.[330] Marie was hired as a servant by Martin Dumollard after meeting him in Lyon when he asked her to point him towards the bureau de placement where he could hire a new servant girl. The young woman enquired about the position he had vacant, which Dumollard described as having excellent wages and living conditions. Marie said to the man, 'Just the place to suit me'.[331] As the pair walked across an open field toward the chateau Marie felt that something was wrong and insisted that they return to Lyon, crying out, 'you have been deceiving me; I will go no further'.[332] Dumollard replied, 'We have already reached the spot'. Martin Dumollard would not let his victim go and produced a rope with which to strangle her. Marie was a strong woman and was able to escape her attacker. She ran to a nearby house, where the frightened girl had the owners raise the alarm. Police officers arrived at the scene and Marie told them her story, including a description of Dumollard in which she described him a having a scar and a tumour on his top lip.[333]

The local judge and gendarmes went to the Dumollards' home, where a search uncovered clothing stolen from their victims. Martin Dumollard was arrested and Marie Pichon brought in to identify him. She saw the man in the cell and promptly fainted.

Forty-seven year old Marie Dumollard[334] was quick to turn on her husband and told the judge of the murders. She claimed, 'my poor husband, it's all his mother's fault, she made him promise to do what he did'.[335] Marie Dumollard claimed that her husband, as a 5-year-old child had seen his Hungarian-born[336] father executed by being broken on the wheel and then quartered by horses for similar crimes.[337] Dumollard's mother had made her son promise that he was avenge his father's death. She also pointed out the graves of several of the victims. Martin denied his wife's story and called her a liar.[338] She responded with, 'I despise him too much'.[339]

The trial took place at the Bourg in January 1862, whereby the motives of the crimes were described as 'gratifying the lust of the male prisoner, and then … enabling the female prisoner to wear the clothes and … trinkets of the victims'.[340] Several other servant girls testified, stating that they had, like Marie, escaped the clutches of the morose and savage temper of Martin Dumollard. During his trial, after losing 'his self-assurance', Dumollard confessed to murdering three girls between 1852 and 1853 and throwing their bodies into the Rhone.[341] In total, he was tried for the murders of six women and the attempted murder of nine more,[342] though evidence was brought before the court of clothing belonging to seventy women.[343] He hissed at Marie Pichon as she took the stand, threatening her with, 'Oh unfortunately, but for me you would not have been here now'.[344]

After being found guilty of murder, 52-year-old Martin Dumollard[345] was sentenced to death at Court of Assize in Ain.[346] He was beheaded ten days later on 8 March 1862. Marie received a twenty-year sentence to be served on the galleys.[347]

In 1952, ninety-two years after the crimes, another victim's body was found.

Gerald and Charlene Gallego

'I want you to get me a girl' *Gerald*

Gerald Armond Gallego Junior was born on 17 July 1946, and spent most of his childhood being violently assaulted by his parents, and then his mother's boyfriends. His father, Gerald Gallego Senior was executed in a Mississippi gas chamber in 1955 for the murder of a marshal and an acid attack on a prison guard.[348] The senior Gallego represented himself through his trial, as later his son would.[349] Gerald Gallego Junior's criminal record started at the age of thirteen. In the beginning it was petty crimes before he moved on to more sexually violent crimes. By the time he met Charlene he had been married five times and had a daughter. His daughter and one of her friends would be sexually abused by Gallego.

Charlene Gallego was born Charlene Williams on 10 October 1956. Her father was a respectable businessman and his wife was a homemaker who was also the perfect hostess whenever her husband entertained or travelled. Charlene was a shy child but once a teenager in the grip of the

1960s she began experimenting with drugs. She married but divorced a wealthy man who also was a drug addict like Charlene. It was not long before Charlene met Gerald. It would mean death for at least ten victims.

When Charlene and Gerald went out on their first date, Charlene would recall later that he was the perfect gentleman. He brought her roses and complimented her parents. He was the typical clean-cut, responsible young man. Charlene had been married twice before, both marriages ending badly, so her parents welcomed Gerald Gallego with open arms. Little did her family know but Charlene was to be his sixth 'wife'.[350]

Charlene Gallego claimed that her husband sent her out to procure for him 'sex slaves' to fulfil his fantasies.[351] He had told her in 1978 that he wanted to build a home in the woods that contained a cellar where he would keep a sex slave to abuse and rape 'at his disposal'.[352] He murdered at least eight victims in the search for the 'perfect sex slave'.[353]

In September 1978, 16-year-old Kippi Vaught and 17-year-old Rhonda Scheffler were abducted from a Sacramento shopping centre, Country Club Plaza. In what would become their signature, Charlene lured the girl's to the couple's van before Gerald appeared with a knife and forced them into the vehicle.[354] The bodies of the two girls were found two days later. They had 'suffered blows to the head, they died of gunshot wounds. Vaught's hands were tied behind her back. Scheffler, who had been raped, died clutching a piece of cord similar to that used to bind Vaught's hands'.[355]

In June 1979, two young girls, 14-year-old Brenda Judd and 13-year-old Sandra Colley went missing at the Reno fairground. Charlene enticed them to the car with the promise of earning some money handing out flyers. Once in the van, both girls were raped repeatedly by Gerald while Charlene drove to a vacant area. Once alone, Gerald took a shovel from the van and struck Sandra in the back of the head. In her testimony,

Charlene said, 'it was the sound of a loud splat, like a flat rock hitting mud and the girl sank to her knees and slowly toppled over'.[356]

In April 1980, the couple kidnapped 17-year-old Stacey Redican and Karen Twiggs. The teenagers were at a Sacramento shopping mall when Charlene lured them to the couple's van. Once at the van, Gerald produced a gun and forced them inside. Stacey and Karen were raped and tortured before being dumped in a canyon where they were found three months later.[357] Both of the girls had been bludgeoned and like the previous girls they had their hands bound behind their backs.[358]

In June 1980, a 21-year-old from Oregon disappeared while hitchhiking and in July 1980, a 34-year-old woman disappeared.

At trial Charlene would recall the night of 1 November 1980, when her husband Gerald told her, 'I want you to get me a girl'.[359] Charlene went out into the night and found 21-year old Mary Beth Sowers with her boyfriend, 22-year-old Craig Miller at a fraternity dance at Sacramento State University.[360] The couple were seen getting into the Gallego's car at gunpoint, where a witness was able to note the licence number of the van. The couple drove the two young lovers to a secluded spot in Eldorado County. Craig was shot three times in the head. His body was found later the following day. Mary Beth was taken back to the couple's apartment where she was raped and tortured. Gallego then drove her to Placer County where Mary Beth was shot and dumped.

The witness to the abduction was able to give police the details of the couple and their van and a warrant was issued for Gerald and Charlene Gallego. The couple were arrested on 17 November 1980 in Omaha for the murders of Craig and Mary Beth. Gerald was also wanted for the rape of his 14-year-old daughter.[361]

In a plea bargain, Charlene pleaded guilty to the murders of Craig Miller and Mary Beth Sowers in return for her testimony against her husband and a lenient sentence.[362] Gerald Gallego, like his father thirty years earlier, represented himself at his trial. He was found guilty of the murders and sentenced to death. In June 1984 Gallego was found guilty of the murders of Stacey Redican and Karen Twiggs in 1980. He was again given another death sentence. In 1999 his death sentence was overturned, but at a new trial he was again sentenced to death.

Charlene was released from prison in July 1997 after serving thirteen years of her sentence. Gerald died on 18 July 2002 following a long-term illness with rectal cancer.

Fred and Rose West

'You've got the killing all wrong, no, nobody went through hell, enjoyment turned to disaster, well most of it anyway' Fred

Frederick Walter Stephen West was born in 1941 in Much Marcle to Walter and Daisy West. Fred was the apple of his mother's eye while his father was a stern man who beat his children and sexually abused his daughters. Fred was sexually abused by his mother. After the incestuous introduction, a sexual awakening saw Fred spend his teenage years coercing young girls to have sex with him.[363]

Following a motorcycle accident in 1958, West became morose and would fly into a rage, striking out with an unpredictable temper that frightened those around him. Like his father he had a violent streak that was coupled with a voracious sexual appetite. In 1960, West was arrested for impregnating his 13-year-old sister.[364] At his trial, his sister refused to testify against him so West was freed.

In August 1962, 20-year-old Fred met 16-year-old pregnant runaway Catherine 'Rena' Bernadette Costello. The couple secretly married on

17 November 1962 in a registry office in Ledbury before moving to Scotland together. On 22 March 1963, Rena gave birth to Charmaine. While she was in hospital with her baby, Fred was at home having sex with one of Rena's sisters. Within a year Rena was pregnant with Fred's baby and in 1964 Anne Marie West was born. Anne Marie, like her older half sister, would be subjected to a lifetime of sexual torture and abuse at the hands of her father and would become a plaything that West repeatedly raped over the decades to come.

Following the birth of Anne Marie, West met 16-year-old Anna McFall, a teenage prostitute who fell under the spell of West. Anna moved into the home that West shared with Rena and worked as a nanny for the two babies. Fred worked as an ice-cream-truck driver to support his wife, nanny and children. Yet tragedy struck when he reversed the truck over a 4-year-old boy, killing him. Though the death was an accident, Fred packed up his belongings and, along with his lover Anna McFall and the children, he returned home to Gloucester, leaving behind his wife.

When Rena attempted to woo back her husband, she found that Anna McFall had taken the full-time role as 'wife' to Fred and mother to the children, a domestic situation that made Rena furious. She reported the sexual abuse of the children to police but then withdrew her complaint.

In 1967, Anna, pregnant with West's child, demanded that he divorce his wife and marry her. Fred refused. In August 1967, Anna McFall, while eight-months pregnant with Fred's child, disappeared. Fred stabbed her through the heart and buried her in Much Marcle. The body remained hidden until 1994.

Another young girl disappeared a few months later in January 1968. Fifteen-year-old Mary Bastholm disappeared while waiting for a bus, and though Fred never fully confessed[365] to her murder, it is likely that she was murdered by West and buried somewhere near the body of Anna McFall.

Fred's mother Daisy died in February 1968. The death of his mother hit Fred hard. He became more morose and returned to his marital home where he began assaulting and raping his wife and two children excessively. Around the same time he met Rosemary Letts, the young woman who would help shape the man into an even more terrible monster.

Rosemary Pauline Letts was born in November 1953 in Devon, England; she was the fifth child to Bill and Daisy Letts. Her father, Bill, was a sadistic schizophrenic and her mother Daisy was undergoing shock therapy for depression when she fell pregnant with the girl they would call Dozy Rosey.[366] Daisy Lett's depression was related to the violence she suffered at the hands of her husband. Rosemary was known to rock herself so violently she would fall into a catatonic state. The unusual behaviour may have been a result of her conception during her mother's shock treatment, or a result of the violent abuse she suffered at the hands of her father.

Like Fred West, Rosemary failed at school and left with only the basic fundamentals of reading and writing. As her older sisters left home, Rosemary's father turned all of his sexually perverted attentions to his young daughter. By the age of fourteen, Rose had seduced her younger brother. She had groomed him, just as her father had done to her. Rosemary was sexually assaulted by a man who grabbed her from a bus stop while she was waiting for a lift home. The man dragged her into a park where he savagely raped her. Some suspect that it was possible that her attacker was none other than her future husband Frederick West.[367]

In summer 1968 the sexually predatory lives of Fred and Rosemary officially collided; the deviant partnership would prove fatal for the young women of Gloucester. By the early 1970s, Fred started picking up young hitchhikers whom he would then rape and torture before letting them go. At home, Rosemary, pregnant with Fred's baby, would babysit his two young daughters, often spending her days beating and whipping the children.

In June 1971 Rose murdered Charmaine West, Fred's step-daughter. Rose had beaten the child to death. The child was cut up and buried under the kitchen of the home the couple had rented in 25 Midland Road, Gloucester.

In August 1971, Fred decided it was time to get rid of Rena to prevent her questioning Charmaine's disappearance. Fred got his wife highly intoxicated and drove her to Much Marcle where he had buried Anna McFall, then raped her and killed her by smashing her into an iron gate. He dismembered the body and buried her in a shallow grave.

Fred began advertising Rose's sexual services in magazines with photographs of her prominently featured in the articles. Fred allowed Rose to use their bedroom to service her clients, many of them West Indian, as long as he was able to watch through a peephole in the wall. Fred also recorded the sexual exploits of Rose and her clients.

The pair married in January 1972 at a Gloucester Registry Office. At the time, Rose was three months pregnant with Mae. After the birth of Mae[368] in June of that year Fred moved his family into their final home, 25 Cromwell Street in Gloucester. Fred had chosen the home for its cellar, which he planned to use as a torture chamber where he would abuse and sexually torture his victims and his children over the next twenty years.

The first victim that was led to the cellar was Fred's own daughter Anne-Marie. The eight year old was lured to the dark hole by her parents. She was tied up and gagged before being savagely raped by her father.[369]

Caroline Owens was the first girl picked up by Fred. The seventeen year old accepted a job as a babysitter with the growing West family, but by December 1972 she left the job fearing Fred's incessant sexual pursuit. A few months later she accepted a lift from Fred and Rose. She was bound and gagged before being raped and beaten with a belt buckle by the couple.[370] After hours of abuse the teenager was allowed to leave. She reported the attack but the pair were let off with a nominal fine.

Nineteen-year-old Lynda Gough moved into the West house in April 1973. Lynda began her time with the Wests as a willing accomplice in the sex games that a pregnant Rose and Fred shared with her. Then one night Lynda found herself hanging by her ankles from the torture chamber ceiling. 'In the hours, even days before her eventual death, Lynda Gough was reduced to nothing more than a slab of meat'.[371] Before being buried, 113 bones were removed from the remains.

Fifteen-year-old Carol Ann Cooper was picked up by Fred in November 1973. Carol Cooper was hung from the wooden beam in the cellar. Rose placed a large elastic band around the girl's head and face to prevent her from calling out. Hanging helpless from the beam she was beaten and abused for days before she was finally murdered by the couple.

Lucy Partington disappeared on 27 December 1972. Lucy was offered a lift by the couple in their car. She was taken back to the Wests' home where she was made to perform various sexual acts with Fred and Rose before she also was tortured, mutilated and murdered. Four months later the West couple struck again. Twenty-one-year-old student Therese Siegenthaler was picked up by Fred West. Therese was tied up and taken down to the cellar where she was tortured and mutilated before her head was removed from her body and a further thirty-seven bones removed. Her body was buried in a corner of the cellar.

Fifteen-year-old Shirley Hubbard was the fifth girl murdered and buried at 25 Cromwell Street. On 14 November 1974, she ran away and found her way to Cromwell Street. Once inside the cellar Fred West engaged in bondage and covered the girl's face with tape, creating a mask that covered her entire face Fred fed two tubes into her nostrils so she could breath. Shirley was left there, trapped in the cellar for days as the couple took turns beating and sexually assaulting her. Again, they sliced off pieces of her body until she finally died. According to Fred's confession, Shirley 'slipped off'[372] the hook where she was hung upside down.

Juanita Mott was the next to accept an offer to stay at Cromwell Street. In April 1975 she was tied up with rope and abused and tortured before her death from strikes of hammer.[373] The young woman was decapitated and had almost ninety of her bones removed before she was buried in the cellar with the other bodies.

Eighteen-year-old Shirley Robinson rented one of the bedrooms in the West home in Cromwell Street and she quickly became Fred West's lover, often sharing the bed with both Fred and Rose. After Rose became pregnant to one of her Jamaican clients, Fred impregnated Shirley. In June 1977, Fred strangled Shirley as his wife slept. He then buried the young woman and the unborn child that he had cut from her womb in the back garden of Cromwell Street.

In September 1979, the Wests took Alison Chambers to the couple's bedroom where she was tied down. Another belt was tied around her face to stop her screaming and they tortured her for the next several days before they murdered her.

On 19 June 1987, Heather West became the final known victim of Fred and Rose West. Following her death, Fred and Rose continued to threaten the other children with being buried in the garden like Heather if they ever spoke about what went on in their home.

Finally, five years after her disappearance, in August 1992 police executed a search warrant on 25 Cromwell Street after complaints had been raised through child services that claimed that the West children were being kept in the cellar of the home and only brought up to be raped and sodomised. After going through the evidence that they confiscated, police arrived again at the home of Fred and Rose West on Thursday 24 February 1994 with a search warrant to search the back garden of 25 Cornwell Street for the body of Heather West.

The following day, Fred confessed that he had killed Heather and buried her in the garden. Police soon found bones that they assumed were Heather's, yet when they unearthed a third leg bone,[374] they knew they had more questions for the couple. Five days into the investigation, Fred had lost count of the number of murders he had confessed to. When again alone with his lawyers, they begged Fred to give police any further information that he may have had. He was told, if there was more, then he should confess. Fred looked at his defence team and said, 'There is a fucking load more'.[375] He confessed to another five murders. What had begun as the search for a murdered young girl ended up unearthing a pair of sadistic serial killers.

Fred West eventually sat down and wrote out a confession. In the childish scrawl of an illiterate labourer he wrote, 'I Frederick West ... wish to admit to a further (approx) 9 killings, expressly, Charmaine, Reena [sic], Linda Gough, and others to be identified'.[376] He was very matter of fact about everything he had to tell them. When asked why he had killed so many young girls, he was adamant that murder was not his ultimate goal in *most* cases: 'You've got the killing all wrong, no, nobody went through hell, enjoyment turned to disaster, well most of it anyway'.[377]

On New Year's Day 1995, just before noon, Fred West was found dead. He had hanged himself with strips of his bedsheet, thus escaping the mounting murder charges against him, leaving Rose to face them alone. Rose's trial for the sexual abuse, torture and murder of ten of the victims opened in October 1995. After a lengthy trial the serial killer was found guilty of the murders. Rose was sentenced to ten life terms for her part in the sexually motivated murders.

Serial killer couples are a deadly combination. Many of the killers, particularly the female partners, may have never committed murder had it not been for the influence and sexually abusive nature of their male partners. Most of the murders were sexually motivated and were ways in which the couples increased their own sexual pleasure. Through the abuse and murder of their, mostly female, victims, the couples cemented their relationship.

The same can be said for the tandem killers explored in the next chapter, partners in crime who murdered victims together, though the two killers were not usually sexually involved.

TANDEM KILLERS

The most interesting and least understood type of serial killer is the tandem killer, those killers who work in pairs or in groups. The term 'tandem killers' was penned by an Australian criminologist, Paul Wilson in 2002, in his book, *Tandem Killers*. The ability to commit murder in the company of another requires a great deal of trust and accord and is also often the reason that tandem killers are caught.

In most cases of tandem killings one of the killers is the dominant partner and seduces the other into his or her murderous fantasies. 'Individually, these people have backgrounds that are not unusual. But when they get together, a sadistic chemistry comes into play' that sets the wheels in motion for torture and death, according to criminologist James Alan Fox.[378] The dominator rarely concerns themselves with the state of the victim after death; the follower is generally left to deal with the aftermath.

However, the follower is usually the one that brings the team to justice. The weaker partner will often confess if pressured and will identify the main killer. Tandem killers rarely continue a friendship or relationship beyond their apprehension and incarceration. Most Tandem killers, like Bianchi and Buono, become enemies once incarcerated.

Kenneth Bianchi and Angelo Buono

'I could be the Hillside Strangler and you'd never know it' *Bianchi*

Kenneth Bianchi was born in Rochester, New York, in 1952 and was raised by foster parents before moving to Los Angeles in 1977 at the age of twenty-five to live with his cousin Angelo Buono, who was seventeen years his senior. Bianchi admired his older cousin immensely and was quickly seduced into Buono's life of sexual perversion, with an endless stream of prostitutes coming into the house. However, within months of Bianchi arriving in LA, the two cousins went on a killing rampage in which ten women would lose their lives to the predators that the media dubbed the 'Hillside Strangler'.[379]

Kenneth Alessio Bianchi was born on 22 May 1951. The son of a teenage prostitute, he was adopted by the Bianchis in August of the same year. Kenneth's mother was aunt to Angelo Buono. Bianchi, even as a child, was a compulsive liar[380] and daydreamer. The lines between reality and his dream world were blurred from very early on and he would regularly be found in a trance-like seizure state. He was also a chronic bed-wetter, and when his mother sought help for his condition, the doctors believed it was her, as an over-protective mother, who needed help.[381]

Angelo Buono Junior was born on 5 October 1934, and his parents divorced when he was five. His mother took him and his sister to a new home in California. By fourteen the killer was already a prolific rapist. His idol was serial rapist Caryl Chessman[382] but he realised soon that raping was not enough and by seventeen he was already fantasising about murder. Buono was arrested several times for petty theft and was incarcerated in a juvenile detention centre.

At twenty-one, Buono married his pregnant girlfriend, but the marriage lasted a week before the man walked out, leaving his wife to raise their son alone. The following year he married another woman, Mary Castillo, after she bore him a son that they named Angelo Buono III. Over the next six years, Mary gave birth to another four children. However, she had to raise the children alone while Buono was incarcerated several times. She then divorced him in 1964, citing violence and sexual abuse during their marriage. Buono moved in with another woman who also bore him two children. By 1971, Buono was raping the woman's teenage daughter on a regular basis. The woman left Buono and within a year he married another woman.

Bianchi began a relationship with 23-year-old Sheryl Kellison. The couple were introduced by Buono, who told the young woman that Bianchi was a talent agent. She was also told stories that he was a psychologist and was dying of cancer.[383] The couple stayed together for two years during the height of the murders. The woman was confused by the man and his stories. Her friends also thought he was rather odd. One of them recalled talking with Bianchi who had said, 'I could be the Hillside Strangler and you'd never know it'.[384]

Between 6 October 1977 and 17 February 1978, the bodies of naked young women were found dumped on hillsides around LA.

All of the young women had been brutally raped and police would discover that two types of semen would point to two killers working in tandem. However, this scary fact was kept out of the press for quite some time—hence the singular name the Hillside Strangler.

On 6 October 1977, 21-year-old Lisa Kastin became the first victim of the killing cousins. She was lured to Buono's house where she was subjected to repeated acts of rape and sodomy; she was also beaten before being killed, Bianchi claimed that 'Angelo didn't have sex with her. I did. When she was being strangled she struggled a bit. I had started the strangulation. I got tired and Angelo completed it. I assisted'.[385] Her body was dumped on Chevy Chase Drive, a street near Buono's house.

On 18 October the killers struck again; this time they chose a black prostitute, Yolanda Washington. The woman was working on Hollywood Boulevard when she was picked up by Bianchi and Buono. After being raped and beaten to death by the men, her dead and defiled naked body was found at the Forest Lawn Cemetery near Ventura Freeway. The piece of cloth that had been used to strangle her was still around her throat. There was, however, something artificial about how she was found: she had been posed grotesquely, displaying her genitals like a showpiece. The ritual was another part of the killers' calling card.

Next to die was fifteen-year-old Judy Miller on 1 November 1977. She was a runaway that had fallen into the hands of the killer pair. Her abused and naked body was found in La Crescenta, a suburb near Glendale. She had had been raped and sodomised before being strangled. Her feet and hands were also shackled.

Eighteen-year-old Jill Barcomb died on 9 November after been raped and beaten by the two men.

On 20 November 1977, the men performed a triple act. They first killed twelve-year-old schoolgirl Dolores Cepeda and fourteen-year-old

Sonja Johnson and dumped the bodies in Elysian Park. The killers then continued on to kill twenty-year-old Kristina Weekler and dumped her naked body in Highland Park.

As more bodies began to turn up, police saw the pattern emerging. Most, though not all, of the girls had been part-time prostitutes and they had been bound and gagged during their ordeal that consisted of rape and sodomy. The victims' bodies were then cleaned after death to avoid detection and then dumped on roadside hills.

The day of 23 November saw another victim of the Hillside Strangler dumped. This time, it was Jane King, a 28-year-old Scientology student who was found on the exit ramp of Golden State Freeway. She had been raped and murdered and her stockings were still around her throat.

Police were getting frantic as the body count grew. Eighteen-year-old Lauren Wagner was the next young woman murdered. However, the killers had upped the stakes; this time, burns on her hands suggested that Lauren had been tortured before being strangled.

A piece of vital evidence was given to police but its significance was not realised until later. A neighbour saw Lauren being abducted from outside her house. The neighbour could describe the two men she saw. But the next day she received a phone call from a man telling her to keep quiet or she would be dead too.

What police did not realise was that to get the witness' phone-number someone would need to have inside information from the telephone company. Had they checked, the police would have found the identity of one of the Hillside Stranglers. Angelo Buono had worked at the local telephone exchange and had heard that there was a witness to the abduction.

Seventeen-year-old part-time prostitute Kimberley Martin was raped and murdered by the men on 15 December 1977. Her body was found posed grotesquely on a vacant block near City Hall. She had gone to the Tamarind Apartments in Hollywood after being requested by Buono from the call-girl agency where she had worked. Bianchi was suddenly one of the two-hundred suspects that they were trying to investigate, but due to police resources was a low-priority possibility.[386] He was working as a junior real-estate agent and was placing advertisements on people's car windscreens. Similar ones had been found near other murder scenes. A witness had seen Bianchi near both sites and he had threatened them into silence. The witnesses went to the police, but with mounting evidence against other possible suspects, Bianchi was questioned but little else was done.[387]

The attention was enough to scare the killers and everything went quiet. The escalation of the killings worried police, but the quiet period that followed worried them even more. Had the killers been caught somewhere else? Had they just decided to stop? Had they died? No one knew. The police followed up any information they received but nothing was of any value.

Another body was found two months later. Twenty-three-year-old Cindy Hudspeth was found naked in the trunk of a car on 17 February 1978. Again, the body and car had been immaculately cleaned before being pushed over a cliff. The cleaned crime scene left no clues for police.[388]

Then, again there was nothing from the killers. After a few months, the special taskforce set up to catch the killers was disbanded after no further information or leads came through.

Little did they know but Bianchi had grown weary of Buono and the filth he chose to live in. So he had moved back to Washington State and began work as a security guard. However, the killings were always on his mind. And this time Washington would be in the killer's grip.

On 12 January 1979, in Bellingham, the bodies of Karen Mandic and

Diane Wilder were found in the boot of a car. The night before, Karen had told her boyfriend that she had been offered 5100 dollars by Ken Bianchi to housesit for him; it was a crucial mistake for Bianchi. He had given his victims his real name and now police had a prime suspect.

Bianchi was immediately arrested. Evidence found at his house proved that he had been the killer. A pubic hair found on the steps that led to the basement of the house matched Bianchi's, and he had menstrual bloodstains on his underwear that had come from Diane Wilder.

Police from LA quickly made their way to Bellingham to question Bianchi about the Hillside Strangler murders.

Bianchi was ready for them. He feigned a split personality, claiming his alter ego was responsible for the murders and meaning he could possibly plead guilty by reason of insanity in the hope of getting a more lenient sentence. In addition, he was their only hope of charging Buono with the Hillside Strangler crimes in LA. Therefore, if Bianchi was declared insane, the case would fold. Thankfully, experts quickly dispelled Bianchi's story. In October 1979, Bianchi was declared sane and able to stand trial. Therefore, Bianchi needed to try something else. Knowing he would go the electric chair if convicted in LA, he quickly pleaded guilty to the two murders in Bellingham so he could begin his plea-bargaining. He then agreed to plead guilty to five of the ten murders in Los Angeles as long as the death penalty was taken off the table. He then was the star prosecution witness against his cousin Buono.[389]

However, it was not successful. After hundreds of witness and evidence exhibits both men were sentenced to life imprisonment. Bianchi's sentence was handed down on 21 October 1983. The judge said, 'I wish I had the power to run the sentences consecutively, but in this state they must be merged as a matter of law'.[390] Angelo Buono, after one of the longest trials in American history that lasted over two years, was found guilty of nine of the ten LA murders and received his life sentence on 9 January 1984. When asked what his punishment should be, Buono, who had been silent during most of his interrogation and trial, said, 'My morals and constitutional rights has [*sic*] been broken. I stand mute. I am standing mute to anything further'.[391]

This, however, is not where the story ends. There have since been two more twists in the case.

While serving his sentence in prison Bianchi was contacted by a strange 23-year-old Los Angeles screenwriter named Veronica Lynn Comton who was seeking information for a book about a female serial killer. Together they hatched a plan to free him in which Veronica would take a sample of his sperm, kill a woman and deposit the sperm sample in her. Though a good idea, it never worked. She tried to strangle a woman but the victim was too strong and overpowered Veronica. Instead, it landed Veronica in jail and Bianchi refused to speak to her ever again.

Bianchi has also been raised as possible suspect in the three 'Alphabet' murders that were committed by an unknown serial killer in Rochester during the early 1970s. To date, no arrest has been made in the case.[392]

On 21 September 2002, 67-year-old Angelo Buono was found dead in his cell at Calipatria State Prison, having suffered a heart attack during the night.

Liao Chang-Shin and Hsui Chang-Shan

'People are always disappearing these days' Chang-Shin

In the small town of Changshow, China, seventy-nine people disappeared between April and July 1945. When the local police interviewed the people of the town, they were quite afraid. They too had noticed that people had gone missing. In contrast, when interviews, local innkeeper Liao Chang-

Shin just shrugged his shoulders in response and told the officers that 'people are always disappearing these days'.[393] Days after interviewing the local community, an anonymous letter arrived at the police station that pointed them towards Liao Chang-Shin and an accomplice Hsui Chang-Shan.

When confronted by police, Liao Chang-Shin confessed that he and accomplice, Hsui Chang-Shan murdered and robbed the victims who had stayed at the inn, with the regularity of almost one victim per day. One victim was a prostitute. She had often worked from the inn and when she uncovered the killers' spree, she blackmailed them in return for her silence. She soon found herself one of their victims.[394] Another was a wealthy student who was staying at the inn with a large sum of money. When he asked Chang-Shin to put the money in the inn's safe, he soon found himself a victim of the killer pair.[395]

Both men confessed at their trial and were found guilty of the seventy-eight murders in crimes that were described as 'ruthlessness unequalled in the annals of crime in Szechwan province'.[396] The men were sentenced to death.[397] Both men were executed in late 1945.

Alton Coleman and Debra Brown

'I wish I didn't flip out. I'm screwed up mentally. I'm glad I could stop when I did. Do you think I'd be here if I didn't want to be here?' Coleman

Alton Coleman was sentenced to death for a murder crime spree during which eight woman and girls were killed in Ohio, Illinois and Indiana in 1984. The victims include a 9-year-old Kenosha girl who was kidnapped from her home. Debra Brown who travelled with Coleman was also convicted in two of the murders.

The FBI commenced profiling the killer soon after the first victims were found. They concluded that the killer hated his mother and the violence inflicted on his victims was a result of that.[398]

Coleman's mother, Mary Bates, had given birth to her first child at the age of fourteen and was institutionalised in a mental facility at the age of seventeen. She had two more children to soldier, Herbert Coleman, before he deserted her in 1954, sending her back to the streets to earn money to support her children. Alton Coleman was born on 6 November 1955 in Waukegan, a rat-infested residential area and red-light district. His father remains unknown.[399] Two more children were born to Mary Bates, who would spend the majority of her welfare cheque on gambling and playing cards. Alton was shipped off to family members while still small. Whenever Mary had the children they would end up with welts and bruises from regular beatings.[400] Alton spent most of his childhood with his grandmother, a voodoo practitioner, Alma Hosea, where he frequently wet the bed or soiled himself. She would often remind Alton that his mother was no good and that she had deserted her children.

At the age of five, Alton Coleman was arrested for the theft of a watch. He had been with his mother, who was entertaining a man when Coleman saw the opportunity to take it.[401] By eleven, Alton had also learned to gamble; like his mother and would use his winnings to buy drugs and alcohol.

By 1974, at the age of nineteen, Coleman was sentenced to two six-year terms for armed robbery. The sentence was part of a plea bargain. He had raped and kidnapped his victims, but for pleading guilty to the robbery charges the prosecution agreed to drop the rape and abduction charges.[402] While Coleman was in prison, his mother died of cancer. He was allowed to attend the funeral, but from then on the man changed.

From 1976, he commenced raping women, and was found responsible for six attacks. He served another six-month jail sentence for one sexual assault, but for the others the charges were either dropped or dismissed. In 1978, Coleman started dating Beverly Perkins. The couple lived at Coleman's grandmother's home and on 1 July 1980 the couple married. But they divorced a year later after Coleman was arrested for rape. He was not single for long, as he proposed to another girl. But that engagement ended when Coleman met Debra Brown. The couple lived at his grandmother's house, along with other family members. In 1983, Coleman was charged with raping his 9-year-old niece, but again the charges were dropped.[403] He was again arrested; this time he had raped a 14-year-old girl.

When Coleman was released on bail, he and Brown fled. Coleman kept Brown incarcerated in their home where he routinely beat and assaulted her. She claimed to have been scarred during one particular beating.

On 19 June 1984, the rapes escalated to murder. The first victim was 9-year-old Vernita 'Tracy' Wheat. She was found in an abandoned building in Waukegan. She had been missing since 29 May, when she had said she was going to meet someone called Robert Knight and help him with a stereo system. Another two victims were found the same day as Tracy. Seven-year-old Tamika Turks and 9-year-old Annie Hilliard were found in swamplands in Gary Indiana. Both of the girls had been raped before being murdered by strangulation.

Ten days later, the couple broke into the home of Palmer and Margie Jones in Dearborn Heights, Michigan. The elderly couple were beaten before Coleman and Brown left in their car, taking with them anything of value that they could find. They then headed to Detroit where they raped and assaulted Mary Lee Billups and beat her friend Marion Gaston. They then broke into another house and assaulted the occupants, Frank and

Dorothy Duvendack in Toledo on 7 July 1984. They also ransacked the home of 79-year-old Millard and Kathryn Gray. They left the couple alive, but would return later.

That same day, the bodies of victims Virginia Temple and her daughter, 9-year-old Rachelle were found on 7 July, two days after they had met Coleman at a fast-food restaurant. Their bodies were hidden in the attic of their own home. After assaulting and raping them for two days, Coleman then strangled them. He let Virginia's four other young children live.

Four days later, another body, that of 25-year-old Donna Williams, was found in Detroit in an abandoned house. Two days later on 13 July, the couple again broke into a home. The Cincinnati home of Harry and Marlene Walters was the scene of the killers' next crime. They appeared on the Walters' doorstep to enquire about the campervan they had for sale in their driveway. Marlene opened the door, only to be marched back inside and down into the basement where she was killed. She had been struck on the head twenty-five times and stabbed repeatedly in the face. She was to be Coleman's only Caucasian victim; all of the others were African-American. Harry was brutally assaulted but survived the attack. Coleman and Brown return to the Gray home in Dayton on 17 July and beat the elderly couple with a crowbar, but they survived the attack after Coleman told them that he was not going to kill them.[404] Two days later, the decomposing body of Eugene Scott was found in Zionsville. The man had been shot seven times and stabbed repeatedly. On 20 July, the day after Eugene was found, the body of 15-year-old Tonnie Storey was found in Cincinnati.

That same day Coleman and Brown were arrested in Chicago. Their faces had been plastered all over the news when a friend spotted them and informed the police. Once in custody Brown quickly confessed to helped in the murder of Tamika Turks. Coleman was a little more calculating.

He wanted to confess, but only to someone who would write a book about him. He was dramatic in his confession to the FBI, saying, 'I wish I didn't flip out. I'm screwed up mentally. I'm glad I could stop when I did. Do you think I'd be here if I didn't want to be here?'

Coleman was described in his trial as a sexual sadist who derived pleasure from the torture and raped he carried out on his victims. Coleman was sentenced to death for the murders. He remains on death row. Brown was found guilty and sentenced to death. Her sentence was later commuted to life in prison without parole.

Simon Majola and Themba Nkosi

'I'm the Bruma Lake Killer' Nkosi

On 21 May 2002, Simon Majola and Themba Nkosi were given multiple life sentences for the murders of eight people in suburbs of Johannesburg between 29 April 2000 and 7 February 2001.

Thirty-four-year-old father Simon Majola, the ringleader in the murder spree, was sentenced to eight life sentences with an additional 422 years for other crimes including assault and robbery. His partner, 22-year-old Themba Nkosi was sentenced to four life sentences and an extra 375 years for robbery and assault charges. At his trial, the judge claimed that Nkosi enjoyed terrorising his victims before they killed them.

The pair murdered eight people that the killers had forcibly stopped on the side of the road. The victims were robbed of their valuables in the affluent suburb of Rhodes and Bruma Lake before being beaten, tied up and strangled. The bodies were then thrown into Johannesburg's Bruma Lake with rocks tied to their feet. However, several of them floated to the surface.[405] Most of the remaining bodies were found after the lake was drained and dredged in February 2001. Nkosi and Majola were arrested after Nkosi assaulted his girlfriend and threatened to throw her into the lake, boasting: 'I'm the Bruma Lake killer that everyone was looking for'.[406]

On 21 May 2002, the two killers were sentenced to almost one thousand years in prison for the murders.

In tandem killings, one of the killers is the dominant partner and seduces the other into their murderous, often sexual, fantasies. Had the pair not met or come together, they may have never gone on the murderous sprees. It is 'a sadistic chemistry that comes into play'.[407] The dominant killer usually leaves the cleaning up to their submissive partner, and it is often this, rather than the killings themselves, that sends the submissive killer to authorities to confess.

The dominance of the killer over the victim is also often a driving force in black widow killings. The black widow killer will dispatch of anyone who gets in her way.

THE BLACK WIDOW

Black widow killers are named after the black widow spider found in North America. The female of the species is extremely toxic, whereas the male and juveniles are completely harmless. Contrary to popular belief, the female black widow spider rarely kills and consumes the male after mating. Yet, it is that legend that has seen the spider lend its name to the female serial killers who murder their husbands or lovers, children and relatives, often for financial gain.

The black widows are extremely patient killers. The murders they commit can take years: some victims are slowly poisoned, others are dispensed of more quickly, but these killers will bide their time before they kill. Regardless of any close relationship with the victim, black widow killers rarely show true remorse for their crimes. They can calmly watch a family member die in agony, only feigning concern to elude suspicion.

Margie 'Velma' Barfield

'When I was taking drugs, I was like a zombie'

The second child in a family of nine siblings, Margie Velma Barfield was born on 29 October 1932. She was the eldest daughter of Murphy and Lillie Bullard who lived with the large family in Wade, North Carolina on a small farm that had neither running water nor electricity. The family shared the bedrooms and Barfield shared a bedroom with her volatile and abusive father and her mother. She feared her father, who was prone to go on alcoholic binges that often resulted in him assaulting his wife and children. To stay away from her father's violence she threw herself into her schooling, and teachers nurtured the bright student who achieved good grades.

When she was at home she was delegated most of the household chores, including the cooking and all of the laundry for the entire family. When this took so long that she was unable to attend school she secretly seethed at her father who would force her, as a ten year old, to stay home until it was done. She also spent several weekends a year at a Presbyterian bible school.

At the age of thirteen, in a moment that Velma defines as the best of her life, her father bought her an expensive dress. She had hoped he had changed in his attitude towards her but months later she was proven wrong. When the teenager stayed home from school with the flu, her father raped her.

To escape her home life, Velma soon met Thomas Burke and at sixteen her father allows her to date the teenager. A year later, in 1949 Velma ran away with Thomas and the two were married. The couple moved in with his parents and the four regularly attended the local Baptist church.[408]

In October 1951, Velma gave birth to a son and the new family moved to a home in Parkton were they also welcomed a daughter in September 1953. Two years later, while crossing the street, Velma was struck by a drunk driver. She was hospitalised for a significant amount of time, which consolidated the depression that she had fought for several years. She later had a hysterectomy when symptoms from her previous injuries returned.

By 1963, as the couple built a new home on a piece of land given them by her husband's parents, Velma complained that she constantly felt stressed and nervous. Both of them worked long hours and their relationship had begun to crumble. Thomas joined the local Jaycees chapter and their many social events saw Thomas start drinking. This reminded Velma of the abuse by her father. Velma hated alcohol and seeing her husband drunk became the basis of many of their arguments that, as Thomas' drinking got heavier, resulted in violent altercations.[409]

Velma had her husband admitted to hospital for treatment of his alcoholism, which resulted in him being fired from his job and further arguments between the couple. Thomas left the hospital only days into his treatment and Velma was forced to get a second job to support them. At home, Thomas threatened their son with a knife and this caused even further distress for the hardworking mother, who collapsed after hearing about the violence in her own home against her children. By November 1968 she had suffered a complete nervous breakdown. On her discharge from hospital she was prescribed many tranquilisers to help her regulate her moods, but she increased the doses exponentially. As her drug intake increased, it did nothing to help with her depression and she began shopping around for different doctors to find further drugs.

On 21 April 1969, Thomas died. Having dropped a cigarette in bed, his death was attributed to smoke inhalation. In her grief, Velma increased her drug taking further and began to receive intravenous injections from her doctor. Though in a deep depression and apparently mourning the tragic death of her husband, she then married a co-worker's brother, Jennings Barfield on 23 August, 1970. Jennings Barfield was a sickly man, suffering from diabetes and emphysema. Velma became the man's main caregiver, but the pressure of his illnesses took a toll on her own health and twice in a year Velma overdosed on prescription medication. Jennings Barfield regretted his decision to marry the unstable drug-abusing widow, and in February 1971 he discussed with his family the decision to leave his wife.

On 22 March 1971, Velma poisoned her husband. Jennings was vomiting and suffering terrible diarrhoea. He was rushed to hospital but died from the arsenic ingestion. Velma later said that she had only tried to make him sick so he would see her nurse him back to health and decide to stay, but unfortunately the dose had been lethal.

Seven months later, Velma had another overdose of prescription medication that required almost a month's hospitalisation. Due to her decreasing health she was fired from her job and lost her house. Reluctantly, she moved back in with her elderly parents and within four months her father had died from lung cancer complications and Velma had again overdosed on medication.

In 1974, Velma took out two loans against her mother's home and wrote several cheques using her late husband's account. When her mother received letters regarding the loans she had taken out against her home, Velma purchased poisons and gave her mother a dose. On 30 December 1974, after suffering days of cramps and vomiting, Velma's mother Lillie died in hospital. Her death was declared the result of a heart attack.

After her mother's death, Velma moved in with her adult daughter but authorities turn up at the mobile home to talk to Velma about the various bad cheques she had written. The woman again took an overdose of prescription medicine.

On her release from hospital, Velma was arrested for cheque fraud but again overdosed on medication while in jail. Once back in front of the courts she was sentenced to six months and served four before being released for good behaviour.

Once back home, Velma stole a cheque from her son-in-law and used it to buy more prescription medication, before her daughter stepped in and demanded that her doctor no longer give her mother any access to medication. Velma was also asked to leave her daughters home.

In November 1975, Velma took a job as a live-in caretaker for an elderly couple, 93-year-old Montgomery and 83-year-old Dollie Edwards. Both required round-the-clock care. Though Montgomery liked the 45-year-old woman, his wife Dollie did not and the two women clashed. On 20 January 1977, Montgomery died, followed by his wife on 1 March.

The following month, Velma was hired as a caretaker for John and Record Lee. Within a week, she had forged cheques from her new employer, and to hide her deceit she poisoned John Lee, who died after a week of suffering from the arsenic's effects.

Barfield quickly left Record Lee's employment and moved in with 53-year-old Stuart Taylor, the nephew of her previous employer, Dollie Edwards. The relationship soured quickly when Stuart found out that his partner had been in prison. After forging several cheques in Stuart's name she also poisoned him and he died on 3 February 1978 after being ill from repeated poisoning for more than three months.[410] An autopsy carried out on Stuart Taylor's body showed that he had been poisoned with arsenic.

On 10 March 1978, police arrested Velma Barfield and questioned her regarding Stuart Taylor's death. She was placed in prison. She tried to commit suicide with an overdose of medication that was brought to her by various people including her attorney and the prison doctor. Following her suicide attempt, she was sent to a mental health hospital for assessment, where she remained for several weeks. Once found to be competent she was returned to prison where she again attempted suicide before seeing an evangelist on television and believing that God was going to save her.

Velma was tried for the first-degree murder of her boyfriend Stuart Taylor.[411] She also confessed to the murder of her mother, John Lee and Dollie Edwards.[412] The killer claimed that it was her addiction to barbiturates that made her a different person, 'a person who could slip poison into food and beverages and then watch the victims die'.[413] She said, 'when I was taking drugs, I was like a zombie'.[414] Velma was found guilty of murder and sentenced to death. After six stays of execution, Velma Barfield was executed by lethal injection in Raleigh's Central Prison on 2 November 1984.

Judy Buenoano

'If I did it, it was an accident'

Judy Buenoano was a black widow serial killer who poisoned two of her husbands. She also drowned her son when the poison she had given him did not work quickly enough.

Born Judias Welty on 4 April, 1943 in Quanah, Texas. Judy, the third of four children, was born into tragedy, with her mother dying from tuberculosis when she only two. When she was twelve her father remarried and his new wife had children of her own. Judy and her siblings were forced to do all of the family chores. The killer also claimed that she was abused and tortured. At the age of fourteen, Judy attacked her stepmother and her step-brothers and was sent to a juvenile detention centre for two years.

In 1961 her first son, Michael, was born. He was partially paralysed and required lag and arm braces to help him walk.[415] A year later Judy married Air Force Sergeant James Goodyear. The couple had a son and a daughter within two years of their marriage. Then, in 1971, after taking out a large life insurance policy on her husband, Judy gave James a lethal dose of arsenic.[416] Foul play was not suspected and Judy received the payout of 85,000 dollars.

Two years later, Judy married her second husband, Bobby Joe Morris. The couple, along with Judy's three children move to Trinidad, Colorado, where Judy burned down their home to again collect a large insurance payout.

In 1978, when again falling on financial hardship, Judy poisoned her second husband with arsenic. Again she received a large insurance payout.

In 1980, Judy drowned her handicapped 19-year-old son Michael while on a boating trip in Florida. She killed him after poisoning had not worked. Again, life insurance was paid out following his death.[417]

In 1981, Judy set her sights on her third husband. Judy and John Gentry moved in together in August 1981 and in June 1983, Judy tried to murder her partner by blowing up his car. The man survived the attack and police investigated the explosion. A month later, Judy was arrested for the attempted murder of John Gentry and, realising that the woman had outlived two other husbands and a son, further investigation commenced.

On 10 January 1984, Judy Buenoano was charged with the murder of her son Michael, as well as the insurance policy fraud. Two months later she was found guilty of her son's death and received a sentence of life imprisonment. A second trial began for the attempted murder of John Gentry and again the killer was found guilty after she had called the trial a witch-hunt, claiming that 'If I did [poison Gentry], it was an accident'.[418] In October 1985, she faced a third trial for the murder of her first husband, James Goodyear. She was again found guilty and was sentenced to death for his murder. On 30 March 1998, Judy Buenoano was executed by the electric chair.

Mary Ann Cotton

'Not Guilty, not guilty, oh no, not guilty'

Mary Ann Cotton was born Mary Ann Robson in Durham, in October 1832. Her father was 17-year-old Michael Robson, a coal miner; her mother was 19-year-old Margaret. Mary Ann would go on to become one of the most prolific poisoners in Britain.

When she was nineteen, Mary Ann fell pregnant and swiftly married 26-year-old William Mowbray in Newcastle, England on 18 July 1852.

The couple eventually had six daughters in six years, all of them died from gastric upsets and fever.[419] A son, John, was born to the family but also died before his first birthday. The children's deaths were only the beginning.

Mary Ann's husband, William Mowbray, died from gastric upset and fever on or about 19 January 1865. The man had injured his foot at work and could no longer support Mary Ann. After taking out an agreeable insurance policy of 35 pounds on her husband, Mary Ann killed him with arsenic.[420]

With her husband having been dead for only seven months, Mary Ann married her second husband, George Ward, on 28 August 1865.[421] The pair had met while Mary Ann was working in the House of Recovery in Sunderland. George had been a patient. The marriage lasted a little over a year, ending with George's death. He died of severe gastric upset on 21 October 1866. His wife had poisoned him with arsenic.

In November 1866, Mary Ann took on the job of housekeeper to widower James Robinson and his five children in Sunderland. After marrying her employer, Mary Anne began dispensing of her new husband's children.[422]

When Mary Ann had to go and look after her ill mother, Margaret Robson, the pair had a volatile argument after which Mary Ann bought arsenic. Her mother died a few days later on 15 March 1867 with severe gastric symptoms. Mary Ann then returned to her matrimonial home where she murdered three children who would die in the same circumstances.

Mary Ann's stepson, 6-year-old James Robinson, died of gastric upset on 21 April 1867 after being given several doses of arsenic. On 26 April 1867, just five days after 6-year-old James Robinson died of poisoning, his sister, 8-year-old Elizabeth died of similar gastric upset—brought on by arsenic poison administered by her step-mother Mary Ann.

On 2 May 1867, Mary Ann killed her daughter Isabella. She had killed her two step-children over the past fortnight and decided that her own daughter also had to go. The young girl was given arsenic in her food until she finally died in agony.

Mary Ann gave birth to a baby daughter, Mary Isabella Robinson on 18 February 1868, but the little infant died on 1 March 1868. The symptoms were the same as the rest of the family—severe gastrointestinal pains and fever—brought on by arsenic administered by Mary Ann.

Soon after the baby's death, Mary Ann's husband James found out that she had taken the money from all of his accounts and still not paid the home loan. He told her to leave. When he came home one day, Mary Ann had left and taken their surviving daughter with her.

The serial poisoner found life as a single mother hard, and so left Robinson's daughter with a friend and never returned. James was later reunited with his daughter.

Soon after, Mary Ann met Frederick Cotton though her friend, Margaret Cotton. The man had two children and was struggling to look after them alone after his wife and two other children had died. Mary Ann found the situation perfect. She soon moved in with him and the couple married. On 25 March 1870, Mary Ann Cotton dispatched of Frederick Cotton's sister Margaret in the same manner that she had every other person. She poisoned the woman with arsenic.

Mary became pregnant with Frederick's child and yet still continued her search for the next victim. She gained employment as a housekeeper for a doctor. When the doctor did not accept Mary Ann's sexual advances she tried to poison him. The man survived the attempt and sacked her.

Mary Ann married Frederick Cotton on 17 September 1870. However, she was still legally married to James Robinson Snr.

Mary Ann gave birth to a son, Robert Robson Cotton, in January 1871, and soon afterwards Mary Ann rekindled her affair with an ex-lover Joseph Natrass.

On 19 September 1871, Mary Ann Cotton's husband Frederick went off to work feeling fine. By the time he arrived he was in incredible pain, doubled over with excruciating stomach pains. He was sent home where he died soon after. His death was later believed to have been caused by arsenic poisoning, like her other victims. But when it came to exhume the body, it could not be found.

Three months after the death of Frederick, Joseph Natrass moved in with Mary Ann. However, Mary Ann tired of Natrass again and, though he remained part of the family, becoming a father to Frederick's three sons, Mary Ann found better company in John Quick-Manning.

On 10 March 1872, 10-year-old Frederick Cotton Jnr died of gastric upsets brought on by arsenic administered by his stepmother, Mary Ann Cotton.

The next to die was baby Robert. His death was put down to problematic teething but in fact his mother had murdered him.

On 1 April 1872, Mary Ann Cotton murdered Joseph Natrass by giving him arsenic-laced food. It had taken the man longer to die than any other victim as she had tried to kill him over such an extended amount of time that he grew almost immune to the poison.

After the death of Natrass, Mary Ann found she was pregnant with John Quick-Manning's child. However, John would not marry her as she still was looking after Frederick Cotton's son, Charlie. To Mary, the problem could be solved quickly. Seven-year-old Charlie Cotton died on 12 July 1872. His stepmother, Mary Ann Cotton, had poisoned him with arsenic. An inquest was held into Charlie's death and afterwards a second chemical test was done on the boy's stomach contents and it was found to contain arsenic.

Mary Ann Cotton was arrested for the murder of the boy. Soon after, the bodies of Joseph Natrass, Frederick Cotton Jnr and Robert Cotton were exhumed; all were found to contain arsenic. The body of Frederick Cotton Snr could not be located. While awaiting trial Mary Ann Colton gave birth to a baby girl, Margaret.

On 21 February 1873, Mary Ann was charged to face trial. Yet with the damning evidence in front of her—the stomach contents of several of her victims—the woman still attempted to claim her innocence. When the judge turned to her and asked, 'have you anything to say before I pronounce the [sentence], in a hoarse voice the poisoner exclaimed, 'not guilty, not guilty, oh no, not guilty'.[423] At trial she was found guilty of the murders of at least twenty-one people and sentenced to death.

On 24 March 1873, Mary Ann Cotton was executed. She did not have a last meal but only accepted a cup of tea at 5.30 a.m. She was lead to the gallows in Durham Gaol crying hysterically. At 7.50 a.m. the hood was placed over her face and the noose put around her neck. The executioner pulled the trap door and Mary Ann fell through. She did not die instantly with a broken neck, but slowly strangled at the end of the hangman's rope. It took her three minutes to die.

Martha Marek

'Other people also became sick after meals'

Martha Marek was born in Hungary in 1898. As a child born out of wedlock, she lived most of her life on the streets of Moedling, Vienna with her mother.[424] By the age of thirteen she married for the first time. Her husband was a wealthy 62-year-old man, Moritz Fritsch. His family were outraged by the arrangement and refused to speak to him again.[425] With no interference from his family, Martha quickly made herself comfortable in her new wealthy life and soon went through most of the man's money, until in 1923 he died under 'mysterious circumstances'.[426] At her husband's funeral, Martha met Emil Marek who would soon become her next husband.

In 1927, while falling on hard times, 23-year-old Emil Marek convinced his wife, 29-year-old Martha, to help him gain 30,000 dollars fraudulently from an insurance company. His plan was to take out an insurance policy, then allow Martha to cut off his leg and claim it had been severed while 'shaping a life-sized model on the terrace of his idyllic villa near Vienna'.[427] However, what had actually occurred was that after Emil had drunk a large quantity of whisky for courage, he told his wife to get an axe. Martha took an axe from the yard in their Vienna home and struck the man's leg. The axe badly damaged Emil's leg but did not sever it. It took another two blows of the axe to finally cut the leg off. Though in excruciating pain, Emil was pleased with Martha's work and set in motion the plan to con the insurance company. Emil contacted his insurer who sent a doctor to examine the man's wounds. The doctor was not convinced by Emil's story and on the doctor's advice the insurance company refused to pay the man's claim, particularly with the evidence that the injury had taken four strikes.[428] Martha Marek was furious with her husband for having failed in his attempt to get thirty thousand dollars from his insurance company. She had a new baby daughter and the family needed money.

Martha decided to get the insurance money herself. By July 1932, Emil died. His death certificate claimed he was suffering from tuberculosis. However, in hindsight, it is believed he died at the hands of his wife.

This time the insurance company paid the policy. Martha inherited 30,000 dollars once her husband was dead. The plan seemed too easy, and a month later, after insuring her baby daughter, she too died. Martha again received a princely sum.[429]

The next person to die was an elderly family member, an aunt. Martha had gone to visit the spritely 67-year-old Susanna Loewenstein. Within six months the woman had become frail and her hair had all but fallen out.[430] Before the woman died, Martha insured her for a large sum, and also found out that the woman's will gave Martha the house and a substantial sum of money.[431] Once the financial plans were in place, Martha killed the old woman with thallium.

Martha decided that she could continue her successful campaign of receiving insurance policies by taking in lodgers into her now empty house. The first lodger to die was Felicitas Kittsteiner. The man had been concerned for his wellbeing for quite some time and suggested to his family that Martha was poisoning him. He claimed to have felt sick every time he ate something she had made. The family dismissed the man's ranting, especially when Martha reminded them that 'other people also became sick after meals',[432] but had recovered. It was only when he died that they realised that he had been right.

The Kittsteiner family checked into the man's claims and found that before his death, Martha had insured her lodger for a large sum, with herself as the beneficiary.

The evidence was overwhelming and the family took their suspicions to police. The body of Felicitas Kittsteiner was exhumed, along with the bodies of Martha's husband, baby daughter, and elderly relative who had made the mistake of telling Marek that she would leave her a large inheritance after her death.

Traces of the poison thallium were found in all four bodies. Martha Marek was immediately arrested in Vienna in 1938 and faced trial for the murders of all four victims. Once in the dock the red-haired poisoner, dubbed the 'Modern-day Lucrezia Borgia', gave the court a piece of paper that claimed that she was deaf and mute.[433]

She was found guilty and sentenced to death; the death penalty having been reinstated earlier by Hitler. The prosecutor called her 'a creature living only to kill, heartless and powerless love, cruel beyond belief'.[434]

On 6 December 1938, Martha Marek became the first woman in Vienna to be executed in more than thirty years. She had become crippled while incarcerated and so was wheeled from her death cell, in a catatonic state, to the guillotine.[435]

At the platform, the executioner had planned to tip the chair forward with Martha's body falling into place on the chopping block. However, on the platform Martha began fighting with her guards and attempted to flee. She was quickly subdued and tied down; the guillotine's blade swiftly severed her head. A far better job than she had done six years earlier to her husband's leg.

Maria Velten

'It is nonsense, not true!'

Maria Velten, known in the press as the 'Poison Witch from the Lower Rhine', was born in 1916. She grew up in extreme poverty in the Lower Rhine. Her father left her mother when she was very small child. As a young woman, Velten married her first husband and they had four children together. However, the marriage was an extremely unhappy one; her husband was a chronic alcoholic who was prone to beating his young wife.[436] He was conscripted into World War I where he was missing in action. At home, Velten gave birth to two more children to different men. Destitute, the woman and her children, who lived in homeless shelters, made the decision to find a wealthy husband to take care of them.[437]

In 1959, she met widower Peter Pesch, a father of eight children. The couple married after a short courtship and Velten commenced looking after the large tribe of children. In 1960, her absent father arrived on her doorstep; he was haggard and ill with cholera and begged her to also look after him. He was in receipt of a handsome pension that was attractive to the now middle-aged woman. However, looking after the man became an incredible burden and would be the catalyst for the five murders that would occur over the next seventeen years from 1963 to 1980.[438]

Velten's first victim was her father in 1963. In the news at the time was the sensational serial killer case of poisoner Christa Lehman in Germany during the 1950s. The woman had used a pesticide E605 to murder her husband, father and a neighbour. Velten decided that the easily accessible poison would be an acceptable way to dispatch of her father. He died after she gave him a dose of the cyanide-like poison. He was buried soon after without any suspicion being raised. In 1970, as money become tight once more, Velten decided to murder her bedridden aunt, after having her sign over her money to her niece. Again the death was attributed to her ill health and she was buried without any cause for suspicion. As the children moved out of home, Velten was left with a marriage to a man that she no longer cared for. She had also found out that Peter had squirreled away a large bank account of money without her knowledge. In 1976, Peter Pesch was poisoned after he asked for a divorce from Velten. He was admitted to hospital with severe stomach cramps, but no poison was noted in his blood samples as Velten had been poisoning him slowly over a long period of time. One of Peter's sons raised the suspicion that his father was being poisoned. The doctor questioned Velten who denied the accusations. No further investigations were made and the man died soon after eating a large serving of blueberries given to him by his wife. She had chosen blueberries, as the poison, E605 changes anything it touches blue. The blueberries hid the distinctive colour in their own hue.[439]

At the age of sixty, Velten found herself in the company of another man, Heinrich Uckerseifer. The man's family were highly suspicious of the woman, and so, in 1978 he was dispatched of quickly with several servings of blueberries laced with E605. An 85-year-old widow became the next victim to die at the hands of Velten.

Bernhard Velten was the killer's fourth husband. His 1980 murder, after a year of marriage, raised the suspicions of his daughter, who went to police to complain that her stepmother had been draining her father's account.[440] Police exhumed his body and found that it contained E605.[441]

Velten, who was working as a housekeeper for a wealthy widow,[442] was arrested in 1983. She claimed that the accusations were false. She exclaimed, 'It is nonsense, not true!',[443] until the exhumation of Bernhard had proven that he had died from poisoning, then Velten confessed to his murder. The other people who had died in the care of Velten were also exhumed and poison was also detected in the bodies of her other husbands. The deaths of her father and aunt could not be determined.[444]

Velten was charged with three murders and six attempted murders. She was found guilty and sentenced to three life sentences. At the age of ninety-two, and suffering severe dementia, she was released from prison to serve the rest of her sentence in a nursing home.

Many of the black widows in this chapter could also have been included in the Poisoners chapter. However, these cases merit being placed separately because these women not only dispatched of elderly family members and children, but they also killed several husbands. Black widows are often portrayed in the media as femme fatales who lure men, often wealthy men, and then kill them, usually through poisoning them when they are ready to move on to the next victim. They are sociopaths with a desire to better themselves at the detriment of lovers and husbands.

Coupled with the black widow killers are the parents who kill. The following chapter will examine those women, who, like their black widow counterparts, rid themselves of children who they believe are a detriment to their own lives.

PARENTS WHO KILL

Like poisoners and black widows, parents who kill their children or the offspring of partners are often some of the cruellest and coldest killers. They, usually mothers, are often patient and will spread the killings out over a number of years.

Parents who murder are usually self-centred and kill out of the need to feel free from the burden of children. They often find that they have lost their identity through becoming a parent. This is highly significant in this chapter, in that the cases chosen are all mothers. They all felt that they were devoid of love and, through the murders of their children or those in their care, thought it would somehow bring them the love they wanted and desired.

Ellen Etheridge

'He lavished his attention on the children'

The daughter of a Baptist minister, John Walker, Ellen West was born in 1889. In Spring 1912, Texan widower J. D. Etheridge married 22-year-old Ellen, who took over as mother to his eight children. The marriage began well but Etheridge soon became increasingly jealous of her husband's devotion to his children. She decided that her only choice was to eliminate the children. In June 1913, Etheridge, using arsenic, poisoned two of the children.

On 2 October 1913, her husband's devotion to his remaining children increased her jealousy and led to the deaths of two more children and the attempted death of another. The fifth potential victim, a 13-year-old boy had run to a doctor after Ellen had poured lye down his throat.[445]

Authorities were quickly dispatched to the home and ordered autopsies of the two dead children. Their suspicions were confirmed when lye was found in all four bodies during the post-mortem. Etheridge was arrested on 15 October 1913 and confessed to the poisonings during police questioning, she told police that her reason for killing the children is that her husband, 'lavished his attention on the children'[446] and not on her. She received a life sentence for her crimes.

In 1930, after serving seventeen years behind bars, the longest sentence at the time, for a female convict, the killer petitioned the state for a pardon, hoping to die a free woman. At the time, she was allowed to leave the prison walls each day but was still locked up each night. There is no known date of death.

Kathleen Folbigg

'She left—with a bit of help'

Australian serial killer Kathleen Folbigg was born Kathleen Megan Donovan on 14 June 1967 to Thomas Britton and Kathleen Donovan.[447] Her parents spent little time with her as a baby and she was instead often left with her aunt and uncle, Mr and Mrs Platt. The couple attempted to adopt the little girl as their own, but her mother refused to sign the papers. In 1969, the Platts were able to adopt Kathleen, after her father murdered her mother by stabbing her twenty-four times. After the trauma it was discovered that Kathleen's father had molested her. The evidence was displayed in the young child's constant masturbation and sexually inappropriate games, as well as incessant crying and horrific tantrums.

By the end of 1970, her behaviour as a three year old became uncontrollable to the point that she was placed into care. She remained with another family, the Marlboroughs, until 1985 when again she became uncontrollable after finding out about the truth about her mother's death at her father's hand. She began stealing and ran away from home. By the age of seventeen she left the Marlborough family permanently and soon met Craig Folbigg. The couple spent most of their time together and married in September 1987.

Their first baby, Caleb, was born on 1 February 1989. At 3.30 a.m. on February 20, Kathleen was standing over the cot when she screamed out for her husband.[448] Craig went scrambling to the baby's room. Kathleen screamed that the baby was dead. The baby's death was declared a tragic accident, with Sudden Infant Death Syndrome (SIDS) as the cause.

More than a year later, Craig and Kathleen welcomed another son. Patrick was born on 3 June 1990. On 17 October, Kathleen again went to the baby's room in the middle of night. She smothered the baby as she had done to Caleb, before again screaming for her husband. Craig picked up the baby and held him to his ear. He listened and could hear a faint sound.[449] The baby was still breathing, though faintly. Craig began CPR on the four-month-old as he told his wife to call an ambulance. Patrick was rushed to hospital where he was put onto oxygen. The boy recovered but had long-lasting complications. He was diagnosed as epileptic and required extensive care. Kathleen resented the baby and the attention he required. She wrote in her diary that she wanted to run away from Patrick. On 13 February, 1991, a little over two years after the death of Caleb, Folbigg finally killed Patrick. Kathleen smothered the little baby as he slept in his cot. She again covered his mouth and nose until he stopped breathing. This time, she made sure he was dead before calling for help. The baby's death was attributed to a cardiac arrest, but again authorities believed it was a tragic accident.

On 14 October 1992, Sarah was born. She was subjected to every conceivable test and was to sleep with an apnoea monitor to ensure she would not succumb to the syndrome that had supposedly taken her brothers. Eleven months later it was decided to switch off the machine. Then two days later, on 29 August 1993, Kathleen Folbigg suffocated Sarah the same way she had done to Caleb and Patrick. The baby was autopsied and showed signs of suffocation, but death was still attributed to natural causes.[450]

On 7 August 1997, the couple welcomed a fourth child, Laura. Again the baby was subjected to numerous tests to ensure there were no underlying abnormalities that may have attributed to her siblings' deaths. By the time the baby was nineteen months old, Kathleen had grown weary of the baby and the incessant alarms from the monitor. She spent little time at home, and if she did, she would hit the baby, or yell at her. On 1 March 1999, Kathleen, suffocated the toddler while Craig was at work. The woman then called for an ambulance and paramedics attempted to revive the baby, without success. The final murder was the woman's undoing. To lose a baby to SIDS was tragic; to lose two was incomprehensible. But by the time the fourth baby died, it was impossible to look to more sinister reasons for the babies' deaths.

Police began to look at the deaths of the babies. No one could believe that a woman could have killed her own children, but most suspected that there had to be more to the story than coincidence. One day the truth came out after Craig Folbigg called the police. He had come across a series of diaries owned by his wife. The diaries were a disturbing look into the mind of a murderer. Though Folbigg had not mentioned the murders specifically. She had written about her resentment of the children and how they hindered her life.

Several comments in the diary stood out for police who read the woman's thoughts on the pages in front of them.

'I had mixed feeling this day [the day of Patrick's birth] ... I often regret Caleb and Patrick, only because your life changes so much ...'[451]

'I know the main reason for all my stress before and stress made me do terrible things[452].

'Seem to be thinking of Patrick, Sarah and Caleb ... my guilt of how responsible I feel for them all, haunts me, my fear of it happening again haunts me ...'[453]

'One day it [the baby] will leave, the others did ...'[454]

'wishing someone else was available with me ... purely because of what happened before ...'[455]

'Monitor is a good idea. Nothing can happen without the monitor knowing and since I'm not game enough to not plug it in because theyde [sic] want to know why I hadn't'[456]

'I'm starting to take it out on her [Laura]. Bad Move. Bad things and thoughts happen what that happen ...'[457] Referring to her escalating violence against her children.

'With Sarah, all I wanted was her to shut up. And one day she did'.[458]

'I lost it with her [Laura] ... Scared she'll leave me know, Like Sarah did ... I don't want to ever happen again ...'[459]

'Obviously, I'm father's daughter'.[460]

'... I knew I was short-tempered, and cruel, sometimes, to her [Sarah], and she left—with a bit of help ...'[461]

The diary entries pointed to only one conclusion. Kathleen Folbigg had killed her babies. Folbigg was questioned by police about her involvement in the babies' deaths. The woman coldly explained that she was not responsible. She talked about going into the babies' rooms and finding them dead. Police tried again and again to get Folbigg to confess the murders of her babies, without success.

The bodies of the babies were checked again, and murder could not be ruled out. Though many had hoped that this wouldn't be what had occurred. It was now inevitable. Folbigg was one of the country's worst serial killers. The woman was arrested and charged with her babies' murders.

A battery of experts were brought out to diagnose the woman with a number of illnesses, from abandonment issues to post-natal depression. In the end she was just found to be a cold-blooded killer. The jury at trial found her guilty of the manslaughter of her first-born son Caleb, and guilty of the murders of Patrick, Sarah and Laura. She was sentenced to forty years in prison for her crimes.

Theresa Knorr

'When Mom's done with me she's gonna kill you' *Suesan Knorr*

Theresa Knorr was born Theresa Jimmie Cross on 14 March 1946.[462] She was the youngest of three children born to James and Swannie Cross. The family lived in Sacramento, California. Though her father was diagnosed with Parkinson's disease the family still managed. At the age of fifteen, Theresa was shopping with her mother when her mother suddenly had a heart attack in the grocery store. Theresa held her mother as she died in her arms. The tragic event had a profound effect on the teenager and she became morose and depressed for years after her mother's sudden death.

Still mourning her mother, Theresa married her first husband, Clifford Sanders, on 29 September 1962. It had only been eighteen months since her mother's death; Theresa was a 17-year-old bride. A year after the marriage she gave birth to a son, Howard. But a year later tragedy struck again. According to Theresa, she aimed a shotgun at her husband and fired, killing him instantly in an act of self-defence. She was arrested for the murder but was acquitted.[463]

Six months after her husband's death, in March 1965, Theresa gave birth to a daughter, Sheila. In July 1966, the 21-year-old widowed mother of two married Robert Knorr after falling pregnant with her third child. Suesan was born in September 1966, followed by William in September 1967 and Robert Junior in 1968. The family was completed by the birth of Theresa, known as Terry, who was born in 1970.

However, the Knorr marriage was not a happy one and soon after the birth of Terry, Theresa and Robert divorced.

By March 1971, Theresa had married Ronald Pulliam, but again the marriage was an unhappy one and the pair divorced nineteen months later.

At the age of thirty, with six children to care for, Theresa married 59-year-old Chester Harris. The union lasted four months and they divorced in December 1976.

Looking after six children on her own was hard and Theresa took out her frustration on her children, brutally beating them on a regular basis. Her eldest child, 13-year-old Howard, was enlisted to help with the beatings of the younger children.

On one occasion, Suesan told a counsellor about the abuse and she was taken to the hospital where police interviewed her and notified her mother. When Theresa arrived she gave police a different story that was backed up by her other children. Suesan was returned to her mother that night where she was violently attacked. The beatings continued. When Suesan turned seventeen, Theresa noticed that she was turning into a beautiful young woman and so she began force-feeding the teenager large quantities of pasta and cheese to make her put on weight. If Suesan vomited up the copious amounts of food she given she was then forced to eat her own vomit.

In June 1983, during one violent episode, Theresa shot Suesan in the back. The bullet lodged deep in her flesh and, when Theresa was unable to pull it out, she left Suesan to writhe in pain in the bathroom for more than a month. The other children were forced to keep watch. Suesan was only allowed out of the bathroom once the infection had gone.

The following year, Theresa forced both Suesan and Sheila to work as prostitutes to help the family survive.

On one occasion, Theresa incorrectly believed that Sheila had fallen pregnant and she received an extremely brutal beating. Suesan, sick and exhausted from the beatings at the hands of her mother, begged to move out of home. Surprisingly, Theresa agreed but said she wanted to get the bullet out of Suesan's back once and for all. She forced the young woman to drink a large amount of alcohol in an attempt to dull the pain. She then made her daughter lie on the floor of the kitchen. Theresa made the other children hold their sister down. Theresa dug the bullet out while Suesan writhed in pain. For eleven days Suesan remained on the kitchen floor in pain and with infection setting in. She lapsed in and out of consciousness before Theresa decided to get rid of her.

On 16 July 1984, with the help of the older children, Theresa put the unconscious Suesan in the car along with her all of her belongings and drove to a secluded wooded area. There, they dumped her body and her boxes of possessions. Theresa then doused her daughter in gasoline and set her on fire before driving away.[464] Suesan's body was later found, but was not identified until 1993 when Terry went to the police.[465]

Before Suesan died she told her younger sister Sheila that it would be her turn once Suesan was dead, she had said to Sheila, 'When Mom's done with me she's gonna kill you'.[466] Suesan's premonition soon came true when in May 1985, believing Sheila to be a witch, Theresa locked her in a small cupboard without food or water. The temperature inside the cupboard was intense and Sheila removed her clothes in an attempt to avoid the soaring temperatures in the summer heatwave. After a week, there was a thud inside the cupboard but Theresa refused to open the door for more than a month after. She only opened it once the body's smell became unbearable. [467]

Again, the other children were made to pack up the young woman's possessions and she was also dumped in the woods where she was found a few days later. Again, her body remained unidentified until the case unravelled.

To try to hide what had occurred in the house, Theresa forced Terry to set fire to their house. However, the fire brigade was called quickly and little damage was done. The trauma of what had occurred in that house took its toll on the remaining children and most of them moved from the house.

Robert shot dead a man in a bar and went to prison, while Terry developed a drug problem in an attempt to erase from her mind the horrors she had seen, until one evening she saw a true crime program on television and decided to go to police. The story was so incredible that police did not believe her.[468] It took another three years before she again tried to get police to listen. On 28 October 1993, Terry went to the police with her story. The description of the deaths of her sisters matched that of the two unidentified bodies found in 1984 and 1985. [469]

On 10 November 1993, while on the run, Theresa Knorr was arrested for the murders of her two daughters. William and Robert Junior were also arrested and confessed to their part in their sisters' deaths. Robert received an additional three-year sentence to be served concurrently with his sixteen-year murder sentence and William was given a probationary sentence.

Theresa Knorr pleaded guilty to both murders and was given two life terms. She is serving her sentence in the Chow Chilla State Prison for Women.

Marybeth Tinning

'When I look back I see a very damaged and just a messed up person ... there is no words that I can express now. I feel none. I'm just, just none'

Marybeth Tinning was born Marybeth Roe to parents Alton and Ruth on 11 September 1942 in Duanesburg, New York. The eldest child, Marybeth spent most of her childhood being told by her family that she was unwanted and unloved, while her younger brother was lavished with attention. An aunt repeatedly told her that she was unwanted.[470]

She was often locked in her bedroom for days at a time. The only attention she received was when her father would beat her.[471] 'My father hit me with a flyswatter because he had arthritis and his hands were not of much use. And when he locked me in my room I guess he thought I deserved it'.[472]

At school she was also lonely, with most students finding her odd. Tinning graduated from Duanesburg High School where her only achievement was being elected president of the Future Homemakers of America Club,[473] a social club for those who wanted to be stay at home mothers following their education. After high school, she worked in several lower-paying jobs including employment as a nurses' aide, a waitress and a bus driver.[474]

She said later that there were only two things that she ever wanted in life, 'to be married to someone who cared for me and to have children'.[475] Her wish was to come true by the time she was twenty-two, when she went on a blind date with Joe Tinning. By 1965, the couple had married and in May 1967 they were blessed with Barbara, the couple's first baby. In January 1970, the Tinnings welcomed a second baby, a son they named Joseph Junior. However, though Tinning now enjoyed the attention received from others who came to coo over her baby, she still desired the adoration from her parents, which never came.[476]

In October 1971, while Tinning was heavily pregnant with her third child, her father died of a massive heart attack. Having been cold and abusive toward Tinning her entire life, she had hoped before the end her father would show her love, and though she begged for his attention it never came. However, the attention she received at his funeral was the attention that she had yearned for her entire life. It was then that she learned that death brought her, a true narcissist, what she desired most: attention.

Again, family and friends flocked to be around the 29-year-old woman who mourned her father's death. The attention she received from those around her switched on a desire to continue that attention. The day after Christmas, 1971, Marybeth gave birth to her third child, another daughter, named Jennifer. After the visits from well-wishers stopped, Tinning came up with a diabolical plan.

On 3 January 1972, the Tinnings rushed their newborn baby girl to hospital where the tiny baby was diagnosed with meningitis.477 Multiple congenital brain abscesses were also found.478 The 8-day-old baby would not survive and died in hospital. Once back at home, and before the funeral, Tinning washed all of the Jennifer's clothes and packed them away. She also disassembled the cot and packed up the baby's toys. The cleaning and packing up would later become part of Tinning's post-death ritual.479 The death of Jennifer was deemed non-suspicious. Again, friends and relatives flocked to console the heartbroken woman and help with her two surviving children.

Yet as the attention waned, tragedy struck the Tinning family once again. Seventeen days after Jennifer's death, Tinning rushed her two-year-old son Joseph Junior to the hospital. She told staff that he had had a seizure. When nothing could be found, Joseph was discharged home. Several hours later, Tinning returned with Joseph's dead body in her arms.480 Again she returned home to wash the toddler's clothes and pack away all of his belongings.

On 1 March 1972, Tinning again rushed to the hospital with another child in her arms. Four-year-old Barbara had had several convulsions at home, but when nothing could be found the child was discharged, before Tinning again returned the next day with the child.

Barbara was unconscious and remained comatos. She later died without ever regaining consciousness. Doctors diagnosed the rare disease of Reyes Syndrome that can cause encephalopathy (swelling of the brain).

Timothy was born on 21 November 1973. However, the joy and elation of the new baby was short lived, when the couple rush the 9-day-old Timothy to the hospital where he was pronounced dead on arrival. His death was declared as being due to Sudden Infant Death Syndrome (SIDS).

The strain of the deaths took their toll on the couple and soon they were fighting over money and Marybeth's failing mental health. Joe convinced his wife to seek psychiatric attention and she was admitted to hospital. However, soon after her admission, she escaped and returned home. Feeling that she had now also been abandoned by her husband, she attempted to poison him with the barbiturate, phenobarbital. However, her husband survived and told doctors that he had attempted suicide.[481]

The couple called police in January 1974 claiming that they had been burgled, but suspicion soon fell on Marybeth following another theft of a family member's money. In late 1974, she confessed to a co-worker that she was pregnant again and that 'God told her to kill this one too'.[482]

On 30 March 1975, Tinning gave birth to her fifth child, Nathan. While everyone around them hoped that the misfortunes of Tinning's previous four children would spare Nathan, it was not to be. On 20 September 1975, Nathan was also killed. She drove to St Clare's hospital with the dead baby in her arms. Like Joseph, Nathan's death was attributed to SIDS.

In August 1978, the couple commenced adoption proceedings for newborn Michael and then in October the couple had their sixth biological child, Mary Frances. At three months old, unconscious Mary Frances was rushed to hospital where doctors were able to revive her.

Her condition was listed as 'aborted SIDS',[483] and she was released from hospital only to be rushed back a month later in cardiac arrest. Doctors revived the child once more, but she was left with permanent brain damage. Mary Frances remained on life support and fought for two days before dying.

On 19 November 1979, Tinning gave birth to Jonathan. At four months old, he was rushed to St Clare's Hospital in an unconscious state. He was revived and discharged only to return a few days later. He held on for a month before dying.

Tinning's adoptive son Michael was the next to die. The two year old was taken to a paediatrician on 2 March 1981. Tinning claimed that the child would not wake up. The toddler was already dead when the doctors examined him. Suspicion now fell on Tinning. No longer could genetics be blamed when their adopted son also died in similar circumstances to the others.

For the next four years, the couple remain childless, and the rumours and innuendo died down. Then on 22 August 1985, Tinning gave birth to Tami Lynne, but four months later the baby was dead. Finally, after the deaths of nine children in thirteen years, police were called to investigate. In April 1986 after tests were done on the baby's corpse, Tinning and her husband were arrested and questioned over the baby's death. Tinning, broke down and told police that she believed that she was nothing and that she wasn't worth 'anything in life',[484] Tinning confessed to three of the murders, but vehemently denied murdering the others. In her handwritten confession she wrote: 'I did not do anything to Jennifer, Joseph, Barbara, Michael, Mary Frances, Jonathon. Just these three, Timothy, Nathan and Tami. I smothered them each with [sic] pillow because I'm not a good mother'.[485] She was charged only with the murder of Tami Lynne.

After a six-week trial, Tinning was found guilty of the murder of Tami Lynne and sentenced to twenty years to life for the killing. According to experts that testified at her trial, she was a narcissist who was motivated by the attention she gained from their tragic deaths.

She has been refused parole since her eligibility in 2007. At a 2011 parole hearing she was asked what insights she had into herself, to which she replied, 'When I look back I see a very damaged and just a messed up person and I have tried to become a better person while I was here, trying to be able to stand on my own and ask for help when I need it … sometimes I try not to look in the mirror and when I do, I just, there is no words that I can express now. I feel none. I'm just, just none'.[486]

Parents who kill, or more accurately in the preceding chapter, mothers who kill, are often mentally unstable women who blame their children for changes in their lives. They abuse and harm their children to make themselves feel better. When they are able to get away with one murder they turn again to killing when they find their life spiralling out of control. They use the murder of their children or children in their care as way to find control.

THE BREAKDOWN OF THE SERIAL KILLER SPECIES

Moving away from the umbrella term of 'serial killer' allows us to examine the precise nuances of the various types of killers who murder more than two victims. The preceding chapters have shown, even by only looking at only ten types, that there are a diverse range of killers that, although collectively can be called serial killers, have a variety of different motives and desires that lead them to kill.

Though most readers interested in serial killers will quickly think of the likes of Ted Bundy and Jeffrey Dahmer, it can be pointed out that even these two killers do not fit into the same category, with Bundy being a spree killer and Dahmer coming under the description of torture killer. Those discussed in this book are also varied. Attempting to compare the brutal murders conducted by Theresa Knorr, a woman who killed two of her daughters, and the sexually motivated child murders by John Wayne Gacy or Dean Corll makes no sense. The killers under the sub-categories of child sexual killers and parents who murder children are at different ends of the paediatric victimology spectrum.

This example shows that the singular term, serial killer, is far too vague to encapsulate the various types of multiple murderers, as well as providing possible subcategories that are more definitive than the umbrella term of serial killer.

Since the term serial killer was penned in the 1970s, many more killers have come under the broad definition, and since then there have been attempts to redefine the term as well as indentify the traits of the various types of killers that come under the banner. This book has looked at ten types of serial killers, their motives, backgrounds and in most cases, the reasons for killing from the mouths of the killers themselves.

As we continue through the twenty-first century, the classification of serial killers has commenced a metamorphosis and serial murderers, though still defined as serial killers, require a more specific classification that defines them by their various subcategories. This book has opened a dialogue to question the reclassification of serial murderers, based on various traits including victimology, pre- and post-death actions, modus operandi, signature and motive.

BIBLIOGRAPHY

Books

Adams, D., *Hitchhikers Guide to the Galaxy a Trilogy in Four Parts*, Pan Macmillan, 2009.

Britton, P., *The Jigsaw Man*, Random House, 2013.

Canter, D., *Criminal Shadows*, Authorlink Press, 2000.

Eckert, A., *The Scarlett Mansion*, iUniverse, 2000.

Gibson, D., *Serial murder and media circuses*, Greenwood, 2006.

Howard, A., *A Killer in the Family*, New Holland, 2013.

Howard, A., et al *River of Blood*, Universal, 2004.

Lowe, G., *Escape from Broadmoor*, History Press, 2013.

Milkins, N., *Who was Jack the Stripper*, Rose Heyworth, 2011.

Rule, A., *A Rose for Her Grave*, Simon and Schuster, 1993.

Vronsky, P., *Female Serial Killers: How and Why Women Become Monsters*, Berkley Books, 2007.

Vronsky, P., *Serial Killers: The Madness of Monsters*, Penguin, 2004.

Wambaugh, J., *The Blooding*, Open Road Media, 2011.

Wansell, G., *An Evil Love: The Life of Frederick West,* Headline, 1996.

Williams, S., *Invisible Darkness*, Random House, 2009.

Documentaries

Cracking the Code Documentary

Deadly Woman: The Sacred Bond Documentary

Do Not Kill, TVN24 Documentary

Fred and Rose: The West Murders, Channel 5 Documentary

Fred West's own words, Fred and Rose: The West Murders,
    Channel 5 Documentary

Instinto assesino—El Monstruo de los Canaduzales—Discovery
    Documentary

Most Evil, Murderous Women Documentary

Wicked Attraction ID Documentary

Newspapers

The Adelaide Chronicle

Adelaide News

Aurora Daily Express

Boca Raton

The Bryan Times

The Bulletin

The Canberra Times

Corsicana Daily Sun

The Courier Mail

The Daily Bhaskar

Daily Mail and Empire

Daytona Beach Journal

The Deseret News

The Dispatch

Ellensburg Daily Record

Eugene Register Guard

The Evening Independent

France Soir

The Freelance Star

Freeman's Journal

Gadsden Times

Glasgow Herald

The Hartford Weekly Times

Herald Journal

The Hindu

The Kentucky New Era

Kingman Daily Miner

The Independent

Lakeland Leader

Lawrence Journal

The Lewiston Daily

Lewiston Evening Journal

Lodi News Sentinel

Ludington Daily

The Mail

McCook Daily Gazette

The Meriden Morning Record

Miami News

The Michigan Daily

The Milwaukee Journal

Milwaukee Sentinel

Mohave Daily Miner

The Montreal Gazette

Moscow Pullman Daily News

NaTemat

The News and Courier

The Newcastle Chronicle

New Strait Times

The Norwalk Hour

Oscala Star Banner

Ottowa Citizen

The Palm Beach Report

Panapress

Pittsburg Post-Gazette

Reading Eagle

The Sarasota Herald Tribune

Schenectady Gazette

Der Spiegal

Spokane Daily Chronicle

St PetersbergTimes

SP Times

The Sun Sentinel

Sydney Morning Herald

The Sumter Daily Item

Times Daily

The Times of India

Toledo Blade

The Tribune

The Tuscaloosa News

Veja

The Victorian Advocate

The Western Mail

Journals

Australian Police Journal

Criminal Law Quarterly 413 (1999)

Time Magazine

Websites

Asif Shahzad, Lahore: The story of a pampered boy, www.dawn.com

Bernardo and Homolka case, http://bernardo-homolka.tumblr.com/

Dubious court defences, http://civicadvocator.net/dubious-court-
defenses

Maniacs of the CIS countries and USSR, http://www.serial-killers.ru/

Pasarmiedo, http://www.pasarmiedo.com

The Poisoner Anna Zwanziger, http://www.geschichte-verbrechen.de/
zwanziger/zwanziger.html

The Child Who Killed Children, https://suite101.com/a/the-child-who-
killed-children-the-twisted-tale-of-harold-jones-a374051

The speech of the murderer Eusebius Pieydagnelle before the Circuit
Court, http://eblox.bplaced.net/die-rede-des-morders-eusebius-
pieydagnelle-vor-dem-schwurgericht/

TruTv, http://www.trutv.com/

The Unknown Misandry, http://unknownmisandry.blogspot.com.au/

The X Dossiers, https://wikispooks.com/ISGP/dutroux/Belgian_X_
dossiers_the_accused.htm

Radford University Timelines

When Women murder, http://www.boen-end.de/velten.htm

Court Transcripts

Gacy v Welborn 61 USLW 2665

People v Gacy 468 N.E.2d 1171 (Ill. 1984)

Pitchfork, R v [2009] EWCA Crim 963 (14 May 2009)

R v Birnie

R v Folbigg [2003] NSWSC 895 (24 October 2003)

News Programmes

ABC

BBC

NBC

ENDNOTES

Child Killers

1   Stephen A. Egger, *The Killers Among Us*, Prentice-Hall 1998.
2   R. Morton (Editor), FBI Serial Murder Multi-Disciplinary Perspectives for Investigators'.
3   'Brazilian, likened to Dahmer, confesses to 14 killings', *The Tuscaloosa News*, February 24, 1992.
4   Ibid.
5   'Veja', February 26, 1992.
6   'Brazilian, likened to Dahmer, confesses to 14 killings', *The Tuscaloosa News*, February 24, 1992.
7   Ibid.
8   Ibid.
9   'Serial killer Arthur Bishop is executed', *Schenectady Gazette*, June 11, 1998.
10 'Disturbing portrait emerges of "quiet" Arthur Bishop', *The Deseret News*, July 27, 1983.
11 'Serial killer Arthur Bishop is executed', *Schenectady Gazette*, June 11, 1998.
12 Amanda Howard, *A Killer in the Family.*
13 The X Dossiers. https://wikispooks.com/ISGP/dutroux/Belgian_X_dossiers_the_accused.htm.
14 Ibid.
15 'Child Abuse tapes seized', *Pittsburg Post-Gazette*, August 24, 1996.
16 Ibid.
17 Next Boa, http://www.peoples.ru/state/criminal/manyak/golovkin/ (translated from Russian).
18 Ibid.
19 Ibid.
20 'Man drowned boy because of thrill', *The Canberra Times*, September 22, 1987.
21 'Court told man played with hundreds of boys', *The Canberra Times*, September 23, 1987.

22   Ibid.

23   'Man drowned boy because of thrill', *The Canberra Times,* September 22, 1987.

24   Ibid.

25   'Court told man played with hundreds of boys', *The Canberra Times,* September 23, 1987.

26   Det Insp Aarne Tees, *Child Murders in Griffith,* Australian Police Journal vol 44, No 1. 1990.

27   'Court told of virtual rape of boy', *The Canberra Times,* September 24, 1987.

28   'Lockhart guilty in slaying', *Toledo Blade,* October 5, 1988.

29   'Did all American Boy become a killer', *The Toledo Blade,* June 26, 1988'.

30   Ibid.

31   'Lockhart guilty in slaying', *Toledo Blade,* October 5, 1988.

32   'Youngest daughter reckless after tragedy', *St Petersberg Times,* July 27, 2007.

33   'Lockhart guilty in slaying', *Toledo Blade,* October 5, 1988.

34   'Death Row inmate expresses remorse', *The Bryan Times,* December 8, 1997.

35   Ibid.

36   'In the name of his sister', *SP Times',* http://www.sptimes.com/News/012300/news_pf/ Floridian/In_the_name_of_his_si.shtml.

37   'Says 9 were slain on murder farm', *Lawrence Journal,* December 4, 1928.

38   Ibid.

39   'Gordon Northcott scoffs at the Charges of killing', *Spokane Daily Chronicle,* September 21, 1928.

40   'Cyrus Northcott abandons Gordon', *Spokane Daily Chronicle,* September 28, 1928.

41   'Says 9 were slain on murder farm', *Lawrence Journal,* December 4, 1928.

42   Ibid.

43   Colin Pitchfork Radford University timelines.

44   Pitchfork, R v [2009] EWCA Crim 963 (14 May 2009).

45   Ibid.

46   Paul Britton, *The Jigsaw Man.*

47   Cracking the Code Documentary.

48   Pitchfork, R v [2009] EWCA Crim 963 (14 May 2009).

49   Joseph Wambaugh, *The Blooding.*

50   Britton, *The Jigsaw Man.*

51   Pitchfork, R v [2009] EWCA Crim 963 (14 May 2009).

52   Tim Lambert, *The Case of Colin Pitchfork,* http://www.localhistories.org/pitchfork.html.

53   John Straffen, *Serial Killer Timelines.*

54   Ibid.

55   Gordon Lowe, *Escape from Broadmoor,* 2013, p. 15.

56   'Murder Trial Evidence', *Glasgow Herald,* July 24, 1952.

57   Ibid.

58   'Straffen sent for trial', *Glasgow Herald,* May 16, 1952.

59   Ibid.
60   'Murder Trial Evidence', *Glasgow Herald,* July 24, 1952.
61   'Date of Straffen execution set', *Glasgow Herald,* August 28, 1952.
62   'Death for serial killer', *New Strait Times,* December 10, 2003.
63   Ibid.

The Known Stranger

64   'Medical Examiner testifies to cause of death of youths', *Star News,* July 9, 1974.
65   Ibid.
66   'Torture board viewed at trial', *Times Daily,* July 8, 1974.
67   Ibid.
68   Ibid.
69   Colin Wilson, *A Plague of Murder.*
70   'Suspect in Deaths proves puzzling', *Spokane Daily Chronicle,* August 14, 1973.
71   'Double Life of Corll begins to unravel', *Lakeland Leader,* August 19, 1973.
72   'Henley gives Statement on Manner of Killings', *Lewiston Evening Journal,* July 9, 1974.
73   Ibid.
74   'Four killings bred by aged Sadist slayer', *St Petersburg Times,* March 1935.
75   Ibid.
76   Ibid.
77   'Albert Fish executed for 8-year-old Crime', *The Post,* January 15, 1936.
78   'Curing Killers with Love', *The Evening Independent,* May 26, 1949.
79   Ibid.
80   'Albert Fish xray', *Daily News,* April 4, 2013.
81   'Curing Killers with Love', *The Evening Independent,* May 26, 1949.
82   'Four killings bred by aged Sadist slayer', *St Petersburg Times,* March 1935.
83   An interesting fact is that a charge of sodomy in Iowa includes oral sex.
84   People v. Gacy, 468 N.E.2d 1171 (Ill. 1984).
85   'Death toll rises', *Chicago Tribune,* August 12, 2001.
86   People v. Gacy, 468 N.E.2d 1171 (Ill. 1984).
87   Ibid.
88   Ibid.
89   Gacy v. Welborn 61 USLW 2665.
90   'Top 50 serial killer moments', YouTube documentary, http://www.youtube.com/watch?v=qNtTeuXHwew.
91   'The Boston Belfry Murder', *The Hartford Weekly Times,* May 13, 1876.
92   Trynkiewicz victim was fishing on the lake. Do not kill, 'when there were no conditions', TVN24 (translated from Polish).
93   Ibid.
94   Ibid.

95 'The paedophile murderer out of prison', *NaTemat,* January 2014, (translated from Polish).

96 'Mariusz Trynkiewicz is free in February', *NaTemat,* January 2014, (translated from Polish).

97 'Barcelona Shadows', *Telegraph,* February 4, 2014.

98 'Story of Sorcery', *The Evening Independent,* March 29, 1912.

99 Enriqueta Marti Pasarmiedo, http://www.pasarmiedo.com (translated from Spanish)

100 'Story of Sorcery', *The Evening Independent,* March 29, 1912.

101 'The eight crimes that rocked Barcelona', *ABC,* February 1, 2014, (translated from Spanish).

The Thrill Killer

102 'Great Crimes of the twentieth', Century *France Soir,* (translated from French).

103 Jean Noel Kapferer, *Rumours: Uses, Interpretations and Images,* Transaction, 2011.

104 'Great Crimes of the twentieth Century', *France Soir,* (translated from French).

105 Ibid.

106 Ibid.

107 *Der Spiegal,* July 17, 1967, (translated from German).

108 Ibid.

109 Ibid.

110 Ibid.

111 Ibid.

112 Ibid.

113 Ibid.

114 'Marquette tells his story of murder night', *The Bulletin,* December 8, 1961.

115 Ibid.

116 Ann Rule, *A Rose for Her Grave,* p. 470.

117 Ibid.

118 'Convicted killer suspect in 2nd mutilation death', *Eugene Register Guard,* April 23, 1975.

119 'Marquette leads police to victim's missing head', *The Bulletin,* July 3, 1961.

120 'Convicted killer suspect in 2nd mutilation death', *Eugene Register Guard,* April 23, 1975.

121 'Marquette admits 3rd murder', *Eugene Register Guard,* June 3, 1975.

122 Maniacs of the CIS countries and USSR, http://www.serial-killers.ru/karts/mihasevich.htm, (translated from Russian).

123 Ibid.

124 Ibid.

125 Ibid.

126 'Victim Shot, stabbed, mutilated and violated,' *The Canberra Times,* June 1, 1994.

127 'Witness A says Milat produced black revolver', *The Canberra Times,* November 9, 1994.

128 'Serial Kill count to rise', *The Canberra Times,* November 5, 1993.

129 'Ropes and underwear found in Forest', *The Canberra Times,* October 26, 1994.

130 'Victim Shot, stabbed, mutilated and violated', *The Canberra Times,* June 1, 1994.

131 Ibid.

132 Amanda Howard et al, *River of Blood,* Universal 2004.

133 Ibid., p. 245.

134 'Trial begins for Ukrainian accused in Murders of 52', *Reading Eagle,* November, 24 1998.

135 Amanda Howard et al, *River of Blood,* p. 246

136 'Man accused of 52 murders goes on trial in Ukraine', *The Day,* November 23 1998.

137 'Trial begins for Ukrainian accused in Murders of 52', *Reading Eagle,* November 24, 1998.

138 Ibid.

139 'Ukranian man sentenced to death for 52 killings', *Ocala Star Banner,* April 2, 1999.

140 Amanda Howard et al, *River of Blood,* p. 245.

141 Ibid., p. 246.

142 'The inside, described in the Con's own words', *The Sumter Daily Item,* December 30, 1970.

143 Ibid.

144 Amanda Howard et al, *River of Blood,* p. 249.

145 Ibid.

146 'Ask report on mental condition of Panzram', *Lewiston Daily Sun,* November 16, 1928.

147 'Says he murdered boy', *The Montreal Gazette,* October 27, 1928.

148 'Kansas ready for Execution first since '70', *The Miami News,* September 3, 1930.

149 Ibid.

150 'Killer', *Boca Raton News,* November 8, 1970.

151 'The inside, described in the Con's own words', *The Sumter Daily Item,* December 30, 1970.

152 Vronsky, Peter, *Serial Killers: The Madness of Monsters,* (ebook).

153 The speech of the murderer Eusebius Pieydagnelle before the Circuit Court, http://eblox. bplaced.net/die-rede-des-morders-eusebius-pieydagnelle-vor-dem-schwurgericht/.

154 Ibid.

155 Ibid.

156 Ibid.

157 Ibid.

Killer Kids

158 'The case of Mary Bell', *The Milwaukee Sentinel,* December 25, 1973.

159 Ibid.

160 Ibid.

161 Ibid.

162 'Young killer Mary does intend to be forgotten', *The Montreal Gazette,* March 24, 1975.

163 'No one wants Little Mary Bell', *The Norwalk Hour,* December 18, 1968.

164 Amanda Howard et al, *River of Blood,* p. 37. Errors in original.

165 'English Youngster of 11 begins lifetime behind bars', *Reading Eagle,* December 18, 1968.

166   Amanda Howard et al, *River of Blood*, p. 37.

167   'Young killer Mary does intend to be forgotten', *The Montreal Gazette*, March 24, 1975.

168   Ibid.

169   '2 girls charged in Slaying Case', *The Tuscaloosa News*, December 11, 1968.

170   'How much as Mary Bell changed in 11 years', *Herald-Journal*, May 16, 1980.

171   'English Youngster of 11 begins lifetime behind bars', *Reading Eagle*, December 18, 1968.

172   'Young killer Mary does intend to be forgotten', *The Montreal Gazette*, March 24, 1975.

173   'Child Killer Escapes', *The Evening Independent*, September 13, 1977.

174   Ibid.

175   'Mary bell held after tip off', *The Glasgow Herald*, September 14, 1977.

176   13-Year-Old Nigerian Girl, Jummai Hassan, Confesses to Series of Ritual Murders, 2001, http://unknownmisandry.blogspot.com.au/2011/09/13-year-old-nigerian-girl-jummai-hassan.html.

177   'Nigerian girl arrested over cult killings', *BBC*, July 27, 2001.

178   13-Year-Old Nigerian Girl, Jummai Hassan, Confesses to Series of Ritual Murders, 2001, http://unknownmisandry.blogspot.com.au/2011/09/13-year-old-nigerian-girl-jummai-hassan.html.

179   'Teenager killed 47 in ritual murders', *The Guardian*, July 28, 2001.

180   13-Year-Old Nigerian Girl, Jummai Hassan, Confesses to Series of Ritual Murders, 2001, http://unknownmisandry.blogspot.com.au/2011/09/13-year-old-nigerian-girl-jummai-hassan.html.

181   'Nigeria Trial of Murder Accused stalled', *All Africa*, December 20, 2001.

182   'Teenager killed 47 in ritual murders', *The Guardian*, July 28, 2001.

183   'Print links Heirens to Ex-Wave's Death', *The Spokesman-Review*, July 13, 1946.

184   'Youth said near Degnan Home after Kidnapping', *The Tuscaloosa News*, July 16, 1946.

185   'Youth seen at Kidnap Victim's home', *Kentucky New Era*, July 15, 1946.

186   'Three Chicago murders solved by Confessions', *Eugene Register Guard*, August 6, 1946.

187   'Youth said near Degnan Home after Kidnapping', *The Tuscaloosa News*, July 16, 1946.

188   'Heirens Loses Plea in Court', *The Miami News*, July 2, 1946.

189   'Young student held in Degnan Kidnap murder', *St Petersburg Times*, June 29, 1946.

190   Ibid.

191   Ibid.

192   Ibid.

193   'Seek a Showdown', *Lawrence Journal-World*, July 17, 1946.

194   'Youth said near Degnan Home after Kidnapping', *The Tuscaloosa News*, July 16, 1946.

195   'Seek a Showdown', *Lawrence Journal-World*, July 17, 1946.

196   Harold Jones, http://www.abertillery.net/oldabertillery/tales/haroldjones.html.

197   Ibid.

198   Child Murder Drama, *The Adelaide Chronicle*, August 26, 1921.

199 The Child Who Killed Children, https://suite101.com/a/the-child-who-killed-children-the-twisted-tale-of-harold-jones-a374051.

200 'Child Murder Drama', *The Adelaide Chronicle,* August 26, 1921.

201 'Boy 16 Sentenced to Death', *The Adelaide Chronicle,* November 12, 1931.

202 The Child Who Killed Children, https://suite101.com/a/the-child-who-killed-children-the-twisted-tale-of-harold-jones-a374051.

203 Ibid.

204 Neil Milkins, *Who was Jack the Stripper?.*

205 'Negro confesses another assault', *The News and Courier,* June 7, 1938.

206 'Negroes accused of killing Woman', *The Freelance-Star,* May 30, 1938.

207 Ibid.

208 'Chicago Negro confesses brick slayings of five', *The Lewiston Daily Sun,* June 3, 1938.

209 'Admits Five Murders', *Lawrence Journal World* June 3, 1938.

210 'Negro boy who used bricks in Murders to Die', *Sarasota Herald-Tribune,* August 5, 1938.

211 'Bereaved husband assaults accused', *The Montreal Gazette,* June 7, 1938.

212 'Negro convicted of brick slaying', *The Owosso Argus Press,* August 5, 1938.

213 'Jesse Pomeroy today', *The Evening Independent,* February 2, 1917.

214 'Sadistic young killer spent life in prison', *St Petersburg Times,* August 2, 1953.

215 'Torture attacks stirred fear in Boston', *The Palm Beach Report,* August 2, 1953.

216 'Sadistic young killer spent life in prison', *St Petersburg Times,* August 2, 1953.

217 'The Boy fiend', *Lewiston Evening Journal,* July 20, 1874.

218 'Jesse Pomeroy Served Forty years in Solitary', *Times Daily,* September 27, 1932.

219 Ibid.

220 'Jesse Pomeroy talks', *Meriden Morning Record,* May 3, 1911.

Poisoners

221 'Big time nineteenth century mass murderer began at U', *The Michigan Daily,* December 4, 1973.

222 Amanda Howard, The Crime Web website .

223 'Heir vindicates Mudgett name', *The Michigan Daily,* December 6, 1973.

224 Allan Eckert, *The Scarlett Mansion.*

225 'His one chief object in life', *Aurora Daily, Express* April 13, 1896.

226 'Murder Most Foul', *Daily Mail and Empire,* July 16, 1895.

227 'Big time nineteenth century mass murderer began at U', *The Michigan Daily,* December 4, 1973.

228 '20 Bodies found in Worst Mass Slaying of Century', *Ludington Daily,* May 28, 1971.

229 'How many did Dr Holmes Kill in his murder Castle?', *The Milwaukee Journal,* June 23, 1938.

230 'Another Disappearance', *Daily Mail and Empire,* July 29, 1895.

231 Ibid.

232   Amanda Howard, *River of Blood,* p. 180.

233   'Murder Most Foul', *Daily Mail and Empire,* July 16, 1895.

234   Ibid.

235   'The Pitezel Case', *Daily Mail and Empire,* July 24, 1895.

236   'Famous Last words', *The Milwaukee Journal,* January 11, 1964.

237   'Heir vindicates Mudgett name', *The Michigan Daily,* December 6, 1973.

238   'Meet India's female serial killer', *Daily Bhaskar,* October 27, 2013.

239   Ibid.

240   'Cyanide Mallika in Kysore police custody', *The Hindu,* April 19, 2008.

241   'Life term for serial killer Cyanide Mallika', *The Times of India,* October 30, 2013.

242   'Serial Killer Cyanide Mallika gets lifer', *Karnataka News,* October 30, 2013.

243   'Cyanide Mallika bashed up in jail', *Times of India.*

244   'Murdered 300 husbands', *The Montreal Gazette,* March 26, 1909.

245   'Woman Kills 300 at Wives' Behest', *The Bryan Times,* September 21, 1909.

246   Ibid.

247   'Murdered 300 husbands', *The Montreal Gazette,* March 26, 1909.

248   Ibid.

249   San Francisco Del Rincon, *Reading Eagle,* November 1, 1964.

250   '17 found dead in Probe of Prostitution ring', *Daytona Beach Morning Journal,* January 18, 1964.

251   Ibid.

252   Ibid.

253   Ibid.

254   Dubious court defences, http://civicadvocator.net/dubious-court-defenses.

255   '2 sisters guilty of slaying of 80 girls', *The Miami News,* October 17, 1964.

256   'When death rode in with the factory tea wagon', *Ottawa Citizen,* January 6, 1979.

257   'Compulsive poisoner is placed in asylum for tests of parents', *The Milwaukee Journal,* July 6, 1962.

258   'When death rode in with the factory tea wagon', *Ottawa Citizen,* January 6, 1979.

259   Ibid.

260   Ibid.

261   Ibid.

262   'German Detective solves crimes', *The Milwaukee Sentinel,* May 7, 1937.

263   The Poisoner Anna Zwanziger, http://www.geschichte-verbrechen.de/zwanziger/zwanziger.html, (translated from German).

264   Ibid.

265   Ibid.

266   Ibid.

Mass Child Killers

267   Instinto assesino—ElMonstruo de los Canaduzales—Discovery Documentary 2010.

268   'Cape Rapist murderer who claims to be the cane fields killer', BBC.

269   'Bermudez is not a psychopath: Legal Medicine', *BBC,* July 31, 2003.

270   'Man accused of killing 42 boys is sentenced', *NBC News,* October 25, 2006.

271   'Suspect Admits killing dozens of youngsters', *Eugene Register Guard,* October 30, 1999.

272   'Colombia outraged, horrified by mass murder of children', *Lawrence Journal,* October 31, 1999.

273   Ibid.

274   'Alleged child killer claims he was abused', *Boca Raton News,* November 1, 1999.

275   Asif Shahzad, 'Lahore: The story of a pampered boy', www.dawn.com. (Accessed March 2008).

276   Ibid.

277   One of the boys that Iqbal routinely abused and used to procure further victims

278   Asif Shahzad, 'Lahore: The story of a pampered boy', www.dawn.com. (Accessed March 2008).

279   Peter Popham, 'Child Killer's accomplice leaps to death', *The Independent,* December 9, 1999, www.independent.co.uk. (Accessed August 2005).

280   Peter Popham, 'Child killer sentenced to be throttled, cut up and immersed in an acid bath', *The Independent,* March 17, 2000, http://www.independent.co.uk/news/world/asia/child-killer-sentenced-to-be-throttled-cut-up-and-immersed-in-an-acid-bath-722013.html. (Accessed March 2008).

281   Seamus McGraw, Javad Iqbal, http://www.trutv.com/library/crime/serial_killers/predators/javed_iqbal/7.html. (Accessed February 2008).

282   Execution of Pak child killer ordered, http://www.tribuneindia.com/2000/20000317/world.htm#1. (Accessed March 2008).

Killer Couples

283   'Had a problem, Bernardo admits', *Toledo Blade,* August 19, 1995.

284   Bruce MacFarlan, 'Horrific Video Tapes As Evidence: Balancing Open Court And Victims' Privacy', *Criminal Law Quarterly* 413, 1999.

285   Williams, Stephen, *Invisible Darkness,* Bantam Books, 1998, p. 64.

286   Ibid., p. 109.

287   Bernardo and Homolka case, http://bernardo-homolka.tumblr.com/.

288   Stephen Williams, *Invisible Darkness,* Bantam Books, 1998, p. 183.

289   Peter Vronsky, *Female Serial Killers: How and Why Women Become Monsters,* Berkley Books, 2007.

290   'Bernardo sentenced to life', *Kingman Daily Miner,* September 3, 1995.

291   'Man sentenced to life in prison for 2 deaths', *Lakeland Ledger,* September 2, 1995.

292   'Man convicted in sex slayings', *The Freelance Star,* September 1, 1995.

293   'Bernardo admits to raping 14 women', *Lakeland Ledger,* November 4, 1995.

294   'Killer of 2 Canadian girls sentenced', *Pittsburgh Post Gazette,* September 2, 1995.

295   'Town destroys house of horrors', *Reading Eagle,* December 7, 1995.

296   'A loving letter from a mother', *Sydney Morning Herald,* March 4, 1987.

297   Based on conversations with David Birnie (2005).

298   Ibid.

299   Ibid.

300   Ibid.

301   Ibid.

302   Ibid.

303   Ibid.

304   'Sex shock confession', *Sydney Morning Herald,* November 16, 1986.

305   Based on conversations with David Birnie (2005).

306   R v Birnie.

307   'No remorse by killer says judge', *Sydney Morning Herald,* March 4, 1987.

308   Ibid.

309   Douglas Adams, *Hitchhikers Guide to the Galaxy: a Trilogy in Four Parts.*

310   Wicked Attraction ID Documentary.

311   Ibid.

312   'Jury gets bizarre murder case', *Gadsden Times,* January 20, 1983.

313   Wicked Attraction ID Documentary.

314   'Jury gets bizarre murder case', *Gadsden Times,* January 20, 1983.

315   Wicked Attraction ID Documentary.

316   Ibid.

317   'Jury gets bizarre murder case', *Gadsden Times,* January 20, 1983.

318   'Accomplice of Sunset Slayer given 52 years to life sentence', *The Bulletin,* June 1, 1983.

319   Wicked Attraction ID Documentary.

320   Ibid.

321   'Jury gets bizarre murder case', *Gadsden Times,* January 20, 1983.

322   'Accomplice of Sunset Slayer given 52 years to life sentence', *The Bulletin,* June 1, 1983.

323   'Limping monster and the 71 women', *Adelaide News,* May 20, 1954.

324   Ibid.

325   Ibid.

326   'A French Wolfe', *Empire,* September 9, 1862.

327   'Limping monster and the 71 women', *Adelaide News,* May 20, 1954.

328   'Extraordinary trial for murder', *The Age,* April 17, 1862.

329   'Limping monster and the 71 women', *Adelaide News,* May 20, 1954.

330   'Extraordinary trial for murder', *The Age,* April 17, 1862.

331   Ibid.

332   Ibid.

333 Ibid.

334 Ibid.

335 'Limping monster and the 71 women', *Adelaide News*, May 20, 1954.

336 'A monster', *Freeman's Journal,* April 30, 1862.

337 'Limping monster and the 71 women', *Adelaide News*, May 20, 1954.

338 Ibid.

339 'English Extracts', *The Newcastle Chronicle,* April 26, 1862.

340 'Extraordinary trial for murder', *The Age,* April 17, 1862.

341 'Dumollard', *Petersberg Times,* December 14, 1984.

342 ' Ibid.

343 'A French Wolfe', *Empire,* September 9, 1862.

344 'A monster', *Freeman's Journal,* April 30, 1862.

345 'Extraordinary trial for murder', *The Age,* April 17, 1862.

346 'A monster', *Freeman's Journal,* April 30, 1862.

347 'Extraordinary trial for murder in France', *The Mercury,* April 28, 1862.

348 'Son may follow father's grim path', *The Milwaukee Journal,* April 12, 1983.

349 'Convicted murderer follows father's legacy', *Lawrence Journal-World,* April 12, 1983.

350 'The couple were never officially married', 'Son may follow father's grim path' *The Milwaukee Journal* April 12, 1983.

351 'It's husband vs wife in double murder trial', *The Free Lance Star,* January 12, 1983.

352 Ibid.

353 'Sex slave killer faces death', *Mohave Daily Miner,* June 10, 1984.

354 Gallego v E k McDaniel [1997] USCA9 2693; 124 F.3d 1065 (4 September 1997).

355 Ibid.

356 Amanda Howard, *River of Blood.*

357 'Sex slave killer faces death', *Mohave Daily Miner,,* June 10, 1984.

358 Gallego v E k McDaniel [1997] USCA9 2693; 124 F.3d 1065 (4 September 1997).

359 'It's husband vs wife in double murder trial', *The Free Lance Star,* January 12, 1983.

360 'Gallego found guilty of murder', *Lodi News Sentinel,* April 12, 1983.

361 'Convicted murderer follows father's legacy', *Lawrence Journal-World,* April 12, 1983.

362 'It's husband vs wife in double murder trial', *The Free Lance Star,* January 12, 1983.

363 Geoffrey Wansell, *An Evil Love: The Life of Frederick West,* Headline, 1996, p. 27.

364 Fred West, Wikipedia (Accessed July 2007).

365 Fred had confessed and recanted the confession to Mary's murder multiple times.

366 Geoffrey Wansell, *An Evil Love: The Life of Frederick West,* Headline, 1996, p. 85.

367 Ibid., p. 89.

368 Mae was born May June West on June 1, 1972.

369 Geoffrey Wansell, *An Evil Love: The Life of Frederick West,* Headline, 1996, p. 107.

370 Ibid., p.129.

371 Ibid., p. 143.

372   Ibid., p. 189.

373   Ibid., p. 196.

374   Ibid., p. 12.

375   Fred West's own words, *Fred and Rose: The West Murders,* Channel 5 Documentary, England.

376   Ibid.

377   Ibid.

Tandem Killers

378   'Torture killers often involved in deadly friendship', *The Lewiston Daily Sun,* March 27, 1987.

379   Note that it is singular and not plural. Police believed only one killer was involved.

380   'Kenneth Bianchi, Serial Killer Timelines', Radford University.

381   Ibid.

382   'Angelo Buono Jr, Serial Killer Timelines', Radford University.

383   'Prosecution witnesses testify confessed Hillside Strangler introduced as talent scout', *Gadsden Times,* March 9, 1982.

384   Ibid.

385   'Hillside Strangler described murders', *The Miami news,* July 7, 1981.

386   'Hillside Strangler Evidence prepared', *The Victoria Advocate,* April 24, 1979.

387   'Hillside strangler named to police a year before his arrest', *Tuscaloosa News,* February 4, 1979.

388   Ibid.

389   'Still emotional about the LA Murders', *Schenectady Gazette,* March 31, 1989.

390   'Confessed strangler given 6 life sentences', *The Dispatch,* October 23, 1979.

391   Dirk Gibson, *Serial murder and media circuses,* Greenwood Publishing group, p. 83.

392   'Bianchi may be linked to the Alphabet Murders', *Ellensburg Daily Record,* July 9, 1981.

393   'Foreign News A Murder Day', *Time Magazine* July 2, 1945.

394   'Innkeeper, Aide put to death for Wholesale Murders', *The Evening Independent* June 21, 1945.

395   Ibid.

396   Ibid.

397   'Chinese Pair found guilty of killing 78', *The Milwaukee Journal* July 21, 1945

398   'Killer described as angry', *Toledo Blade,* April 14, 2002.

399   Ibid.

400   Ibid.

401   Ibid.

402   Ibid.

403   Ibid.

404   Ibid.

405   'I'm the Bruma Lake Killer brags boyfriend', *IOL,* May 20, 2002.

406   Ibid.

407   'Torture killers often involved in deadly friendship', *The Lewiston Daily Sun,* March 27, 1987.

The Black Widows

408   'Barfield led troubled life', *The Times News,* October 31, 1984.

409   Ibid.

410   'Barfield's victims died slow painful deaths', *The Times News,* October 31, 1984.

411   Ibid.

412   'Barfield led troubled life', *The Times News,* October 31, 1984.

413   Ibid.

414   Ibid.

415   'Black Widow scheduled to die', *McCook Daily Gazette,* February 9, 1998.

416   Ibid.

417   Ibid.

418   'Woman Denies poisoning Husband', *Sun Sentinel,* October 30, 1985.

419   'Wholesale poisoning at West Auckland', *The Glasgow Herald,* October 5, 1872.

420   Ibid.

421   Ibid.

422   Ibid.

423   'An Amazing female criminal', *The Advertiser,* October 16, 1915.

424   'The Flaming haired Borgia', *The Milwaukee Sentinel,* August 28, 1938.

425   Ibid.

426   Ibid.

427   'Alleged insurance fraud', *The Mail,* April 2, 1927.

428   Ibid.

429   'Murdered for Money', *The Courier Mail,* May 21, 1938.

430   'The Flaming haired Borgia', *The Milwaukee Sentinel,* August 28, 1938.

431   'Poisoned four persons', *Newcastle Morning Herald,* May 20, 1938.

432   'The Devil in Petticoats', *The Milwaukee Sentinel,* April 24, 1948.

433   'Woman's shocking crime', *Western Mail,* May 26, 1938.

434   'Cruel beyond belief', *The CourierMail,* May 23, 1938.

435   'Austria beheads woman who slew four in Family', *St Petersburg Times,* December 7, 1938.

436   When Women murder, http://www.boen-end.de/velten.htm (translated from German).

437   Ibid.

438   Ibid.

439   Ibid.

440   Ibid.

441   Ibid.

442   Ibid.

443   Ibid.

444   'Police search for more victims of the plump poisoner', *The Deseret News,* August 2, 1983.

Parents Who Kill

445   'Woman gets life', *Corsicana Daily Sun,* December 23, 1913.

446   'Jealous Wife Kill Children', *The Gazette Times,* October 15, 1913.

447   R v Folbigg [2003] NSWSC 895 (24 October 2003).

448   Ibid.

449   Ibid.

450   Ibid.

451   Kathleen Folbigg Diary entry (03.06.90).

452   Kathleen Folbigg Diary entry (14.01.97).

453   Kathleen Folbigg Diary entry (04.02.97).

454   Kathleen Folbigg Diary entry (17.02.97).

455   Kathleen Folbigg Diary entry (16.05.97).

456   Kathleen Folbigg Diary entry (25.08.97).

457   Kathleen Folbigg Diary entry (8.11.97).

458   Kathleen Folbigg Diary entry (9.11.97).

459   Kathleen Folbigg Diary entry (28.01.98).

460   Ibid.

461   Ibid.

462   'Father blames mom for two killings', *Lodi News-Sentinel,* November 9, 1993.

463   'Murder suspect killed husband', *Lodi News-Sentinel,* November 8, 1993.

464   Ibid.

465   'Woman accused of killing children arrested in Utah', *Moscow Pullman Daily news,* November 12, 1993.

466   Deadly Woman: The Sacred Bond Documentary.

467   'Woman accused of killing children arrested in Utah', *Moscow Pullman Daily news,* November 12, 1993.

468   'Murder suspect killed husband', *Lodi News-Sentinel,* November 8, 1993.

469   'Father blames mom for two killings', *Lodi News-Sentinel,* November 9, 1993.

470   'Marybeth Tinning: Radford University Serial Killer Timelines'.

471   Most Evil—Murderous Women Documentary.

472   Marybeth Tinning's Sentencing, Court Transcript, October 2, 1987.

473   Most Evil—Murderous Women Documentary.

474   Robert Boorstin, 'Schenectady Child Suffocation Case Goes to Jury', *New York Times,* July 16, 1987.

475   Robert Gavin, 'Rare Glimpse into child killer's mind', *Times Union,* February 11, 2011.

476   Most Evil – Murderous Women Documentary.

477 James Leggett, 'Grand Jury Investigating Deaths of At Least Two Tinning Children', *Schenectady Gazette,* June 18, 1986.

478 'Marybeth Tinning: Radford University Serial Killer Timelines'.

479 Most Evil – Murderous Women Documentary.

480 'Marybeth Tinning: Radford University Serial Killer Timelines'.

481 Ibid.

482 Joyce Egginton, *From the Cradle to the Grave,* Mass Market, 1990.

483 'Marybeth Tinning: Radford University Serial Killer Timelines'

484 Most Evil – Murderous Women Documentary.

485 James Leggett, 'Grand Jury Investigating Deaths of At Least Two Tinning Children', *Schenectady Gazette,* June 18, 1986.

486 Robert Gavin, 'Rare Glimpse into child killer's mind', *Times Union,* February 11, 2011.

UK £12.99
US $16.99